# Employee Benefits

## Plain and Simple

# JAMES M. JENKS AND
# BRIAN L.P. ZEVNIK

Collier Books
Macmillan Publishing Company • New York
Maxwell Macmillan Canada • Toronto
Maxwell Macmillan International
New York • Oxford • Singapore • Sydney

# Employee Benefits

## *Plain and Simple*

**THE COMPLETE
STEP-BY-STEP GUIDE
TO YOUR BENEFITS PLAN**

## AUTHORS' NOTE

The information contained in this book is, of necessity, general in nature and does not provide solutions for specific individuals' situations. It is not intended to substitute for the professional advice of lawyers, accountants, financial advisors, and other consultants. This is especially true in light of the constant changes in federal and state laws, IRS regulations, and judicial decisions.

Collier Books
Macmillan Publishing Company
866 Third Avenue
New York, NY 10022

Maxwell Macmillan Canada, Inc.
1200 Eglinton Avenue East
Suite 200
Don Mills, Ontario M3C 3N1

Macmillan Publishing Company is part of the Maxwell Communication Group of Companies.

Library of Congress Cataloging-in-Publication Data
Jenks, James M.
Employee Benefits : plain and simple : the complete step-by-step guide to your benefits plan / James M. Jenks and Brian L. P. Zevnik.—1st Collier Books ed.
p.    cm.
Includes index.
ISBN 0-02-052295-9
1. Employee fringe benefits.    I. Zevnik, Brian.    II. Title.
HD4928.N6J46    1993
658.3'25—dc20                      93-19471
                                          CIP

Macmillan books are available at special discounts for bulk purchases for sales promotions, premiums, fund-raising, or educational use. For details, contact:

Special Sales Director
Macmillan Publishing Company
866 Third Avenue
New York, NY 10022

10    9    8    7    6    5    4    3    2    1

Printed in the United States of America

# CONTENTS

# INTRODUCTION

Lots has been written about the expanding choices that employers have when it comes to *offering* benefits to their workers. But what about the choices of employees when it comes to *accepting* those benefits?

Actually those two words are misnomers in the new benefits partnership among employers, employees, and Uncle Sam. It's no longer a question of employers giving and employees receiving. You no longer have to sit back and take what "they" give you. You've now got a chance to stand up and make your benefit voice be heard—as an active participant, not a passive receiver.

Changes in the benefit scene aren't new, just as benefits themselves have a little gray in their sideburns. Back in 1636, Plymouth Colony settlers had a military retirement program; American Express put together a private pension for its people in 1875; and Montgomery Ward boasted group life, health, and accident insurance in 1910.

But never have benefits played a more vital role in your compensation. And never have you had to play such a vital role in getting the most out of the benefits available to you.

Getting top value for those benefits takes time, thought, and effort. Your time, your thought, your effort. But it can save you hundreds of dollars in taxes every year, put thousands more into your nest egg, and make sure that if disaster strikes, you're not left holding an empty bag.

Many workers sit idly by, wringing their hands and complaining that their benefits are shrinking. But you're taking your benefits future into your hands with this book. It's up to you to understand the options, up to you to decide on personal priorities, up to you to tailor available packages to your needs.

This book gives you a personal blueprint for:

1) making more intelligent choices in your benefits;
2) wangling the most bang for the buck out of what you're offered;
3) tailoring company benefits to your individual needs;
4) saving money by refusing coverages you don't need;
5) putting more money in your pockets through tax-favored features.

You're now in a period of do-it-yourself benefits. Self-service. If you don't take charge, who'll do it for you? Not your employer anymore. Most employers are passing off major responsibility for benefits to their employees. Prime evidence: the switch from traditional, defined-benefit pension plans to defined-contribution plans.

You'll read more on this later, but simply put, with **defined benefits**, employers promised specific payouts at some future date. Your company would sock away money for you, and depending on a formula that took into account your years of service and salary, it would then hand over after retirement a monthly reward for loyal service. A specific monthly award.

Now it's a new ball game. **Defined contributions** means just that. The company kicks in specific amounts based on a formula. But it no longer guarantees specifically how big your pot will be at the end of your retirement rainbow.

*The old promise*: Work for us for twenty-five years, make $65,000 in your final go-round, and we'll make sure your pension stuffs, say, 50% of that final salary in your pocket every month, with Social Security on top of that.

*The new promise*: We'll help you build up tax-deferred assets in a 401(k) fund with matching funds and spice up your future with a profit sharing account. And we may even offer a nonspecific pension that we'll contribute to when we feel it's appropriate.

## MANAGING YOUR BENEFITS BEST

It's actually not a very complicated process. Just three steps:

• First you lay a foundation of knowledge with this book.
• Then you get to know every detail of your current employer's plans.
• Finally, you sort through the options and seize the opportunities that make sense to you.

No one else is going to do it for you. Benefits are no longer sacrosanct, so you have to do as the ancient Romans recommended: Seize the day.

Working at full throttle with you at the wheel, an employee benefits package can carry you away from economic disaster and deliver you to a financially secure future. Without your input, guidance, and control, it can idle by the side of the road and leave you behind the pack when it comes to economic stability and peace of mind.

One last thought (okay, so a couple of last thoughts): Normally you'd see a disclaimer at the start of a book, or in the credits of a movie, that states something to the effect that all characters and incidents in the book/movie have no relation to reality and any resemblance to real events or people is coincidental.

That's not true of this book. Every incident and every situation may have a direct relationship to a living person—**YOU**. The various characters who are puzzling out their benefits' problems should definitely resemble an actual person—**YOU**. When you read about Bill Ticknor and Kathy Crowley and all the others, you should be imagining another person in their predicaments—**YOU**.

You'll find a lot of repeat topics as you read along. That's because almost every benefit is tied to another one in some way. Health and medical care may tie in with life insurance. Disability links up with government options. Financial investing offers parameters for everything from personal IRAs to company-sponsored 401(k)s. And flexible-benefits programs circumscribe them all. So use the cross-references to build your own personal data bank little by little on each topic . . . until your benefit confidence level zooms right off the scale.

A lot of the information will someday—in one way or another—have an impact on how you live your life. So put your benefits "game face" on, and get involved. It'll pay off in championship benefits for you in the end.

# 1
▼

# BASIC BENEFITS

*Taking a Snapshot of Your Employee Benefits Picture*

*THE CASE OF THE HEALTHY CURIOSITY*

**K**athy Crowley considered herself pretty bright when it came to her job. She knew how to handle just about every situation she had ever been confronted with. But that was on-the-job stuff.

She had never really had time to check out the "extraneous" points of her employment. Just too busy. She wanted to know how much money she could count on taking home every week. When her next opportunity for a raise or promotion was scheduled. And whether she could get a piece of her regular medical and dental checkups paid for by insurance.

Kathy never really worried about more than that until a friend had a serious accident and got stuck holding the bag on a handful of huge medical bills. That started her thinking. So she decided to investigate her own benefits package to find out just where she stood.

Before you focus your viewfinder on the specific details of a complete employee benefits package, take a couple of moments to quick-check the big picture.

Just to whet your appetite, figure 1 below is a checklist of potential benefits that can add color to your employment life. If you're going to start making intelligent choices about what to do with them, you've got to get a better view of what they really are.

What is a benefit, anyway? It's any kind of compensation provided in a form other than direct wages and paid for in whole or in part by an employer, even when it's provided by a third party. You're familiar with the most common benefits, like health insurance, life insurance, and pension plans. But government-provided Social Security also falls in the bailiwick of benefits, as does pay while you're on jury duty, parking spaces, and a company box at the ball park.

In fact, you may be surprised at what's considered a fringe benefit these days. Employees at a major U.S. airline ranked the company's **suggestion system** as their second most valuable benefit, behind profit-sharing. Reason: The program paid out more than $25 million over a five-year period and induced some three hundred suggestions per day.

Generally, though, benefits fall into three main categories. You've got those required by law, like Social Security and Workers' Compensation. (Note that pensions, while regulated by law like Social Security and Workers' Comp, aren't mandated.) You've got time-oriented benefits, such as holidays, vacations, sick days, maternity leave. (Note again, vacations are not a mandated benefit.) And you've got supplementary benefits, with such items as insurance, productivity bonuses, etc.

*Figure 1. Checklist of potential benefits*

### Educational Reimbursement

- personal development
- scholarships for children of employees
- training in literacy/job skills
- tuition

### Travel/Transportation

- preferred rates
- frequent flier miles
- mass transit subsidy

- van pool
- carpool match-ups
- moving expenses
- relocation services
- housing allowance
- company car
- car allowance

## Employee Incentive/Convenience

- matching gifts
- volunteer recognition
- anniversary programs
- parking
- direct deposit
- automated teller machines
- food services
- bonuses for productivity
- profit sharing
- overtime
- payroll deduction for auto
- legal services
- loans or salary advances
- severance
- discount program (company products/other)
- credit cards with reduced interest and membership fees

## Health

- physical exams
- employee assistance program
- fitness center
- wellness incentives
- health screenings/seminars
- sickness/accident insurance
- short- and long-term disability insurance
- dental care
- vision care
- sick days
- club membership
- PPOs and HMOs

## Recreation
- competitive teams
- picnic grounds
- country club membership
- cultural events program
- entertainment tickets

## Government
- Social Security retirement/disability
- Medicare/Medicaid
- Workers' Compensation
- Unemployment Insurance
- Supplemental Security Income

## Family
- child care
- dependent care resource/referral
- dependent care reimbursement account
- family/maternity leave
- sabbaticals
- flextime
- spouse job search
- psychiatric or marital counseling
- parental leave
- home purchase assistance
- accident insurance for children/spouse
- eldercare milestone program (births, deaths, anniversaries)

## Savings
- U.S. Savings Bond purchase
- credit union
- employee stock ownership plan
- employee stock option plan
- 401(k) or 403(b)
- matching savings plans
- deferred compensation bonus plan
- cash accumulation funds
- thrift savings

## Life/Lifestyle

- life insurance
- supplemental options
- vacation
- paid holidays
- home entertainment allowance
- financial counseling and tax return preparation
- computer
- survivor income benefits
- dependent life insurance
- funeral leave
- jury duty/military leave
- reimbursement accounts
- flexible spending accounts

## Retirement

- pension plan
- salary deferral plan
- Simplified Employee Pensions
- IRAs
- supplemental benefits
- post-retirement counseling

This chapter is divided into smaller snapshots to give you a simplified view of the overall picture. First it touches on some wide-angle views of the major categories; then it takes some close-up shots that focus on individual parts of modern plans.

**Benefits alert:** All these subjects will be given closer scrutiny in later chapters. For now, just frame your own montage of the world of benefits. ▼

## MEASURING THE HEALTH OF
## HEALTH BENEFITS

The most important, and most controversial, of all benefits are those involving health insurance and medical expenses. Costs are skyrocketing, so employers are passing on more of these costs to you. You may already have felt that firsthand in the increased paycheck deductions for your share of premiums. You may have experienced the higher deductibles you have to accept when you make a claim and the chopped-down coverages you've been offered.

Basic health plans usually cover those expenses associated with hospitalization, from room/board, medical supplies, and nursing to physician care and surgery. They can include anything from X-ray coverage to psychiatric treatment to drug or alcohol programs, from ambulance fees to prescription drugs to chiropractic care.

Fee-for-service medical plans pay for specific medical procedures as they are incurred, usually after you pay a deductible amount. They usually have a cap on the maximum amount they'll pay.

A newer trend is away from fee-for-service and toward some type of managed care, mainly Health Maintenance Organizations (HMOs) and Preferred Provider Organizations (PPOs). Both are groups of doctors and other health professionals who offer a range of services at a set fee. Your costs for such options may be less, but so are your choices. Basically, for a lower bottom-line cost, you must utilize the services provided by the specific group to which you belong.

**Note:** Changes in health care seem to be the only constant in an ever-changing field. Hillary Clinton, both houses of Congress, state legislatures, and every point of the private health care system have all stuck their two cents into the debate. New federal mandates and old state requirements both lead to the same conclusion. You must pull a Kathy Crowley and make sure you investigate your health care rights and priviledges constantly.

## SAVING YOUR HARD-EARNED DOLLARS

The good news is that the choices you have today can help off-set some of the bad news. You may be able to lower your share of premiums by choosing a higher deductible. It's similar to the choices you make with your car insurance. If you have an old clunker, you don't buy what's called first-dollar coverage. That means you're not going to fix every little ding and dent. The same goes for health care coverage. You really want to be pro-tected from the big expenses. You just cover your assets for cat-astrophes.

You may also be able to save money on taxes by hitching a ride on the vehicle known as a Flexible Spending Account (FSA). Basically, it enables you to set aside untaxed dollars from your regular paycheck in a fund that you can use to pay for medical expenses not covered by insurance, or to knock down a higher deductible.

Again, you need some careful planning. You need to predict just how much you're likely to spend, which affects how much gets subtracted from your take-home pay every month. While you save big on taxes (check out chapters 4 and 7), there's a catch, as usual: Use it or lose it. If you put $2,500 in the fund over the course of a year and only use up $2,000, that extra $500 reverts to, horrors, your employer.

## WHAT HAPPENS WHEN YOU CAN'T WORK?

Disability is another health benefit consideration. It comes in the shape of short- or long-term plans to continue your income in the case of a substantial illness or injury that keeps you from working. Short-term coverage usually provides salary replace-ment for up to a year, depending on employment level, years of service, and company plan. Long-term typically picks up a per-centage (around 60%) of base salary until age 65. Such plans are coordinated with Social Security and Workers' Compensation (check out chapter 4).

No one likes to think of becoming unable to work. But statistics show that you're more likely to become disabled during your lifetime than to die while you're still on the job. If you're thrown for a loss by a physical disability that keeps you from working, neither private plans nor Social Security by themselves will "make you whole" financially.

Most employers pick up the full cost of the standard disability package, but you usually have an option to buy more and to have payments deducted from your paychecks (check out chapter 4).

## PUTTING NEW LIFE IN YOUR LIFE INSURANCE

Another fairly standard benefit, though it doesn't leave a whole lot of room for maneuvering, is life insurance. Here, you're basically looking for financial protection for your spouse and children in case of your death. But in today's benefit world, there are other considerations, like investment and saving opportunities, as well as accidental death and dismemberment clauses that increase payouts (check out chapter 10).

Many company-paid life insurance plans pay on your death one or one-and-one-half times your salary, up to certain legal limits, and give you the option to buy additional coverage at company rates. You may want to get that extra coverage, but don't automatically jump at your employer's rates. Compare them with low-cost term rates you can get on your own.

## RETIREMENT: WHEN THE LIVING SHOULD BE EASY

Most of the headlines trumpeting change in employee benefits swirl around savings and retirement programs. Your mission, and you're going to have to accept it, is to make choices among a growing variety of options for which retirement accounts you want your money to go into, and how you want it to come out. But be careful. You can self-destruct in the proverbial five seconds unless you plan carefully.

Among the more popular tax-deferred retirement savings vehicles are profit sharing, thrift, and the high-profile 401(k) plans.

Savings or thrift plans basically involve your kicking in a predetermined amount to an account; your employer may match a certain percentage. These "salary reduction" plans give you the double advantage of a lower income tax base and tax-deferred savings.

Profit sharing plans are just that. Your company posts better bottom-line results; you share in the profits; you work harder; your company posts better results. You've heard that song before, right?

---

**Benefits alert:** Don't let all these definitions throw you. They'll be explained fully later in the book. And if you need a quick brush-up, check the glossary.▼

---

With most savings plans, especially the 401(k), your first question will be "Should I?" The almost universal answer is "Definitely." You not only save for the future, but you pay Uncle Sam less. And you often get to use matching money from the company to augment your own. The main drawback is that, with few exceptions, you can't easily dip into your pot of gold until you reach the end of your retirement rainbow.

Most plans these days offer options for the way you allocate your savings among various investment vehicles (check out chapters 5–9). It used to be that you'd toss your money into a pool and forget it, while your employer worried about where to channel it. That hands-off employee role has gone the way of the horse-drawn carriage.

Now it's up to you to kick the tires of those investment vehicles that eventually will be delivering your postemployment paychecks. You decide which ones will take you for the best ride. You may be looking for a very safe, conservative trip; or you could opt to go a little faster in hopes of reaching your personal retirement Disneyland sooner or with a few more bucks to spend.

## *BENEFITS CHECKOFF: BOOSTING YOUR SAVINGS POTENTIAL*

Other savings vehicles that may come into focus as you review your specific benefits package include:

✔ Employee Stock Ownership Plans (ESOPs)—Besides making you an owner of company stock, ESOPs don't put you on the spot for any cash injections. In fact, you most likely will derive cash from dividend payments. Basically, the company's board of directors directs that shares of the company's stock be purchased for the ESOP, and those shares are allocated to employee participants (that's you) according to a set schedule. Sometimes you can take your stock shares with you when you leave the company; often, you must wait for retirement to redeem them.

✔ Incentive Stock Options (ISOs)—Generally only go to higher-level management types and executives as rewards for special services or productivity.

✔ Employee Stock Purchase Plans—Normally, your company gives you a prospectus outlining how much stock you can buy and at what cost. Many companies offer their stock at discount prices, typically at 85% of market value, to their employees. Key point to investigate: the impact on your tax situation of buying or selling the stock.

✔ Individual Retirement Accounts (IRAs)—These are not company-sponsored benefits per se, but they should be coordinated with what you get in the workplace. There are specific restrictions and amount caps, with a maximum $2,000 contribution the most important. Not only does an IRA grow, tax-free, but a portion of your IRA contribution can be deducted from your taxable income base under certain circumstances (check out chapter 9).

## *PUMPING UP PENSION PLANS*

Another area of controversy and contraction, pension plan changes reflect the growing trend away from company responsibility. No single trend better reflects it than the move away from traditional defined benefit plans and toward defined contribution plans, as noted in the introduction.

For both types of plans, the feds make some rules (check out chapter 12) about who can participate, when you become a vested partner in the plan, and how the benefits build up.

When you home in on pensions, you should also know about:

- Vesting—when you become a full partner in a pension plan. Determined by law and spelled out early in every benefits handbook (check out chapters 3 and 12).
- Portability—an important factor in pensions for today's more mobile employee. Allows you to move from one employer to another without losing the source of your pension funds. You just direct a former employer to "roll over" a tax-free lump sum already accumulated in your previous account into either a personal IRA or your new employer's plan.

---

**Benefits alert:** If you do roll over a lump sum, be aware that Uncle Sam's IRS is standing ready to insert its fingers into your pie, to the tune of 20% off the top. The key is how the bucks are transferred. If your employer transfers the funds directly into another account, you pass go and the IRS collects nothing at the time. If the money goes to you first, then the 20% is deducted.

A similar trap exists when your payout includes company stock. You can't just "roll over" a cash sum equivalent to the stock's worth to delay paying taxes. On a stock distribution, you must either sell the stock and invest the proceeds in the roll-over target (IRA or new employer's plan), or roll over the actual stock certificates into a self-directed IRA.▼

---

- Social Security—basically financed by payroll taxes paid by you and your employer, as evidenced by the FICA (Federal Insurance Contributions Act) contribution that gets sucked out of your checks on payday. Payments from Social Security include monthly benefits for retirees, disabled workers and their spouses/dependents, and survivor benefits. Don't count on getting rich on this stipend. Plan on using Social Security as your benefits floor of protection to combine with pensions and other investments, not your cushion of comfort (check out chapter 11).

*Now if you're like Kathy Crowley, your curiosity is still aroused, but it's balanced by an equal amount of confusion. Keep reading. All the snapshots will come together in a focused picture as you go along.*

# 2
▼

# BENEFITS DOCUMENTS

*Reading Between the Lines of Your Benefits Material*

## THE CASE OF THE READY READER

This was almost like a research project in college, Pete Lydecker decided. But the payback was a lot more immediate—and valuable. It began to dawn on him that all those headlines he was reading about regarding increased medical expenses, decreased retirement payments, and investment opportunities gone awry—they all had to do with him and his employee benefits.

Pete had never given a second glance to that first benefits booklet the company had given him. Or to much of the material that crossed his desk thereafter, for that matter. He tossed it all in the "future file" drawer that he cleaned out once a year, usually in a hurry on a Friday afternoon around Christmas.

Now he was having second thoughts. Could his company make him assume higher payments for his health insurance, like the big airline he had read about had done? And what about the steel company that all of a sudden cut the benefits its retirees thought had been promised to them for life?

His next step was certain: He rummaged through that file

*drawer and pulled out every scrap of paper that had anything to
do with benefits. Then he sat down and opened the first booklet
he had ever received, appropriately entitled "Your Benefits and
You."*

They go by several monikers—personal benefits booklet, summary plan description, ESOP statement, pension plan personal
account, employee benefits summary. And they can range from
dozens of pages with dense text and mostly indecipherable
phrases to a six-panel brochure that cuts the legalese to a minimum and doesn't take a rocket scientist to translate. (Hope for
the latter, but be prepared to confront the former.)

Company benefits documents are not exactly beach-reading
material. But if you're going to really benefit from your benefits, you'd better share a blanket with them and make them
your friends.

To do that, check out the forms and phrases in this chapter.
Use the "Find Out" sections to analyze your own company's explanations of your benefits. And don't be afraid to ask more
questions of your benefits rep. No single booklet or statement,
no matter how extensive, will have the answer to every question that every individual employee has. It's part of your job to
make sure you understand. So ask.

All these specific benefit categories are covered in later
chapters. What you're doing here is easing your way into the
benefits document jungle. You'll get the tools to hack away
some of the wordiness in those documents so you can concentrate on your specific interests.

## BEGIN AT THE BEGINNING

If you have a specific area of interest, look it up in the booklet's
table of contents. If you're building a general idea of your
whole benefits package, read the booklet a little at a time. It's
not a novel in which you have to follow character development
or action sequences. The best-prepared booklets have an index
you can use to home in on specific sections that discuss issues
you want to understand.

For example, take the overall subject of your benefits coverage. You need to know when it begins and, just as important, when it ends. Eligibility requirements can cause major nightmares if you think you or a dependent are covered for an accident or illness or medical bill . . . and it turns out you're not.

*Find out:*
- what the definition of a regular employee is, and whether you fit that description;
- when each coverage begins, and when or whether you can buy extra;
- what the continuous service requirements are, and what you must do to meet them;
- how to become eligible for different coverages or plans;
- whether the company has a nonduplication clause that reduces company benefits if you have access to others.

Almost all companies give out a basic employee benefits explanation booklet, no matter what they call it. Here's what else to look for:

## CLAIMING YOUR RIGHTS

One matter often gets buried in or scattered throughout an employee benefits booklet. It is the usually simple but often exasperating problem of filing a claim (check out chapter 4). Many booklets are now devoting an entire section to claims filing.

**Benefits alert:** Don't just read the claims information. Ask for a filled-out sample form (check out figure 8, page 52) that you can refer to when you have to do it yourself. You can save yourself a lot of time and aggravation, not to mention money, if you remember to carry appropriate forms on every visit to a doctor's or dentist's office, to a hospital emergency room, or when you're entering a hospital as a patient.▼

*Find out:*

- What are the dates within which you must file?
- Is your insurance based on payments and deductibles per

person? If so, then keep separate records for each individual covered.

- How soon after you file a claim can you expect to be reimbursed?

## TAKING THE PULSE OF MEDICAL BENEFITS

You need to know what you're covered for, what you're *not* covered for, how much you have to pay for that coverage, and whether or not there are waiting periods. But beyond that, you may have choices to make as outlined in chapter 4.

Before you get glassy-eyed reading the medical/health part of your benefits booklet, look at eligibility. Are your dependents eligible? Do you need to contribute to make them eligible? In most cases, it pays to cover them. Usually the booklet spells out a regular payroll deduction for your portion of medical premiums.

The booklet should show the applicable deductible and the amount you'll have to pay before insurance kicks in. See if the amount is different for medical, dental, chiropractic, etc. When you know the deductible, you'll be able to decide better how much you can afford to have taken out of your pocket, and whether you can choose a higher-deductible plan (if available), which may be cheaper.

*Find out: whether the deductible is per person, per family, per calendar year, or per incident.*

The list of covered expenses is normally fairly straightforward. They include such expenses as:

- hospital services requiring admission or confinement;
- physician's services for a surgical procedure;
- emergency transportation service by ambulance;
- radiation therapy ordered by a physician.

What you really want to comb through is the "expenses not covered" or general exclusion section. When you know what's not covered, you won't be surprised when you get charged for such typically excluded items as treatment of a pre-existing condition, or cosmetic surgery, or artificial insemination.

### Checklist of Exclusions in One Company's Plan

- sickness or injury for which payment is made or available through Workers' Compensation;
- shots to prevent disease, except as specifically provided by name in the plan;
- appliances and splints placed on or attached to the teeth, except if needed due to accidental injury to natural teeth which happens while covered;
- expenses for confinement, treatment, services, or supplies given for or related to any of the following:
  - in vitro fertilization;
  - sex-change surgery;
  - liposuction;
  - tobacco dependency.

## WHAT TO LOOK FOR IN DISABILITY BENEFITS

What are the salary continuation requirements and benefits? You want to know what percentage of your salary you can expect if you become disabled, whether there is a maximum, and how your payments fit into what you may claim from Social Security, Workers' Comp, etc. When do the benefits start and stop? They may start, say, on the first of the month after six months of total disability, and they may end when you recover or die.

There may also be maximum payment periods (such as 48 months if your disability occurs at age 61), and specific disorders, like mental and nervous conditions, may also have caps. You'll always run into some exceptions to your ability to claim disability payments, especially in cases involving drug addiction or alcoholism.

***Find out:***
- Do your disability benefits change if your employment status changes, say from regular to part time?
- What is the cutoff date for mailing a claim (usually a year from date of disability)?

- If you're receiving benefits and die, is your spouse entitled to survivor benefits?
- Can you lay your hands on your profit sharing or company savings plan as soon as you're disabled?

## *YOUR HEALTH WATCH: SPOTTING SPECIFICS*

Some other areas to scrutinize in the medical and health section of your benefits document include the following:

**Pregnancy**—Are expenses subject to the same deductible/payment schedule? Are there uncovered expenses (fertility drugs, for example)?

**Vision care**—Does this have a deductible? Is there a maximum cap? Which expenses are covered, and which aren't?

**Dental**—Is there a difference between regular covered expenses and orthodontics? Are all standard procedures covered, like examinations, X-rays, preventive care, and cleanings? Is there a limit on the number of examinations and cleanings?

**Chiropractic**—What are "reasonable and customary" covered expenses? Maximums? Do the services and expenses of a chiropractor count toward the medical deductible, or does this area have a separate deductible?

**Extended coverage**—Do you have the option to buy extended coverage at your own expense? Are there specific qualifying events (death, termination, divorce) that trigger such options?

**Health Maintenance Organization**—Are HMOs an option? How do benefits compare to company benefits, if the two are separate programs? What is the cost of each? Are there specific periods of "open enrollment" when you are allowed to sign up for an HMO? Are any of your current doctors involved in an applicable HMO?

## *READING BETWEEN THE LINES OF RETIREMENT PROGRAMS*

For most employees, retirement benefits are second in importance only to health and medical benefits. For more information on the pension aspects of employee benefits, check out chapter 12. But as you're reading through your company booklet, keep these points in mind.

*Find out:*
- when normal retirement begins;
- when and if there's an early-retirement date, and what percentage of your pension you forfeit by choosing that option;
- when you become eligible and become a full participant, and how your service gets credited.

## *BENEFITS CHECKOFF: KEY RETIREMENT ISSUES IN YOUR BENEFITS BOOKLET*

✔ When normal retirement begins: This is usually at age 65 and sometimes there is a minimum-service requirement (e.g., five years).

✔ Eligibility for the retirement plan: This usually comes after one year of continuous service and at a minimum age of 21.

✔ Early retirement: Can you opt out of the workaday world early? How much will it cost you? If you get 100% of your pension at 65, you may get 95% at 64, 85% at 63, two-thirds at 60, maybe even down to half at 55.

✔ Breaks in employment: If you leave and come back, does your plan allow for crediting of your initial employment period?

✔ Benefit computation: What is the basis of calculating your actual retirement paychecks? One method uses the average monthly pay you earned over the last five successive calendar years before retirement. Check whether that rate includes overtime, bonuses, and commissions. Then look for the multiplication factor. Many plans take your years of service and multiply them by, say, 1.5%. That percentage is multiplied by your average monthly pay for the last five years of employment to determine your monthly retirement pay. For instance, say you worked for 30 years and your final average pay was $4,000 per month. Thirty years times 1.5% = 45%; 45% of $4,000 = $1,800. That's your monthly retirement pension.

✔ Optimal income payments: What ways can you receive your company pension? Can you ask for a lump sum? Can you get a higher sum of modified income guaranteed for five or ten years and then a lower sum thereafter? Can you get a pension for your life and for the life of your spouse if he/she outlives you?

You're normally given a "Benefits Statement" covering retirement income once each year. But you're entitled to ask for one at any time. You have to make your request in writing to the plan administrator, and you can normally ask for it only once a year (see figure 2).

Some companies will include in their documents your own retirement benefits worksheet, similar to the one in figure 3. You can practice with this one or use it to fill out the one your company offers. Ask for it today.

## GETTING YOUR SHARE OF THE PROFITS

If your company has a profit sharing plan, it will be spelled out in your employee benefits booklet. Breeze through the explanation of how the company is sharing its wealth with you. You'll work hard for every penny you get. What you want to know is how munificent the company is going to be, and what the nitty-gritty details are for your involvement. Once you've read the chapters on investing and the intricacies of such plans (check out chapters 5–9), you'll have a good feel for how to analyze them. Here are some investment investigations to conduct as you're reading your benefits book:

**Investigate:** How and when you become eligible. It may be six months after date of hire, and you may have to elect to participate. It's not always automatic.

**Investigate:** Contributions. Is there a minimum and maximum in terms of both percentages and dollar amounts? How much does the company contribute as its investing amount, if it does? If your company does match, that amount may be subject to a vesting schedule. Your contribution is always vested from

*Figure 2. Sample personal benefits statement*

## ACME SERVICES CORPORATION PENSION PLAN
### A PERSONAL RETIREMENT BENEFIT STATEMENT FOR: (name)

ESTIMATED MONTHLY BENEFITS AT NORMAL RETIREMENT DATE:

YOUR MONTHLY BENEFIT FROM THE RETIREMENT PLAN: $____

YOUR MONTHLY PRIMARY SOCIAL SECURITY BENEFIT:     $ ____

Social Security estimates are based on current laws and the assumed continuation of your present salary to your normal retirement date. Actual Social Security benefits will be based on your actual wage history and Social Security laws in effect when you retire.

YOUR TOTAL MONTHLY RETIREMENT INCOME: $_____

ESTIMATED MONTHLY ACCRUED RETIREMENT BENEFIT: $____

Your monthly accrued benefit is the amount of the benefit earned as of the date of this statement. It will give you an idea of your current status as to Plan benefits, but it is not a guarantee that such benefits are or will become payable. If your Plan participation were to terminate as of the date of this statement and you are fully vested, the accrued benefit is payable monthly, for your lifetime, commencing on your normal retirement date.

YOUR TOTAL MONTHLY ACCRUED BENEFIT TO DATE: $_____

As of the date of this statement you were _____ % vested in your accrued benefit. The Pension Plan provides a vested benefit after five years of service. If you had at least _____ years of service on (date), you will remain 100% vested in your accrued benefit.

DATE OF BIRTH_____ DATE OF HIRE_____

NORMAL RETIREMENT DATE_____

ANNUAL SALARY (date) $_____

This statement was prepared on the basis of the above data and the current terms of the plan. Some of the figures are necessarily approximate. When the time comes for you to receive a benefit, the amount you receive will be based on the provisions of the plan in effect at that time. If any employee data are incorrect, contact the business office.

*Figure 3. Practicing your retirement income calculations*

## MONTHLY RETIREMENT INCOME

1. Estimate your final average monthly income: $ _____

2. Take 1% of that estimated compensation up to $550: $ _____

3. Take 1.5% of that portion of estimated compensation which is over $550: $ _____

4. Add lines 2 and 3 to get the benefit for each year of credited service: $ _____

5. Enter your number of years of credited service at normal retirement date: _____

6. Multiply line 4 by line 5 to get your estimated monthly retirement income under the plan: $ _____

7. Estimate your monthly primary Social Security benefit: $ _____

Example of Normal Retirement at Age 65

1. Final average monthly compensation: $1,500.00

2. 1% of first $550:       $ 5.50

3. Add 1.5% of excess (1.5% x $950): $ 14.25

4. Add line 2 plus line 3:  $ 19.75

5. Years of credited service:  30 years

6. Estimated monthly retirement income at age 65 (line 4 multiplied by line 5): $ 592.50

7. Estimated Social Security at age 65:       $ 647.00

8. Estimated total monthly retirement income at age 65 (line 6 plus line 7): $1,239.50

Example of Early Retirement at Age 62 (using lines 1 through line 6 above)

9. Early retirement income at age 62 (line 6 multiplied by 80%):
$ 474.00

10. Estimated Social Security at age 62:      $ 517.00

11. Estimated total monthly retirement income at age 62 (line 9 plus line 10): $ 991.00

---

day one. But your company may require you to stay employed for a certain period to be eligible for matching funds. For example, it may match your contributions with a 20% contribution after two years, 70% after four, and 100% after five.

**Investigate:** What constitutes the compensation base on which your amount of contribution is calculated. If you can contribute 2% of your compensation base, does that include overtime, bonuses, and/or 401(k) contributions?

**Investigate:** Withdrawals. Some voluntary plans allow for "hardship" withdrawals, with penalties. Make sure you recognize the restrictions before you decide how much you want to contribute. Don't look at this as a liquid savings account. Normally you won't be able to tap into this type of account unless you meet strict hardship definitions (immediate and heavy financial burden for medical needs, house payments, tuition, prevention of eviction or foreclosure), and unless you have used all other available funds first.

**Investigate:** Can you arrange for a series of installments? Lump-sum payments? What is the difference in taxes you pay? Can you roll over the amount into another employee plan or an IRA, and what are the tax consequences? Also investigate how payments are made in the event of your death. Can you name your beneficiary? Must it be a spouse unless both of you sign papers to the contrary?

## LOOKING AT LIFE INSURANCE

Most life insurance sections of an employee benefits handbook focus on death. Your basic interest: how much your surviving beneficiaries will receive if you're no longer around to provide for them. Most company policies are term insurance, meaning they have no cash value and terminate after a specific period, for instance when you leave the company. They also often contain accidental death and dismemberment provisions. Some pay double for accidental death. Some pay scheduled amounts for loss of an arm, a leg, an eye, a hand, etc.

Besides checking how much coverage you have, you should find out if you can get more. A company's group rates may or may not be the best buy for your money. But the booklet should give you a list that looks something like this:

| Supplemental | Monthly Premium |
|---|---|
| $ 10,000 | $ 2.20 |
| 50,000 | 11.00 |
| 70,000 | 15.40 |
| 100,000 | 22.00 |

**Benefits alert:** See if there's a taxable-income explanation. In some cases, the IRS will hold you up for some of the extra amount of coverage you receive. Example: You're 55 and have $55,000 in basic and $50,000 in supplemental. The premium for the amount in excess of $50,000 is considered taxable income to you. Suppose the table shows the cost is $9 per thousand. So your premium for the excess would be $495. Suppose you paid $195 for your supplementary coverage and the company paid the balance of $300. Then $300 is taxable income for you for the year.▼

Accidental Death & Dismemberment insurance is often optional and employee-paid if it's not part of the life insurance policy. Your employer may give you a chart showing costs for extra coverage, but you should decide first if you really need it. You should also note any restrictions (AD&D might not pay for suicide or self-inflicted injury, etc.) and the percentage reductions at certain ages (check out chapter 4).

## CONVERTING YOUR CONVERSION OPTIONS

Portability is an important consideration in the modern world of work. "Cradle to grave" employment has been buried six feet under. So an important part of any company benefit is what you can do with it when you leave (or, heaven forfend, get bounced out of) the organization. That should be spelled out in company documents.

*Find out:*
- whether you can convert your term life insurance to a permanent personal policy, for which you'll have to pay the full premium (you may be able to do that without a physical exam, which could be an advantage);
- the same for voluntary AD&D insurance;
- how much of your profit sharing you're entitled to during the course of your employment, how soon you can get your hands on it, and how it will be paid out;
- when your pension plan will begin payout, and whether you can take it before then or even take it with you to another employer's plan (check out chapter 12);
- what your medical conversion rights are, and what qualifying events (e.g., death of covered employee) permit extended coverage for your spouse and dependents (check out chapter 4).

## INVESTING IN YOURSELF AND YOUR COMPANY

Many employers today are dangling employee stock purchase plans in front of their workers. They serve the dual purpose of giving employees advantages (usually a break in the stock price, an easy way to purchase, no broker fees) as well as tying employees more tightly to the company by giving them bigger stakes in its success.

Participation in such plans is not automatic, and you should beware of tying too much of your financial future to one company, even if it's your own. You may have a soft spot in your heart for your company. Just make sure that soft spot doesn't move to your head when making investment decisions.

*Find out:*

- the discount price of the stock, any annual limits on how much money you can spend on stock, and how many shares you can buy;
- what the prospects are for the company and its industry;
- whether you can dispose of stock as you wish after it is transferred to you;
- how you can cancel a payroll deduction;
- whether you lose future options to purchase if you decrease or discontinue your payroll deduction at any point.

Tax consequences are important in employee stock purchase plans. You'll need to seek professional advice on the specifics of your particular situation. Certain general tax implications are spelled out in chapter 8, which looks at investments. Some benefits booklets will give you an overview of taxes on company stock. Don't depend on it. Understand it, but go further with your research.

## STOCKING UP ON OTHER STOCK PLANS

You get a completely different angle on company stock with the employee stock option plan, or ESOP. If your company offers one, count your blessings. Then count your money. Actually, count your company's money, since in most cases it gives money to a trustee to buy company stock for the ESOP which is then allocated to your account.

You may get a document like figure 4. It's fairly self-explanatory. Your biggest concerns are how many shares you have and what they're worth.

*Find out:*

- when you can tap into your account. Some companies cash you out when you leave their employment; others hold on to your account as a "pension supplement" and dole it out at retirement time.

*Figure 4. Sample ESOP personal statement*

## COMPANY EMPLOYEE STOCK OWNERSHIP PLAN
### Statement of Account as of December 31, 19XX

Employee: _____
Date of Birth: _____
Date of Hire: _____

|  | Cash | Shares of Stock |
|---|---|---|
| ACCOUNT BALANCE (Date) | $0.00 | 400 |
| COMPANY CONTRIBUTION | N/A | 250 |
| FORFEITURES | $0.00 | 0.0000 |
| INVESTMENT EARNINGS | $0.00 | N/A |
| DIVIDENDS | $1,300.00 | N/A |
| DISTRIBUTION OF DIVIDENDS | $1,300.00 | N/A |
| ACCOUNT BALANCE (Date) | $0.00 | 650 |
| TOTAL ACCOUNT VALUE 12/31/XX | | 65,000.00 |
| VESTED PERCENTAGE | | 100% |
| VESTED BALANCE 12/31/XX | | $65,000.00 |

TO: (Name) as an eligible participant in ASC's ESOP as of (Date)

| Number of Shares Added | Total Shares in Your Account | Value per Share | Total Value |
|---|---|---|---|
| 250 | 650 | $100.00 | $65,000.00 |

Your 19XX Dividend = total shares × $2.00 = $1,300

Look over figure 5. It's an explanatory notice that lays out the details of one company's ESOP. You'll see the four events that trigger payment, as well as the "cutoff number" for receiving a vested balance on termination of employment.

*Figure 5. Details of an ESOP*

---

### ESOP: (COMPANY) EMPLOYEE STOCK OWNERSHIP

The purpose of this notice is to advise you of your benefits under (Company) Employee Stock Ownership Plan. Attached to this Notice is a statement of your account as of (date).

Normally, the Plan Administrator will distribute the value of your vested interest not earlier than the occurrence of one of the following events:

(a) Upon your retirement at age 65.
(b) Upon your early retirement at age 55 if you completed five years of service with the company.
(c) Upon your death.
(d) In the event you become totally and permanently disabled.

However, if the value of your vested account balance is $3,500 or less, a distribution of your vested account balance will be made within a reasonable time after you incur five consecutive one-year breaks in service.

It is your responsibility to notify the Employer or Plan Administrator of any changes of address. Otherwise, we will be unable to locate you.

Until a distribution occurs, your vested interest will continue to earn interest income until the end of the Plan Year preceding the date of your distribution.

For the Plan Administrator _____

---

## SUMMARIZING A SUMMARY PLAN DESCRIPTION (SPD)

Much of the information you've just read about is what a Summary Plan Description (SPD), as opposed to a full employee benefits booklet, should contain. When you read an actual Summary Plan Description, look for the same factors and attributes pointed out here.

That SPD will contain another important feature: names and addresses. It will list the people to contact with your questions and tell you who's in charge of different programs, so you can investigate further. It should also tell you how to appeal claims or rights which have been denied, with deadlines and checklists of what kinds of information you're entitled to. Don't skip over this section. Know your rights. Then assert them.

You may also see a legal section in the SPD. Read it too. It provides a condensed version of what you'll read about in chapters 14 and 15. Basically, it tells you that you are entitled to certain rights and protections under the Employee Retirement Income Security Act of 1974 (ERISA). ERISA provides that all participants in employee benefits plans are entitled to:

- examine and copy documents;
- receive summaries of annual financial reports;
- obtain statements on pension rights.

No one, including your employer or any other person, may fire you or otherwise discriminate against you in any way to prevent you from obtaining a pension or welfare benefit or exercising your rights under ERISA.

If your claim for a pension or welfare benefit is denied in whole or in part, you must receive a written explanation of the reason for the denial. You have the right to have the plan administrators review and reconsider your claim.

Now that you have had a brief review of company benefits documents, take a look in the following chapters at the specifics you need to know.

*Pete Lydecker (and you) should be feeling a little more confident about employee benefits now. It may be a jungle out there, but there's some light sifting through. The ensuing chapters will give you personal searchlights for spotlighting exactly what you need to know.*

# 3

▼

# FLEXIBLE
# BENEFITS

*Choosing What You Need from the
Benefits Menu*

## THE CASE OF THE FOODLESS MENU

Janice Wong had heard the rumors for a while. Personnel was brewing up another change in the employee benefits package, and this time it would be a doozy. Not just a new wrinkle in retirement or an added charge for health coverage.

This time it was going to be a dramatic change in the entire system. This time employees like Janice would have no choice but to get involved. Because it was a system of choices that was coming, what the company called a cafeteria system.

Janice had vaguely heard about such programs, and while she knew they had nothing to do with food, she didn't really understand the nuts and bolts of what such flexible benefits programs involved. Now she would need to know.

The subject of flexible benefits deserves its own chapter, although it's not a benefit per se. It's a program that encompasses a variety of other employment benefits, and it has assumed increasing importance in the benefits landscape over the last few years. Some think it will be *the* benefits-delivery mechanism of the 1990s. And why not? According to one employee survey, nine out of ten want input into the design of their benefits program.

Flexible benefits is currently the proverbial nine-hundred-pound gorilla. It can sit anywhere it wants, and it gets called "Sir" at all times. No matter whom you work for over the years, chances are very good that at some time an employer will offer you the options of a flexible or cafeteria program.

Choice, as you've read, is the wave of the future in employee benefits. And the future is now. Choices include what kind of health plan to sign up for, an HMO or PPO or fee-for-service plan; how much life insurance to buy, and whether to get supplemental; how, and how much, to invest in your retirement plan. All those choices and more will be on your menu, which goes by the name of flexible benefits. What you select for your own plate is up to you.

The major advantages in flex are: a) You control your own benefits destiny; b) you feed your own priorities; c) most flex payments you make are in pretax dollars, which lowers your base tax rate; and d) you often get to use your employer's money as well as your own to shape a package custom-tailored to your situation.

The drawbacks are: a) You need to become—and remain—more informed; b) you must accept the challenge of choices; and c) you've got to share more of the risks that result from the benefits choices you make.

## FLEXING YOUR FLEX MUSCLES

*Flex* and *cafeteria* are interchangeable idioms, but basically you get this: a menu and a budget or credits. Sort of like Monopoly money. You decide which benefit to "land on" and how much you'd like to pay. You choose what and how much to "buy" from among your options in medical, dental, life, disability, time off, etc. This makes it a more individual program. So a working single mother, for example, might use some of her credits for child care; a 55-year-old widower doesn't need that, so he might put more of his credits into a pension retirement plan; a young, healthy worker isn't overly interested in those options, so she chooses to spend her credits on extra vacation time.

Figure 6 reflects two typical explanations of flexible benefits package options offered by major companies.

## *MEDICAL BENEFITS TO CHOOSE FROM*

Your variables in a flex plan will usually include several levels of health insurance coverage (from weak to comprehensive) as well as services like HMOs. Turn the mirror on your own situation: Are you single and healthy? Head of household with spouse and three need-their-braces children? Senior employee with a spouse who works part time? Each situation calls for different choices, as you'll see in the next chapter.

Think about the health situation of anyone you want covered. Give some thought to your ability to pay premiums, deductibles, copayments, and any other out-of-pocket expenses. Consider how you'd face a heavy uncovered financial burden caused by poor health.

---

**Benefits alert:** If you and your spouse both have health coverage and one has flexible options, check out double coverage and see if you can divert some flex funds to other needed benefits. But be sure you can return to the flex plan you drop if you need to at some future point.▼

---

If you're the king or queen of the castle and your family's health care bills are rather regal, then you should be leaning toward the more comprehensive coverages—which are, of course, more expensive. But don't immediately jump on such an offering. Check HMOs first. They might offer better coverage at comparable costs. If you can accept the lack of flexibility in such a flex option, take the HMO option.

Singles who don't use many of their medical benefits are likely to do better with less expensive options. Families usually come out better by taking advantage of managed care options that provide more payments and coverages (check out chapter 4).

*Figure 6. Actual flex options at two firms*

## FLEX DECISION: PICK AND CHOOSE

**At (Company), these are your flexible benefits options.**

1. Any of four medical plans. Each offers different combinations of deductibles and copayments; one is specifically tailored to the needs of new parents and includes extra coverage for infants' health care.
2. Dental coverage.
3. Vision care.
4. Dependent life insurance.
5. Either of two long-term disability plans.
6. Life insurance with coverage in the range of one to three times employee's annual salary.
7. Accidental death and dismemberment benefits up to $1 million.
8. Two pretax spending accounts.

In this plan, each employee gets an "allowance" with which to pay for his or her benefits, ranging from $91 to $253.50 per month, depending on the employee's family status. Each of the eight benefit options comes with a price tag, and the employee can use that allowance to pay for the benefits he or she chooses from those offered. If the price of the benefits selected exceeds the employee's allowance, the difference is made up through payroll deductions. If the employee doesn't use the full amount of the allowance, the difference is added to his or her paycheck.

Here's another plan:

| Benefit Area | Options |
|---|---|
| Medical | 1. $150/$450 deductible, 80% coinsurance |
| | 2. $350/$1,050 deductible, 80% coinsurance |
| | 3. $1,000/$3,000 deductible, 80% coinsurance |
| Dental | 1. $25 deductible (for each person covered) |
| | 2. $50 deductible (for each person covered) |
| | 3. No coverage |
| Life/AD&D | 1. 2 x pay |
| | 2. 1 x pay |
| | 3. $10,000 |

| Long-term disability | 1. 66% of pay |
| | 2. 50% of pay |
| | 3. No coverage |
| Spending accounts | 1. Health care |
| | 2. Dependent care |

The options remain the same for all employees. But credits and costs vary by business unit.

The actual number of credits allocated to each employee depends on the financial requirements of the business unit where he or she is working.

---

Example of the medical portion of a flexible plan: Managers at a major telecommunications firm get a $260 monthly allowance that covers complete medical/dental. They can choose a cheaper plan with a higher deductible. That way, they earn credits that they can use to "purchase" nonmedical benefits, like extra days of vacation. They have similar choices in insurance, long-term care, and other categories.

In chapter 2 you read about how to read benefits documents, and in chapter 4 you'll see how to hack your way through health plans. But as a quick barometer, figure out how much you spent on health bills in each of the last three years. Then compare the average to the cost/coverage of your options. You may be surprised to see you can "afford" a lesser option that covers what you need the most, and costs less.

## *LIFE INSURANCE OPTIONS AND OPPORTUNITIES*

Most companies pick up the tab for the lowest-cost option and offer you the opportunity to supplement that option by paying for more yourself. Don't overbuy. However, the more people who depend on you, and the fewer assets you can count as yours, the more insurance you can use.

**Benefits alert:** Don't automatically buy into the company group insurance if you're supplementing. You might get a better deal on term insurance from a personal policy. Shop around.▼

## MORE BENEFITS, MORE CHOICES

Two of the biggest trends to trip down the benefits pike in recent years are 401(k) investment vehicles (check out chapter 7) and flexible spending accounts (see below).

If you have an option to use a 401(k) and don't, you're not just missing the boat. You've fallen overboard and the sharks are circling. It's a deal. You kick in money that lowers your taxable income base. Your employer usually kicks in a certain matching percentage. (It's all gravy, right?) That raises your interest-earning base with no effort at all on your part. All the money then grows, tax-free. You can even make the choices (sometimes) of exactly where the money is invested, when it gets moved, and how much goes where.

So now you've contributed a chunk of your money and watched it mix with your employer's bucks. New information and expanding choices are always popping up, many sparked by government regulations, as you'll see in chapter 7.

## FLEXIBLE SPENDING ACCOUNTS (FSAS)

Also called reimbursement accounts, these work a little like a tax magician to turn ordinary dependent care or health expenses into tax deductions. Basically you store up an untaxed mound of money to pay for costs not covered under other benefits plans or for care of a child or dependent disabled parent. You fund individual accounts (normally $2,500 for a health care FSA and $5,000 for dependent care, the latter being a limit set by law), either with flex credits from your budgeted balance or with payroll deductions.

You can siphon money out of your *health care account* to pay for any expenses considered deductible by the tax code, including dental/vision care and deductibles for your regular medical coverage.

When you use the bucks in your *dependent care account*, the standards are the same as those governing the deductions you can claim on your tax return (e.g., the expense must be incurred so you can work). Note: You can't double dip, claiming the tax deduction and seeking an FSA reimbursement for the same expense.

Your tax savings in an FSA can be substantial. On the federal level, if you're in the 15% tax bracket and you salt away $1,000, you save $150 right off the bat. Suppose your employer sets the max at $3,000 and you're in the 28% bracket. You immediately save $840. Plus, most states give you a break on that money too, so you'll save maybe another 5% to 7%.

Basically an FSA requires that you predict how much you'll spend in a given year for the health or dependent care expenses that you want covered by this vehicle. The amount you designate is then divvied up and funneled out of your paycheck into the FSA, before you pay taxes on it.

Your purchasing power may even be boosted by your employer contributing either a flat amount or a matching amount into your FSA kitty.

---

**Benefits alert:** FSAs are subject to the "use it or lose it" dictum. If you think your expenses will hit $3,000 but they only reach $2,500, you're out the $500. Of course, you most likely have already saved that much in tax reductions.▼

---

## *OTHER FLEX OPTIONS TO BE AWARE OF*

**Dental**—From routine exams, cleaning, X-rays, and fluoride treatment to restorative services (fillings, root canal), major surgery, and orthodontics. This type of benefit, along with vision and hearing, is usually loaded with restrictions, such as mandatory two-year coverage before you can collect, low maximum caps, and "customary and reasonable" definition reins. Usually you get an all-or-nothing choice in these areas, without escalating options. Best bet: Use flexible spending credits to pay for routine dental/vision benefits with pretax dollars if they are a major part of your family's medical future.

**Time off**—While vacation time has long been a staple of benefits, it's now often combined with other time-off benefits or offered as an extra that you can buy with flex credits. Some companies lump sick and personal days with vacation time. You can add to that base amount by "buying" more time. Even holidays have become more "flexible." That's good news for dual-career families whose schedules might not otherwise coincide.

**Education**—Today, with education a prime focus of the new American workplace, you can get educational benefits money for a wide variety of activities. Besides a straight allowance for work-oriented education programs (and sometimes cash bonuses for straight A's!), there are other benefit connections to education, such as scholarships for employees' children.

## BENEFITS CHECKOFF: NEWER BENEFITS ON THE RISE

The basic thrust of flexible benefits is to load your benefits bag with goodies that will appeal to you. That means more and different types of benefits will be available, as employers seek both less expensive and better value options to retain their best employees. Some of the following options you may have seen, some may not be available, and some may be buried in the fine print of your benefits booklet. Root them out. In fact, if they're not offered, see if you can get your employer to plug them in.

Here are some of the latest that might pop up in your benefits "in" box:

✔ Adoption—Some companies will pay expenses associated with adoption for agency, legal, and medical fees, up to a specified amount (usually around $2,000; more for "special needs" children).

✔ Legal services—This is usually an adjunct to a flex program, but one that is attracting more and more flex credits. It covers areas like consumer disputes, wills, and real estate transactions and may offer discounts on professional services. Note: Some plans are called "open panel"; you get to choose your own lawyer. Others are "closed panel"; you must use the attorney designated for you. For more information, contact: The National Resource Center, 1441 I Street NW, 8th Floor, Washington, DC 20005.

✔ Financial education classes—Another rising benefit, these are offered to help you decide what benefits to take, how to invest what you've got, financial-planning moves to make, and strategies to follow; offered either in-house or through professionals. Clamor for this one.

✔ Mass transit—Under a little-known provision of the National Energy Security Act, employers can provide tax-free vouchers, passes, tokens, or tickets up to a certain maximum per month ($60 in 1993) to employees who use mass transit or other qualified transportation (like van pools) to get to and from work; you can't get cash, and if you get more than the maximum amount, it's taxable; otherwise you pay no taxes and don't even have to show it on your income tax return.

✔ Housing assistance—Again the government is involved in trying to help the growing number of employees who are on the move: The Fannie Mae program has come up with a billion-dollar investment effort aimed at employer-sponsored housing-assistance programs.

✔ Sabbaticals—Most are unpaid-time-off deals, many tied to performing some type of community or public service, or training that will positively affect job performance.

✔ Nontraditional-partner benefits—Some companies are redefining what they consider family, especially in light of gay domestic partners and live-in family; a few companies even cover qualified dependents of homosexual employee couples (check out chapter 13).

✔ Little perks—Even these are getting more important.

Among them is direct deposit of paychecks, which can save both the company and employee time and can bump up interest return for the employee.

*Many times when employees are hit with the myriad options of a flexible benefits program, their first reaction is to curl up like a porcupine and repel information. Janice Wong did just the opposite by making like a sponge and soaking up all she could learn. So should you.*

# 4
▼

# HEALTH
# BENEFITS

*Your Prescription for Insuring That
They're Healthy*

## THE CASE OF THE OPEN POCKETBOOK

Nola Olivieri played tennis twice a week, watched her weight with the help of some friendly gibes from her co-workers, and prided herself on rarely missing work because of illness. She considered herself healthy, and lucky to be that.

She had also never had any reason to review her company-sponsored health insurance. Until she came down with a nagging cold.

Not able to shake it, she went to a doctor with whom she often played tennis. A series of tests were scheduled, and completed on consecutive Saturday-morning visits to the doctor's office.

After struggling with the unfamiliar claims form, Nola finally got it filled out and sent in. She knew she paid a premium every month that came out of her salary. And she knew she wasn't going to collect every penny of the bills she had rung up.

What she didn't know was the coinsurance amounts she was obligated to cover, the high deductible that ate away at the total she expected to be reimbursed for, and the individual tests that were excluded from the plan she was covered under.

*She found all that out the hard way, when her health care coverage turned out to leave her pocketbook sorely uncovered. Nola paid for being lulled into a false sense of security by her good health.*

*Moral of the story: Your health insurance coverage may not be as healthy as you are. Conduct a checkup.*

## HOW VALUABLE ARE YOUR HEALTH CARE BENEFITS?

In many cases, the second-greatest source of compensation after your paycheck is your health care benefits plan. But you can't fall back on the old "any health care plan my company offers will take care of me" attitude.

It doesn't work that way anymore. You've got to take care of your health plan. You've got to massage it so it fits you, make sure it's not overweight with excess coverage, give it the proper financial funding so it grows strong enough to take care of your health problems.

**How important is health care?** It's the *numero uno* worry for Americans today, according to one survey, edging out paying taxes, finding a job, and educating one's children.

**How much is it changing?** Irreversibly. You're paying more of your premium. Deductibles are higher. Copayments (where you pay a fixed fee toward the cost of each service you use) and coinsurance (where you pay a percentage of each bill above a deductible, and your insurance company pays the rest) are more popular. Claims payers are tighter with reimbursements, often opening their wallets only for "reasonable or customary" usage (which means that bills flying above a typical range for a specific service in a specific region will be shot down).

**How do you judge your health plan?** By how well it protects you during traumatic injuries and illnesses, not how it handles minor bumps and bruises. In the new scheme of things, the one that protects you best in an emergency is likely better for you than the one that reimburses you the most for a $50 doctor's office visit.

**How confusing is the situation?** You get more selection,

more choices, more responsibility, more trade-offs. You get more restrictions, more costs, more treatment exclusions, more watchdog measures.

**How does the future look?** You'll see even more changes, with trends toward precertification of nonemergency treatment (that means raising your hand and asking for permission from a third party in order to get the okay for surgery or specialists); review firms that pass judgment on the doctors and hospitals you can use based on their efficiency; benefit caps, especially for mental health and drug/alcohol abuse; encouragement of the use of outpatient facilities; and second opinions for non-elective surgery.

---

**Benefits alert:** Health care plans are even being tied to another hot benefits area, 401(k) deferred-tax savings plans. A large food-industry firm sat down at the table with a major union and came up with a network care plan designed to save money through managed care. The twist: The company will make matching contributions to the new 401(k) program based on savings from the health care plan strategy.▼

---

## GETTING DOWN TO THE BASICS

You'll come across more types of health insurance plans than you can shake a stick at on the market today. But basically you've got to get on speaking terms with four kinds of health benefit plans:

1. Indemnity—The traditional way of handling health insurance. Basically, an insurance company agrees to reimburse you (indemnify you) for a specific percentage of your actual hospital and medical expenses. You see the doctors you prefer, pay for their services up front, and send your claims to the insurance company.

2. HMO—The biggest headline generator is today's trend toward managed care. A Health Maintenance Organization provides health services that are paid for by an employer on a flat-cost basis for each person enrolled. HMOs are less ex-

pensive than indemnity plans because they negotiate with a select group of hospitals and physicians to treat you and others in the plan.

3. PPO—A growing managed care option. A Preferred Provider Organization is a group of health care providers in the community which agrees to offer health care to groups of consumers/employees at a negotiated rate. Regular PPOs provide health care consumers with a list of doctors and hospitals to choose from. Exclusive Provider Organizations (EPOs) limit consumers' choices to only a few doctors and hospitals designated by the plan.

**Note:** You should also know about Individual Practice Associations (IPAs), which are associations of independent physicians in private practice who buy memberships in the association, which is usually administered by an HMO. Patients choose from among a list of these association providers but are restricted to hospitals within the network. Patients opting out of the network usually pay their own way.

4. Service—A service plan guarantees subscribers that it will pay for covered health care services. Participating physicians typically send in each patient's claims themselves. A commonly known example is Blue Cross/Blue Shield.

## BENEFITS CHECKOFF: CHOOSING A DOCTOR

The freedom of choosing your own doctor is going the way of sub-six-foot basketball players. Don't depend on it. But if you do get the opportunity, factor in all these conditions before making a choice:

✔ What are your primary health care needs? Will you need a family physician or a specialist most often?

✔ What is the physician's reputation? Check with family, friends, neighbors, or other physicians in the community.

✔ Find out whether the doctor has ever been restricted from

practicing medicine. You can verify this type of information through your state Board of Examiners.

✔ Check whether the doctor has admitting privileges at your local hospital.

✔ Don't stop with just the physician. What about his or her colleagues and staff? Give the nurses a once-over. Is it easy to get in to see the doctor? Will you see that doctor every time, or will you be shuttled around? Is the office open after normal working hours? Does it have an urgent-care facility?

✔ See if the physician has a list of fees for usual services. Are they comparable to other area physicians' fees? Will the physician discuss the cost of medical treatment in advance, so you can make cost comparisons with other area physicians?

✔ Finally, choose a physician who will present you with options for medical treatment and who will allow you to have a role in discussing what should be done.

## THE HOTTEST TOPIC: MANAGED CARE

Employers who adopt managed health care are really taking up an idea that originated in the health care business itself. The Health Maintenance Organization, or HMO, has been called the purest form of managed care.

The U.S. Department of Health and Human Services defines an HMO, along with its more newly arrived cousins, as a "managed health-care plan that provides or arranges for the delivery of comprehensive, coordinated medical services to voluntarily enrolled members on a prepaid basis." Note the word *managed*. Just like a business. In fact, it is a business. It's also the latest prescription in the pharmacy of health-care cost-containment strategies.

In 1973, Congress sought to encourage HMO development with the Health Maintenance Organization Act. This act was adopted as an alternative to the traditional fee-for-service or indemnity plan. The act defined the structure of the typical HMO. Its goal was to deliver services economically, with participants and providers sharing the risk equally.

Participating employers pay fixed fees once a year. In return, employees are entitled to the full range of HMO services as needed. This is a major incentive for the provider to avoid unnecessary treatment and hospitalization. In addition, HMO services are managed in a controlled environment. A physician decides on the factors and criteria necessary for a patient to receive health care services.

## BENEFITS CHECKOFF: SIX POINTS OF COMPARISON

If your employer's plan offers you an option, check out the differences between traditional insurance and HMOs:

- ✔ Choice of provider—optional with traditional insurance, regulated by HMOs.
- ✔ Concentration on preventive health care—not so much with traditional insurance, heavy emphasis with HMOs.
- ✔ The pain of forms filing—constant with traditional insurance, absent with HMOs.
- ✔ Regional restrictions—not present in traditional insurance, a source of employee discontent in HMOs.
- ✔ Copayments—not so much with traditional insurance, possible with HMOs.
- ✔ Reimbursements for routine care—not the case with traditional insurance, often the case in HMOs.

HMOs have their pluses and minuses. On the plus side, they tend to emphasize preventive health care and cover a wide range of services, including well-child care and routine immunizations that are often not covered under indemnity plans. Members are charged only a small copayment for visits. Unnecessary and inappropriate treatments can be prevented by working with a primary-care physician who oversees your total medical care, thus decreasing unnecessary utilization. On the downside, you're very likely to be strictly limited in your choice of doctors.

Figure 7 is an example of how one company explained its various HMO offerings. Notice it starts with a disclaimer and ends by telling the employee recipient to ask for more information.

## *BENEFITS CHECKOFF: CHOOSING AN HMO*

If you have a choice among HMOs, as the employees in figure 7 did, you should investigate these areas:

- ✔ How does the HMO compensate its doctors? Some HMO physicians earn more money if they prescribe less care. Some have money withheld until their record for referrals and hospitalizations is analyzed as over or under target.
- ✔ Can you find any statistics on the complaints about the HMO's doctors or services? Some HMOs do surveys of customer satisfaction, to find out how long is spent in waiting rooms, how courteous a staff is, and whether the members would recommend the HMO to friends.
- ✔ Are any statistics available on doctor turnover within the HMO? That could indicate internal problems.
- ✔ What about accreditation? The National Committee for Quality Assurance is one organization that rates HMOs.

## *PROBING THE PPO ALTERNATIVE*

One of the fastest-growing types of alternative delivery systems or managed care is the Preferred Provider Organization (PPO). It represents a compromise between an HMO and a strict fee-for-service system.

PPOs are generally part of an indemnity medical plan. You get reimbursed for a percentage of your payments to physicians, hospitals, pharmacies, and laboratories. There is a maximum out-of-pocket expense and usually a fixed deductible each year.

PPO plans may cover emergency room treatment without the deductible. Many have optional dental care, eye care, etc. PPOs can be expensive because of high costs, deductibles, and copayments.

*Figure 7. How one company described its HMO options*

## AN ACTUAL HMO EXPLANATION

**While any HMO offered must meet certain requirements of (Company) to be offered, specifically federal qualifications, we do not certify as to the quality of medical care provided by any HMO.**

### What does an HMO offer you?

HMOs offer you a comprehensive benefits package including coverage for "wellness" items such as physical examinations and immunizations in exchange for monthly premiums and usually a copayment each time care is received.

HMO members choose their doctors from a list of physicians contracted with or employed by the HMO.

HMOs have no deductibles and no claim forms to fill out.

### What do you give up?

You give up the right to an unrestricted choice of health care providers. Other than when out of the HMO service area or in an emergency, your care must come from the physicians, hospitals, and laboratories contracted with by your HMO.

It should be noted that some employees who elect HMO coverage will occasionally use physicians or services not contracted with or payable by the HMO. In those cases, however, the employee assumes responsibility for all the expenses incurred.

A summary of the benefits available from the HMOs available in your area is attached.

**Note:** Dental coverage will be offered under some HMO packages either as part of the program or as an optional rider.

Participation is not automatic. You must elect to join either (a) within the open enrollment period or (b) at the time you have completed three months of service (date of employment for exempt employees and officers).

The first payroll deduction commences on the 30th (last day) of the month prior to the effective date of your coverage. If you elect to join an HMO during the open enrollment period, your first payroll deduction will be made on _____.

It should be noted that the benefits are not the same under each HMO the company has contracted with, and some benefits provided under the traditional company policy are not provided under the

HMOs. Similarly, some benefits provided under the HMOs are not provided under the company policy. You should compare the benefits and costs closely.

**Selecting an HMO:** If you are interested in an HMO and think one might be right for you, review the informational packets and provider lists and ask the HMO representative any questions you have.

Confused as to which one might be best for you? Ask your physician or dentist which one or ones they belong to. That way you can keep your same doctors and dentists. Check the hospitals. If you need to go to a hospital, does the HMO offer coverage at the one you like?

---

In some PPOs, each patient can select a primary-physician case manager to serve as a personal physician. That means your regular doctor is also the one to whom you raise your hand to ask for special services.

If a PPO is on your health benefits table, chew on these key characteristics:

- They use a panel of physicians and hospitals that have been designated as "preferred" because they can provide cost-effective service.
- They charge negotiated fee schedules that are usually discounted from prevailing charges.
- You have your choice of providers. You are not required to accept the services of doctors designated by someone else.
- The financial incentives normally include reduced deductibles and copayments to encourage you to use PPO providers. You can still go outside the plan, but you'll usually pay through the nose to do so.

## LOTS OF OPTIONS POPPING UP

While today's managed care offerings usually fall under the HMO or PPO plan categories, there are a number of hybrids taking root in the health-care field.

One new sprout: the "point-of-service" (POS) product. It's a cross between the managed care of an HMO and the freedom of choice of traditional fee-for-service health insurance. Your major choice: in-network or out-of-network.

As the name suggests, in-network means you can use any of the health care providers participating in the company network, at substantial cost savings. If you opt out of the network, you have the freedom to use any physician, thus maintaining relationships with doctors not in the network. But the costs are substantial, compared with those of in-network users.

Plus, if you stay in-network, you avoid the administrative hassles connected with the more traditional coverage.

Even when you opt to stay in-network in a POS, you might be offered optional coverages. One company gave its employees a high/low choice. Among the differences:

- High had a $15 office visit copayment; low was $20.
- High's deductible was $150 single, $300 family; low was $500/$1,000.
- High offered 90 percent coinsurance; low was at 80 percent.

Employees at that firm really needed a road map for their health care choices. They could also get a straight indemnity plan ($300/$600 deductible and 80 percent coinsurance); an HMO with 100 percent coinsurance; or a PPO with a $15 co-payment per office visit, 90 percent coinsurance, and a $150/$300 deductible.

## WANT TO SEE NEW APPROACHES IN ACTION?

A large oil company experimented with a point-of-service managed care program for about 10,000 employees in one region. The company scrapped its former indemnity and HMO options and replaced them with a designated network of some twenty-one hospitals and eight hundred physicians.

Instead of deciding once a year between indemnity and HMO coverage, employees are in two plans simultaneously. Each time they need medical service, they can choose in-network or out-of-network providers. If they stay in the network, the company pays 80 percent of their expenses; if they go outside, it pays only 70 percent.

A major bank developed a similar program. It offered a provider network of doctors and hospitals through a standard insurance carrier, designed to operate somewhat like an HMO.

Employees who chose a network provider would not pay deductibles. There would be a flat $10 copayment for an office visit. Employees would also receive special wellness services, such as mammograms and well-baby care. Employees who went outside the network would be subject to standard deductibles and copayments and would not get the benefit of wellness care.

## TRIPLE OPTION

Some health care experts say they foresee a managed care system that won't limit choices at all. They envision widespread use of a flexible benefits system that gives employees a "triple option." This is a choice of (a) an HMO, (b) a PPO, or (c) traditional indemnity insurance, with the choice made at the point of service.

In this hybrid, employers will agree on a set premium with an insurer and offer employees the ability to select their coverage when they need to see a doctor, rather than at the beginning of each year. If an employee opts for a physician on the traditional indemnity insurance side, it simply will cost more.

## TAKING THE HASSLE OUT OF CLAIMS FORMS

One of the major benefits of managed care is that you get claims forms off your back. But if you're still stuck with the task, you can make it less excruciating. In fact, most insurance companies are trying to simplify the process too.

If you've never filled out a form before, have your company's benefits person walk you through it. After the first time, keep a copy of the filled-out version in your personal file at work.

Figure 8 gives you a potpourri of items you're likely to find on a typical form. Practice on it. Important points:

1. Fill in every nook and cranny. Don't give an insurer an excuse to delay the process by sending back the form, marked "incomplete."
2. In describing the "nature of illness or injury," use the doctor's terms and phrases. Attach his or her medical report. It's a language you may not understand, but insurers do.
3. Make sure the company's policy number is on the form. If you have to fill it in, double-check it.
4. Read the hints carefully. Review your bill with your doctor if necessary to make sure it's complete.
5. Watch out for "assignment" of benefits. If you have to pay your doctor up front, you don't want him/her getting your insurance check too.

## CLAIM DENIED—WHAT THEN?

Suppose you're charged $3,000 for a medical procedure. You carefully fill out the claim, cross the t's and dot the i's, and confidently wait for your reimbursement.

When it comes, you're stunned to see it's for $2,500. Reason: The "reasonable and customary" provision. The three grand was considered too high for ordinary circumstances. Are you stuck? Maybe yes, maybe no. You may not have any recourse, but don't pull a Charlie Brown and meekly accept your fate. Put up your dukes.

## BENEFITS CHECKOFF: GETTING WHAT YOU THINK IS COMING

✔ Be aware of the "reasonable and customary" clause from the beginning. Shop around. Ask up front what the charges will be. Compare several quotes, especially in a nonemergency situation. Then check with your benefits contract to find out

*Figure 8. Components of a typical health claims form*

## CLAIM FOR BENEFITS

1. I HEREBY APPLY FOR BENEFITS FOR ❑ SELF ❑ SPOUSE ❑ UNMARRIED CHILD (❑ UNDER 19, ❑ FULL-TIME STU-DENT UNDER 23) in connection with sickness or injury not aris-ing out of or in the course of any employment. I authorize any insurance company, organization, employer, hospital, or physician to release information with respect to myself or any of my depen-dents regarding benefits payable under this or any other plan pro-viding benefits or services.

2. Employee name:
   Address:
   Social Security number:
   Status: ❑ Active ❑ Retired ❑ COBRA

3. Patient's name:
   Patient's sex: ❑ M ❑ F
   Patient's date of birth:
   Relation to employee:

4. Is claim due to an accident? ❑ Yes ❑ No
   If yes, where did accident occur?
   Describe accident:
   Is claim due to illness or injury? ❑ Yes ❑ No
   Describe:

5. Enter type and dollar amount of your claim: $
   ❑ Chiropractor ❑ Medical ❑ Dental ❑ Vision
   ❑ Orthodontic ❑ Psychiatric

6. Do you wish to assign benefits? ❑ Yes ❑ No
   If yes, please make assignment on reverse side. Assignment made at hospital or doctor's office cannot be reversed.

7. Is this claim the result of a work-related illness or injury?
   ❑ Yes ❑ No
   Pregnancy? ❑ Yes ❑ No
   Employee's (your) marital status: ❑ Single ❑ Married

8. If married, is your wife/husband employed or self-employed?
   Does your spouse work for (Company)? ❑ Yes ❑ No
   Your spouse's employer, if not (Company):

9. Your spouse's date of birth:
   Your spouse's Social Security number:

10. Is this patient also covered under any other group health or government plan? ❑ Yes ❑ No

If yes, give name address of insurance carrier (e.g., Blue Cross, Medicare, Medicaid):

Identification number:

If yes, give details on amount of coverage and amounts paid, if any:

11. Employee's (your) work location:

Telephone number:

12. Employee's (your) signature:_____Date:_____

13. ANY PERSON WHO KNOWINGLY AND WITH INTENT TO INJURE, DEFRAUD, OR DECEIVE ANY INSURANCE COMPANY, FILES A STATEMENT OF CLAIM CONTAINING ANY FALSE, INCOMPLETE, OR MISLEADING INFORMATION MAY BE GUILTY OF A CRIMINAL ACT PUNISHABLE UNDER LAW.

14. Hints for submitting claims:

- If you want _____ to pay benefits directly to the provider of medical services, write "pay directly" prominently on the bill(s):
- Attach your bills to this completed form and mail them to _____ _____ at the address shown above.
- Make sure all bills indicate the reason (diagnosis) for treatment and list the date, type, and cost of each service.
- Send additional bills periodically or when they total $_____ _____ or more.

---

what the company's policy considers reasonable and customary.

✔ Negotiate in advance if there is a discrepancy between what you'll be charged and what you'll be reimbursed. Try to gain a compromise.

✔ If you're already stuck with the bill, check it with a fine-tooth comb. Are all the procedures correctly identified? All the tests explained? Were they all conducted?

✔ Make sure the reason for being denied is an acceptable one, and not due to carelessness, like missing documentation or transposed code numbers. Always check charges for human and computer error, for duplication, for tests that were scheduled but then canceled. Even if your claim wasn't denied, you should still check. The money you save isn't only your employer's. It's yours, especially when you pay premiums, copayments, and deductibles.

✔ Check for extenuating circumstances that might negate the reasonable and customary parameter. Maybe there were medical complications or other logical reasons for higher fees.

There are other reasons besides reasonable and customary charges or inaccurate documentation that may lead to denial of a claim.

An insurer may say that a procedure wasn't a medical necessity. Get your doctor to back you up if that happens. In fact, the more the merrier. Obtain some second opinions.

A pre-existing condition—a disease, disorder, or health condition judged to exist before coverage started—can be a sticking point in a claims denial. You should know right from the get-go how your insurer deals with such a situation.

## *JUDGING YOUR HEALTH CARE PLAN*

So your company offers you a plan—or two or three. How do you tell how good it is, or judge among your choices?

When you are trying to decipher what your plan offers, there are six key sections of the plan you should examine:

1. Summary of benefits—This section sums up, in one or two pages, all your benefits. The summary should provide you with a good overview of the plan. You'll have to read the entire plan, of course, for more specific information and to check the fine print.
2. Premium—The premium is the monthly payment you make to your health insurance company, HMO, or PPO. Usually, your share of the premium is taken directly out of your paycheck. Most employers contribute to the cost of your health insurance as well. Some employers pay all the premium for their employees, but this is becoming less common as costs increase. Insurance companies typically offer different premium rates for single people, married

people, and married people with children. Find out how much you are paying for your monthly premium and who your insurance is covering.

3. Deductibles—This section tells you how much extra you must pay when you actually use the insurance. Your deductible is a specific dollar amount that you must pay for covered services in a year's time before your insurance kicks in.

4. Coinsurance—This is a form of cost sharing between you and your health insurance company. After you meet your deductible, you must pay a percentage of each additional bill you submit to the insurance company. So you pay a percentage of your health costs and your insurance company pays the rest. A typical coinsurance ratio is 20 percent (what you pay) to 80 percent (what your insurance pays).

5. Exclusions—This section tells you what health problems or situations the plan will not cover. Be sure to read it carefully. Many plans will not cover pre-existing conditions— health problems that began before you joined the plan. Many policies limit or exclude coverage for specific diseases or conditions, such as organ transplants or mental illnesses. Or they put a cap on AIDS-related payments, for example.

6. Filing claims—In some plans, you may have to pay for your health care first and then submit your receipts with a claim form to the health insurance company. Some plans will accept a claim directly from your physician. In other plans, the process varies. Many plans nowadays require you to get advance permission before receiving certain types of care, including hospitalization.

## KEY QUESTIONS TO ASK ABOUT YOUR PLAN

Here's a rundown of the key questions you need to answer in order to judge how well your current health plan covers you, and how cost-effective it really is:

✔ How much is your monthly premium? (Can you afford more, to get better coverage? Or pay less, to shift your money to a more cost-effective use?)

✔ How much is the annual deductible? (The higher you make it, the lower your premium.)

✔ What costs count toward the deductible? What costs don't? (The more that count, the faster you use up the deductible and get into the insurance.)

✔ How much is the coinsurance? (Ideally you'd like to pay nothing.)

✔ Is there an annual limit on how much the plan will pay? (Can you "afford" a lower limit?)

✔ What physical health problems are excluded? (Do you or your family need those covered?)

✔ What mental health problems are excluded?

✔ Is there a limit on care you can receive each year or during your lifetime? (Are there foreseeable reasons you'll need extended care?)

✔ Does your insurance cover annual checkups with your doctors? (This is where an HMO comes in handy.)

✔ Does the plan provide the benefits you value most? (If not, does the company offer any options?)

✔ What treatments or procedures require advance approval? (That's where an HMO precertification demand doesn't come in handy.)

✔ Does the plan cover prescription drugs? Is the percentage of coverage the same regardless of the illness? (This is especially important if you or your dependents need them.)

✔ Does the plan offer coverage for your family as well as you? (It had better.)

✔ How are claims filed? Do you file them yourself, or do your health care providers file them? (Nice if it's the latter.)

✔ Is there an appeals process you can use if your claim is denied? (This should be one of the first items you check.)

## HEALTH CARE SPENDING ACCOUNTS

While we're on the subject of cost, remember that one way to defray your overall out-of-pocket health care costs is to take advantage of a health care spending account, or flexible spending account (FSA), which you read about in chapter 3.

Basically you set aside money from your paycheck and earmark it for a special account that reimburses you for out-of-pocket health expenses not covered by other means. You get a double break on taxes because the deductions lower your taxable income and the reimbursements come back to you untaxed.

The downside is that you must predict how much you'll spend in the covered period, and if you don't use it all, you lose whatever is left.

Before you jump into a health spending account, make sure you know:

- minimum and maximum contributions;
- minimum and maximum reimbursement for claims;
- how much and how often money is deducted from your paycheck;
- what expenses are eligible for reimbursement (e.g., medical and dental deductibles and copayments, cosmetic surgery, etc.).

You should also know that:

- you can't start, stop, or change your contributions during the year, unless you have a legitimate change of family status;
- you can't be paid for retroactive or carryover expenses—each twelve-month period stands on its own;
- you use it or you lose it!

## GETTING A HANDLE ON YOUR
## HEALTH CARE COSTS

You can kill two (or three) birds with one stone by taking the time to keep track of your health and medical expenses for an entire year. While the added paperwork may be a pain, your future savings will be a pain-killer.

First, you can home in on whether a flexible spending account would give you an appropriate return on your dollar, and if so, what amount you should set aside. Second, you'll be better able to judge whether you need to augment your employer's plan with a personal one. And third, if you're involved in flexible benefits, you'll be able to focus on those you need, and those you can scrape from your benefits plate.

Use figure 9 to track your health expenses through the year. Transfer the appropriate numbers to the summary to get a quick review of the financial health of your health benefits.

## OVERCOMING THE DETRIMENT OF DISABILITY

Most employees view any health care problem they have as an uncommon occurrence. No one plans to be disabled. It happens. Then what?

Some people can depend on disability benefits from the government (under Social Security) or their employer (with private plans). For some, though, income stops when work stops. Disability income insurance is designed to fill the pocketbook gap when an illness or injury halts your income flow.

Disability insurance comes in two forms:

- A variety of employer-paid and government-sponsored programs, generally cost-free to the recipient, covering certain categories of workers.
- Private policies, paid for by individuals, which can protect income when there are no applicable employer or government programs or when those programs do not adequately meet income needs.

Those people who think they'll automatically be rescued by a big-brother government or a benevolent employer—well, they could have another think coming. Prime example: Only about one-third of the people who seek disability help from Social Security get it.

Many corporate health care plans carry disability provisions. Check to see what your company provides. Factor in accumulated sick leave. Usually short-term disability benefits run anywhere from thirteen to twenty-six weeks and give you 70–80%

*Figure 9. Estimating your health care expenses*

## HEALTH CARE SPENDING CHART
**Potential twelve-month out-of-pocket expenses (for a good baseline, look at last year's health expenses):**

| Date | Services | Physician | Illness/Accident | Cost |
|------|----------|-----------|------------------|------|

Include:
- reason seen
- treatment
- surgical procedure
- site (office, hospital)
- chronic condition (allergies, etc.)
- medications, prescriptions

SUMMARY

Medical deductible expenses    $

Medical copayments    $

Dental deductibles and copayments    $

Medical and dental expenses above plan limits    $

Vision or hearing care expenses (if uncovered by your plan)   $

Other eligible expenses (e.g., unreimbursed physicals)    $

of your salary. Long-term benefits normally drop to 50–60% of your pretax earnings. There may be a monthly cap as well, and the base on which the amount is calculated usually doesn't include bonuses or commissions.

If you do go the Social Security disability route, be aware of its strict guidelines (call your local Social Security office for a copy of the pamphlet entitled "Disability"). For example, you can't collect from Social Security if you expect to be on the workplace sidelines for less than one year, or if you can do certain jobs, even if they don't relate to your previous occupation.

**Note:** If you become disabled, you can get the 10% early-withdrawal penalty waived on your tax-deferred retirement plans.

## ARE YOU COVERED BY GROUP DISABILITY BENEFITS?

After you find out whether your employer offers disability benefits in the event of a disabling illness or injury, check the schedule. Most employers allow some short-term sick leave, which might last from a few days to as much as six months, depending on employer policy and duration of employment.

Typical group long-term disability benefits kick in when short-term benefits are exhausted, and continue anywhere from five years to life. **Important:** Employer-paid disability income is subject to income tax when it is received.

Check with your company benefits office to see if you are covered, how you are covered, and whether more coverage is available to you. Find out how long you must wait before benefits begin, and how long payments will continue during your disability. Find out, too, whether your employer's plan takes other disability coverage (such as government programs) into account when calculating what your long-term disability pay will be. Ask for a booklet describing the disability coverage your company offers.

## BENEFITS CHECKOFF: KNOWING SOCIAL SECURITY DISABILITY BENEFITS

Most salaried workers in the United States participate in the federal government's Social Security program. Social Security is best known for its retirement benefits, but it also administers disability benefits.

Your salary and the number of years you have been covered under Social Security determine how much you can receive.

But you should know that:

✔ You are eligible for benefits after you have been disabled for five months and if the disability is expected to last at least twelve months. You need a thorough medical exam to back your claim. Claims processing may take up to three months, so file as soon as possible.

✔ Social Security payments may be reduced by disability entitlements under other government programs because total combined payments under Social Security, Workers' Compensation, civil service, and military programs generally cannot exceed 80 percent of average pre-disability earnings. A government pension may also reduce Social Security disability payments.

✔ Eligibility is based on being unable to perform **any** gainful employment, not just the job you were performing at the time the disability began.

✔ After twenty-four months of benefits, recipients qualify for Medicare. If you want the medical insurance portion of Medicare, in addition to hospital coverage, you must enroll and pay a monthly premium.

✔ Social Security disability payments are subject to federal income tax if your adjusted gross income (which includes 85% of your Social Security benefit) exceed a total of $34,000 (if you file tax returns individually) or $44,000 (if you file jointly).

## HOW MUCH DISABILITY INCOME WILL YOU NEED?

Make a rough estimate of all the benefits you are entitled to under the public and private programs that apply. Add in any monthly income you could count on from other sources, such as your own savings. If the total approaches your required income after taxes, you can rest a little easier should total disability strike. You should be able to pay your day-to-day bills while recuperating.

If the total from employer benefits, Social Security, and other programs (along with your own resources) will not be close to your pre-disability, after-tax income and will not be adequate to support your family, you will want to consider buying additional disability insurance to make up the difference.

Remember, though, if your employer pays for your disability coverage, or if you purchase it with pretax dollars through a cafeteria plan, your disability payout gets taxed. It can make a big difference. It means if your replacement level is two-thirds of salary, and you paid for the disability so the payment isn't taxed, then that replacement level could ratchet up to 80–90% rather than stagnate at two-thirds.


## MAIN FACTORS IN DISABILITY POLICIES

If you find that you do need an individual disability policy over and above any other income protection you may have, here's what you need to know:

### 1. *Definition of disability*

Some plans pay benefits if you are unable to perform the duties of your customary occupation, others only if you can engage in no gainful employment at all.

When you're analyzing a disability plan, one key point will be whether it uses "own occupation" or "any occupation" to determine your eligibility for benefits. The "any occupation" guideline is much broader and will only consider you disabled if you can't work at a job for which you are qualified by education, training, or experience. For most people, that covers a broad spectrum.

The "own occupation" designation is more limited, and considers you disabled if you can't perform the duties of the job you had before becoming disabled, even if you can do other work.

Another key point to consider is whether a disability policy allows you to earn money at a job other than your "own occupation," and whether benefits are reduced, offset, or terminated if you go back to work in any organization at any job.

Also key: Does the disability policy cover you for sickness as well as accidents?

### 2. *Extent of disability*

Some policies require that you be totally disabled before payments begin. Partial disability sometimes is covered for a limited time.

3. *Size of benefit*

Monthly benefits are calculated in terms of income at the time of purchase. Most insurers limit benefits from all sources to no more than 70 to 80% of monthly income.

4. *When payment begins*

Today's policies allow you to decide when benefit payments begin, anywhere from the thirty-first day to six months or more after the onset of the disability. If you have savings or other financial resources, extend that "elimination" period as long as you can. Go 180 days or even more. You'll save a bundle in premiums.

5. *Length of coverage*

You may elect benefits that are payable for one year, two years, five years, to age 65, or for a lifetime. Since disability benefits are designed to replace earned income, most people do not need benefits extending beyond the working years.

**Note:** Your policy may pay to age 65 for an accident but may only cover you for three years if you're tossed from the employment saddle by illness.

6. *Keeping pace with inflation*

For an additional premium, you can add a cost-of-living adjustment (COLA) to basic disability income coverage to keep pace with inflation. That can be either a simple or compound adjustment. With the simple, the increase is based on the original benefit. With the compound, each year's increase is based on the current successively higher base.

## *BENEFITS CHECKOFF: WHAT ELSE DO YOU NEED TO KNOW?*

You should also know these definitions as they pertain to disability insurance:

✔ *Guaranteed renewable* . . . insurer can't drop you as a policyholder as long as you pay your premiums . . . cost of premiums can increase in line with similar policies.

✔ *Level premiums* . . . they stay the same for the entire length of the policy.

✔ *Rising premiums* . . . they start lower but keep going up each year . . . ask for sets of projections of future increases . . . this type makes most sense for younger workers.

✔ *Elimination period* . . . time before disability payments start . . . the longer you can wait after you are disabled, the lower your premiums will be.

✔ *Additional features* . . . such as COLA riders, which are nice but usually expensive; increased coverage you may be able to purchase without taking an exam; or a waiver of premiums so once you start collecting on the policy, you no longer have to pay the premium.

**Legal note:** As in almost all benefits areas, the courts are having their say in disability disputes. The Supreme Court has ruled that states cannot force employers to provide employees who become disabled with the same health insurance they offer active ones. Usually Workers' Compensation laws prescribe the benefits you get once you've been off the job, depending on your earnings record. The ruling means once you become eligible for Workers' Compensation, you aren't automatically entitled to health benefits equivalent to those of active employees.

## YOU MAY WANT AN ADDED LAYER OF PROTECTION

Another health benefit you'll see involves Accidental Death & Dismemberment or AD&D. It might be explained in a separate booklet from your company as an adjunct to life insurance. It's usually voluntary, with you choosing the coverage and paying the premiums, which will naturally be less for group coverage than for a policy you could get on your own.

When you study an AD&D policy, look for:

1. Eligibility and definition of dependents and beneficiary, so you know when you qualify and who else may qualify for a piece of the benefits.
2. The designation of coverage, so you know what kinds of ac-

cidents will trigger payments. Are you covered for on- and off-the-job accidents? Home and away? Any geographic limitations?

3. Exclusions, which usually include wars, activity in the armed forces, and self-inflicted injuries.
4. Benefits, such as the principal sum that is paid for death, and the percentages that are paid for each type of loss covered, like fingers or a hand or leg.

Also be on the lookout for:

- availability of a "family plan" where dependents get varying percentages of the principal sum;
- a termination clause and conversion options in case you switch jobs;
- a schedule of payments and payroll deductions so you can figure out how much you can realistically afford (you might see a principal sum of $100,000 costing $3.60/month for employee-only payment and $5/month for family, and a sum of $200,000 costing $7.20 and $10/month);
- whether there is a cap on what you can choose as the principal sum, such as ten times annual salary.

Figure 10 is a typical long-term disability claim statement. If you're lucky, you'll never have to learn how to fill one out. But just in case, take a look.

It's very straightforward. Section 9 is the onerous one. You've got to have good documentation to answer all the details. Keep a separate file on each piece of disability income you receive.

## BRIDGING THE COVERAGE CANYONS: MEDIGAP AND LONG-TERM CARE

If health insurance hasn't given you a headache yet, hang in a little longer. Medigap and long-term care policies may sound like subjects for employees looking retirement in the eye.

*Figure 10. An actual disability claim form*

## Long Term Disability Claim Statement

1. Full name_____ male_____ female_____

   Date of employment_____ Date of birth_____

   Occupation_____

2. Employer's name and full address_____

3. Nature of sickness or injury *(if due to accident, explain where and how it happened)*_____

4. Date of first medical treatment for this condition_____ Date on which you were first unable to work because of this condition._____

5. Have you engaged in any work, part-time or otherwise, since your sickness or injury began?

   _____Yes _____ No *If yes, please explain and give dates.*

6. If you have recovered or returned to work, give date._____ If totally disabled, when do you expect to return to work?_____

7. Names and addresses of all physicians who have been consulted because of this condition. Name_____

   Address_____Dates of consultation or treatment_____

8. Have you been confined to a hospital for this disability?

   Yes_____ No_____ If yes, please complete:

   *Name of Hospital_____ Address_____ from__ to__*

9. Are you receiving, or are you entitled to receive, benefits from any of the following sources? *(Each question must be answered)*

   |  | Yes | No |
   |---|---|---|
   | a. Salary, wages, commissions | _____ | _____ |
   | b. Any group insurance, health plan | _____ | _____ |
   | c. Workers' compensation | _____ | _____ |
   | d. Social Security | _____ | _____ |
   | e. Veterans Administration | _____ | _____ |
   | f. Retirement or pension plan | _____ | _____ |
   | g. Any individual insurance | _____ | _____ |
   | h. Any governmental agency | _____ | _____ |
   | i. Other sources (details below) | _____ | _____ |

   *For each questions answered "yes," please furnish the following information:*

   Name and address of source_____ Group or individual_____

   Policy or claim number, if any_____ Exact date benefits began or will begin_____ Length of each period_____

Amount of periodic benefit_____ Total paid_____
10. Marital status:
_____Single          _____Widowed
_____Married         _____Divorced
11. Number of dependent children under age 18 and/or full-time students under age 22_____

I certify to the correctness of the statements above and on the preceding page. I hereby authorize any physician, hospital, or other institution or person to furnish [company name], or its authorized representative, any information they may request concerning my medical history. A photocopy of this authorization shall be considered as effective and valid as the original.

Date_____ Signature_____
Full address_____

**IMPORTANT**

*When you have completed this form, please return it to [name] along with the attending physician's statement.*

---

They're not. You need to start eyeballing them much earlier in your employment career, so you go into either type of situation with your eyes wide open.

Since Congress pulled the plug on catastrophic illness coverage, Medicare supplement insurance (Medigap) has been pushed into the spotlight. Congress has passed Medigap law that seeks to simplify policies by limiting the types of plans that can be sold, and specifying exactly what those plans must contain.

Check out your company's health plan to see if so-called Medigap offerings are available. Look into commercial insurers, Blue Cross/Blue Shield, or senior groups or organizations that have developed Medigap plans. But no matter where you look, you should be investigating the following aspects:

What gets covered? By definition, Medigap is supplementary insurance designed to pay for what Medicare doesn't. Despite its new, increased benefits, you'll still be responsible for sizable deductions, some copayments, and other noncovered charges, especially in light of the low schedules of Medicare payments and the high fees most doctors/hospitals charge.

Having a lot of coverage is a two-edged sword. You want

gaps covered, but you don't want to pay for some coverages twice. Check a Medigap policy to see if it duplicates Medicare coverage. If it does, put those premium dollars to better use, maybe in a long-term care (LTC) protection policy.

Check out Medigap coverage to see if it's based on the same "approved schedules" as Medicare itself. If so, it's less valuable than a more realistically based plan.

Put Medigap under the fine-print microscope to see exactly what it covers. The bottom line: Medigap policies range from bare bones to blanket. The key question: Can you comfortably pay the difference between what Medicare covers and what you estimate you'll get stuck with? If you can, Medigap isn't for you. But if you think you'll eventually be facing, say, five-figure doctor bills, a policy covering 20% of the approved charges not picked up by Medicare could prove a life-savings saver.

## A SHORT COURSE ON LONG-TERM CARE

One item on the employee benefits menu for health care that often gets short shrift is long-term care or LTC.

Long-term care refers to the services required to support an individual who is chronically ill or functionally handicapped. A long-term care benefit may cover a wide range of medical, con-valescent, or custodial care provided by physicians, nurses, and aides.

In essence, when you insure for LTC you're betting that you'll require some extended care for chronic impairment when you get older. That's one way of looking at long-term care. There's another: An LTC policy will guarantee you TLC (tender loving care) when you need it most. You may never need it. But then again. . . .

Basically, long-term care insurance policies cover extended stays in nursing homes or health-related facilities at either skilled, intermediate, or custodial levels, or sometimes home care instead of such confinement.

There's no such animal as a typical policy. And the price rises with age. So the sooner you buy, the better. There's lots being written about long-term care today. Among organizations with material on the subject are:

- United Seniors Health Corp., 1331 H St. NW, Suite 500, Washington, DC 20005;
- Health Insurance Association of America, P.O. Box 41455, Washington, DC 20018;
- The National Association of Insurance Commissioners, 1025 Connecticut Ave. NW, Washington, DC 20036-3998.

## BENEFITS CHECKOFF: QUESTIONS ABOUT LTC INSURANCE

If your company has an LTC policy, or if you're looking at a personal one, have this checklist ready:

✔ How will benefits be paid? Does the plan reimburse for a given service at a fixed rate, or pay a certain percentage of care costs? Is there a deductible?

✔ What is the level of coverage? Is it defined as a daily maximum, a lifetime maximum, or something else? What daily amount is paid for: skilled care, intermediate care, custodial care, home care? How long (days, years) will you receive benefits for each? What is the maximum dollar amount the policy will pay?

✔ What kinds of services are covered? Does the plan just cover nursing home stays, and if so, what kind? Does it cover services such as home health visits, adult day care, or respite care? Is there variation in coverage for inpatient and outpatient services?

✔ Does the plan include an inflation escalator? Does it have options in deductibles, benefit amounts, and length of confinement, so you can control what you get (and pay premiums you can afford!)?

✔ What does the coverage you want cost per month, per year, for five years, ten years, lifetime?

✔ Will the premium continue to be based on your age at enrollment? You don't want one that rises with age.

✔ Are certain diseases and conditions excluded from coverage, such as Alzheimer's, Parkinson's, or senility?

✔ Does the plan take an HMO or PPO approach, encouraging or requiring the use of certain providers?

✔ If it's a company policy and you leave the company, can you convert the coverage to an individual policy?

✔ How many days after you enter a nursing home must you wait to start receiving benefits?

✔ Does this policy contain any restrictive mumbo jumbo like "not medically necessary" or "not reasonable or customary" or "only Medicare-approved expense levels" or "skilled nursing facility" (as opposed to state-licensed, which is what you want)?

✔ How many home visits are allowed, and what type of institution or home health organization may provide such services? Do such facilities exist in your area?

## WELLNESS: BETTER HEALTH WITHOUT HEALTH INSURANCE

One of the major trends in employment health care involves wellness programs. From major Fortune 500 companies to small mom-and-pop operations, everyone seems to have recognized the need for an emphasis on prevention and teamwork.

If your company offers wellness incentives, grab them. They'll be good for you physically and financially. If your company isn't on the wellness bandwagon yet, give it a leg up. Suggest some of the programs you'll read about here.

They don't have to be all-encompassing, and they don't have to be costly. Some companies offer positive incentives, like lower premiums, decreased deductibles, and flexible benefits credits. Others use the stick approach, by sticking employees with higher premiums or a larger percentage of costs if they don't follow a wellness program.

You can get rewards by shunning tobacco, exercising, wearing seat belts, losing weight, lowering cholesterol and blood sugar counts, and a host of other simple activities.

Inventiveness often accompanies good health programs. One company created a "no-belly prize" for losing weight and gave away clothing gift certificates; another offered $500 to those employees who eschewed the elevator every day and climbed the sixteen flights of stairs to the company's main office; still another gave away T-shirts and lottery tickets for walking one hundred miles in one hundred days.

## BENEFITS CHECKOFF: SOME MORE HEALTHY IDEAS

✔ At a manufacturing plant, the carrot is an annual $200 bonus for ten minutes of aerobics three times a week for nine months. Visits to the gym are monitored by computer.

✔ A chocolate maker uses the stick of a loss of up to $720 per year in flexible benefit health care dollars if an employee uses tobacco, is overweight, doesn't exercise, and has high blood pressure or cholesterol.

✔ Employees at an oil company can earn up to $700 in cash per year if they exercise three times per week, don't use tobacco, don't take sick days, and don't submit major medical claims.

✔ A bank offered a $6/month reward for employees who wore seat belts, didn't smoke, and attended wellness seminars. Those who had a fitness evaluation and followed an exercise program received $9/month; employees who did it all received $12/month.

✔ A beer firm gave employees a voluntary health-hazard appraisal questionnaire. The company picked up an extra 5% of the health insurance premiums of those employees rated low-risk and those who climbed on the low-risk bandwagon.

✔ A major computer company offers a voluntary health assessment plan; screening for life-threatening or debilitating illnesses; educational, exercise, and safety courses for employees, spouses, children, and retirees; and tuition reimbursement for health-related courses.

✔ A large regional electric company gives voluntary screening tests, and if an employee makes a certain score, he or she gets a rebate on health-care premium contributions.

## PHYSICAL INVENTORY

In addition to knowing what can help make you healthier, you should try to have a good idea of what your health risks are. That way you can make an informed judgment about whether your health care plan covers the types of services and treatments you are most likely to need. You should remember that it is sometimes hard to predict the treatments you or your family will need as your life progresses. Ask:

- Does your age, race, or sex place you at special risk for any health problems?
- Do you or any of your dependents play sports that have a high risk of accidental injury?
- How frequently do you get regular physicals? Eye exams? Hearing exams? OB/GYN exams? Dental checkups?
- Is there a history of disease or other chronic conditions in your family (heart, cancer, kidney, arthritis, diabetes)?

## WHAT IF YOU STILL WANT MORE INFORMATION?

- Find out who you can talk to at your company about your health insurance benefits. Ask that person to explain areas that aren't clear.
- Attend any staff meetings that your company arranges to explain your benefits. Read all the memos you receive, and keep them in one handy place for easy reference.
- Be sure to ask questions about areas of coverage that interest you. If you don't understand an answer, ask again. Ask what would happen in a hypothetical situation that concerns you: "Suppose my son or daughter . . ."

- If you feel your employer offers a plan that does not provide you with enough coverage or options, find out whether the plan can be changed. Talk to someone who is able to directly influence decisions about the plan. Maybe your employer is open to conducting a survey of employees to find out which benefits they believe are most important.
- Examine the health benefit plans of family members and friends employed in other companies. You might see a plan you like that you can suggest to your management.
- Be aware that your plan's coverage will probably change to some degree from year to year. If you're with the same company for a long time, don't assume your coverage is the same from one year to the next.

## *BENEFITS CHECKOFF: HEALTH BENEFIT SOURCES AND RESOURCES*

Lots of associations, private publishers, and government agencies are standing ready to offer you in-depth advice on various specific aspects of health care benefits today. Here are just a few:

✔ American Association of Retired Persons offers information you can use for planning, no matter what age you are. It offers, among others, booklets on Medicare and HMOs. Contact: AARP, 1909 K. St. NW, Washington, DC 20049.

✔ Your local Social Security office and your state insurance commissioner's office have valuable material available. Call or write.

✔ The National Insurance Consumer Hotline offers health insurance counseling at (800) 942-4242.

✔ Material can be obtained from the Group Health Association of America, 1129 20th St. NW, Suite 600, Washington, DC 20036.

✔ Several booklets on Medicare and health insurance are available from such organizations as Health Care Financing Administration, Office of Public Affairs, 6325 Security Blvd., Baltimore, MD 21207; American Council of Life Insurance, 1001 Pennsylvania Ave. NW, Washington, DC 20004-2599;

Consumer Information Center, Dept. 529-T, Pueblo, CO 81009.

✔ For a fee, some companies will provide you with data to compare coverages and costs. For example, Quotesmith Corp. in Palatine, Illinois, tracks rates, coverage, and safety ratings of insurance companies and Blue Cross/Blue Shield plans; Wilkinson Benefits Consultants in Towson, Maryland, has a one-thousand-plan database it will search to help you match your needs.

*It may not help her forehand, and it won't get any of her lost out-of-pocketbook expenses back. But knowing more about her health care coverage gives Nola Olivieri a warm feeling that has nothing to do with body temperature. She'll be ready to take advantage of her health care benefits the next time she's not healthy. So will you.*

# 5
▼

# FINANCIAL PREPARATION

## *Learning About the Dollar Aspects of Your Benefits*

*THE CASE OF THE ELIGIBLE EMPLOYEE*

**B**ill Ticknor was worried. In fact, he was on the verge of panic. He felt like nearly all people do when asked to make decisions concerning things they know very little about.

He'd received a memo from the benefits person in the company he'd gone to work for less than a year earlier. The memo, he thought, had good news and bad.

The good news was that he'd become eligible for all the company benefits that required a probationary employment period before they kicked in. (Health and medical covered him in the first month he'd joined.) These benefits included supplementary medical, a stock purchase plan, profit sharing, and a 401(k) plan, whatever that was.

The bad news, Bill thought, was that the memo said the 401(k) was a "salary reduction type of pension plan." He wasn't too keen on the words "salary reduction." After all, he'd made a lateral move to this job with only a modest boost over his previous pay. He was looking for an increase, not a reduction. On the *other hand, he'd never been covered by a pension plan. Even though he was only thirtysomething and retirement seemed ages away, Ticknor knew it was time to at least think about it.*

*The memo said that he was automatically included in the profit sharing plan. But he had to sign up for the others. What panicked Bill was the fact that he had to indicate on a form exactly how much he wanted his salary reduced (ugh). And equally upsetting, he had to tell the benefits person how much of this salary reduction he wanted to contribute to buy various kinds of mutual funds, a guaranteed investment contract (whatever that was), etc.*

*The memo contained another piece of good news: For every buck he put in the 401(k), the company would contribute fifty cents, up to a certain amount each year. And he'd save some money on taxes, the memo said.*

*That news nearly swung him over. Still, with a lower salary, his cash flow would be really tight. Bill decided to talk to his boss about the benefits. The boss simply said that the company's plans were "a really good deal." But then, he was management, right?*

*The benefits person wasn't much more help. Ticknor realized that he was really on his own. He'd have to rely on himself to learn about these puzzling plans. So he set out for his local library, which, luckily for him, had a big reference section stocked with books and magazines on business and investments.*

*"Doing it yourself is tough when it comes to money decisions," Bill told his wife one night. "But I'm going to get the maximum I can out of all these benefits plans. That'll make this work—figuring out how to play them to the max—pay off in spades."*

The trend today among companies providing benefits is to put you in Bill Ticknor's place. You get more control over where and how your benefit money is invested. Uncle Sam is urging your employer, and all others, to give you more choices for where and how you can invest it.

That's an important reason for you to learn the ins and outs of investing and financial planning. An even more important reason is to help you get the biggest possible bang out of the benefits bucks that are being set aside in your name.

---

**Benefits alert:** Four chapters on the financial and investment aspects of your benefits may seem like overkill. But if it saves **YOU** $100 in taxes, is it worth it? If it makes it easier for you to decide how to allocate **YOUR** retirement dollars, is it worth it? If it gives **YOU** a bigger postwork nest egg, is it worth it? To paraphrase what the Mets' Tug McGraw said in his team's pennant-winning season: "You Gotta Believe It."▼

---

## GETTING A LEG UP ON FINANCIAL BENEFITS PLANNING

Some very well-known companies like AT&T and DuPont are offering a financial planning benefit to employees to beef up other dollar-in-your-pocket perks like pensions, profit sharing, and stock purchase plans. They usually offer the financial planning benefit under a flexible benefit or cafeteria plan. The employee can choose to take it or leave it. Ask your employer if it has any plans to offer this benefit. You could reap big dividends and avoid the library trips of Bill Ticknor.

---

### ACTION IDEA

The Ayco Corporation, an American Express company, offers organizations a financial planning service for their employees. When a client company includes this benefit, the Ayco Corporation gives a whole kit of materials to each person who signs up. The idea is to help each employee, with the Ayco Corporation's guidance, to:

- Set financial goals
- Get control over spending and debt
- Save on taxes
- Make smarter investment decisions
- Get better understanding of company benefits
- Plan for children's educations
- Have a source for answers to personal financial questions.

If your company doesn't offer a benefit like this one, consider talking it up. Persuade management at least to take a look at a financial planning benefit.

Maybe you've never thought of zeroing in on the financial mysteries of stocks and bonds, brokers and brokerages, and the stock, bond, and commodities markets. The world of investing, though, gives you ways to build bigger and better values in many benefits if you're willing to work on them.

## BENEFITS CHECKOFF: START THINKING LIKE AN INVESTOR

When you look over all the benefits your company has showered on you, and all the new ones that could someday come your way, you may think you're in Fat City. But you're not there yet. You can make that grade, though, when:

- ✔ you appreciate that all benefits have a common connection: MONEY;
- ✔ you whip up your ambition to guarantee that your slice of the benefits pie is big and juicy;
- ✔ you understand fully how money goes into and comes out of each benefit you're qualified for;
- ✔ you quit thinking of yourself as a passive "participant" or "beneficiary," as most benefit plans call you;
- ✔ you jump into the role of INVESTOR, because that's exactly what you are when it comes to your benefits money.

Make your benefit dollars work harder for you by learning how to manage money and how to think like an investor.

## SMART EMPLOYEES MAKE SMART INVESTORS

When it comes to benefits money, you can't put things off, or you'll never get started. Use your time wisely today, and you'll win more benefits money tomorrow.

There's an old Greek myth about three beautiful nymphs who lived on a pretty island. These Sirens sang so sweetly when ships sailed near that sailors would be seduced by their voices. Before the voyagers became aware of danger, their ships would be smashed to bits on the rocky shoals surrounding the island, and the seas would drown them all.

Benefits often sing siren songs too. Just being a participant in them can seduce you into believing you're getting something that's money- and worry-free. Cover your ears. And open your eyes. Don't let time fly by while you neglect to steer your benefits ship to its most profitable destination. Here's how that melody plays:

You're 25 . . . you're just getting started . . . you can't put any money aside now . . . you don't earn a lot . . . you're entitled to have some fun while you're still young . . . besides, there's years and years ahead to learn about steering your benefits investments.

You're 35 . . . your family is growing . . . hey, those mortgage payments are killers . . . when the children get older your expenses will go down and then you can learn how to handle money . . . anyway, you haven't a nickel left over to put aside . . . besides, you'd rather put benefits credits into medical insurance than 401(k)s.

You're 45 . . . you've got two kids in college at the same time . . . those tuition payments are breaking your back . . . this has got to be the most expensive time of your life . . . the only way you think about money is how to lay your hands on more of it right now, not how you can funnel more benefits bucks into the future.

You're 55 . . . yeah, you know you should learn all about money, how to invest . . . retirement is just around the corner . . . but at your age you've got to keep an eye on organizational downsizings . . . you could get caught in the crunch, too . . . time to check out other possibilities, maybe a franchise or consulting . . . you have to sit tight and see how things break.

You're 65 . . . okay, okay, investing money is a great idea . . . you're getting Social Security, which doesn't get all the bills paid . . . yeah, you know you should have started years ago . . . it's too late now.

Don't listen to the Sirens' songs. Get started on learning how to manage your benefits money now.

# MATCH YOUR GOALS TO INVESTMENT STRATEGIES

Before you tackle the tricky task of getting the most out of your benefits, you have to decide what your priorities are. What do you want your benefits to do for you today? Five and ten years from now? At retirement? After retirement? You have to set your goals.

## ACTION IDEAS

1. Lay out your goals—put them in writing, but prepare to change them as needed.
2. Separate your goals into the ones you want to reach right away, ones that are five or ten years up the road, and those you want to reach in retirement and after.
3. Decide how much risk you can take with the money in each benefit category: a sure thing, some risk, risky as all get-out, the sky's the limit!

You should match your choices of investment vehicles with your goals. Those goals differ according to the timing of the result you want. You may want to be able to draw out some cash at any time, even right now. Other goals you'll want to reach much later in life. Use the chart that follows as a model to figure out how to invest money so it matches up with your goals.

## MATCHING INVESTMENTS TO GOALS

| Years | What you want | Trade-offs | Matching Investment Possibilities |
|---|---|---|---|
| 0 | Liquidity | Low payouts | Money-market funds, bank savings accts. |
| 1-2 | Stable prices Short due dates Easy access | Inflation may hurt values | 90-day to 1-year bank CDs |

| 3-5 | Higher income Small price change, regular income | Less safety Inflation will hurt values | Bonds due in 3–5 years Blue chip stocks |
|---|---|---|---|
| Over 5 | Growth potential Very high yield | Big price changes | Stocks, gold real estate |

Make up your own "Matching Investments to Goals" chart. The first column is the time ranging from zero years, which is right now, to over five years. Fill in the second column, "What you want" (these are your goals for your money today and in future years), with the results you want within the time periods of the first column. "What you want" differs from person to person. It varies with age, income, amount of money involved, and how much risk you can live with.

Then consider the "Trade-offs" in the third column. Check them out in light of the more detailed information given in chapters 6–9. Pick out some "Investment possibilities" for the fourth column. Pick ones that match your goals, the "What you want" for each time period. Study carefully the kinds of investment instruments or vehicles (stocks, bonds, CDs, treasury securities, real estate, etc.) to learn their characteristics—yield, safety, growth—and their risk. Make sure you understand the trade-offs of each.

## GET SMART: IT'S YOUR MONEY

You should know what your company's benefits-plan administrators do with the money you and your employer put aside for your benefits. That kind of handle on what's being done with your benefits money keeps your employer on its toes and helps make your benefits bigger and safer.

You may not be able to get yours to make many changes, though the employees of one company squawked so loudly about the poor financial condition of an insurance company that insured one of their benefits that their employer switched to another.

If you don't know where your benefits money goes, ask your

benefits, human resource, or personnel department people. They have no reason to keep the information a secret. In fact, they're obligated to tell you.

Figure 11, a general grouping of benefits, gives you an idea of where your company may be shipping your benefits money.

The insurance companies, banks, investment companies, and brokers who supply benefit services to your company have financial experts on their payrolls. They decide how much of the cash they'll invest in such things as corporate bonds, preferred and common stocks, mutual funds, real estate, and, though rarely, commodities like gold and silver. The trustees of regular pension plans usually allocate a percentage of the money they invest to stocks and the balance to fixed-income securities and cash equivalents.

With many 401(k) and 403(b) plans, you'll be asked to decide what percentage of your money you want to be put into various investment options the plan provider or administrator offers. Most of them give you at least three choices, usually bond and balanced mutual funds, and a fund of guaranteed investment contracts (GICs) (check out chapter 6).

## "TRIANGULATING" YOUR RISK AND REWARD

No matter how you slice it, you'll always be trading off risk against reward when investing benefits dollars. The more risky the ways you manage your benefits money, the higher the reward may be—OR the bigger your loss.

The safer you play the money-handling game, though, the less likely you'll make a big score or take a big loss. That situation sets up what's known as "the risk triangle." In the money game, you have yield (income) in one corner of the triangle, safety in another corner, and growth in a third. You're not alone when you want what everyone else does—safe investments that'll grow fast and pay out high cash returns. But take a look at the triangle.

**Yield**

Nearly
anything you
might invest in can
be found inside this triangle

**Safety**                                        **Growth**

*Figure 11. Knowing your benefits-bucks pipelines*

| Type of benefit | Money usually goes to |
|---|---|
| 1. Life, health, and disability insurance | Money usually goes to insurance companies (some companies don't buy insurance, but self-insure. That's usually riskier for you than if your company buys from a sound and reliable insurance company that's fully set up to handle all types of claims) |
| 2. Regular pension plans that pay amounts at retirement that you can count on; profit sharing plans | Trustees—often a bank or insurance company which invests the money in assets like bonds, stocks, government securities |
| 3. Employee stock ownership plans (ESOPs) | Usually in your employer's stock; some cash equivalents |
| 4. Thrift, savings, salary reduction plans (such as 401(k)) | Plan administrators in your organization who may hire a provider of investment services like a bank, broker, investment company, which will usually invest the money in assets like fixed income, growth, and balanced mutual funds, guaranteed investment contracts (GICs), etc. |

| 5. Simplified Employee Pensions (SEPs) | Plan administators in your company who will invest the cash in savings accounts, mutual funds, insurance contracts, etc. |
|---|---|
| 6. Individual Retirement Accounts (IRAs) | Usually no company involvement; what you do with the cash is up to you; you will get a broker or bank to handle the details for you while you decide which investments are most suitable—bonds, stocks, bank CDs, money funds, etc. |

You must learn this: Move your investments toward one corner of the triangle, like safety, and you'll move away from *two* others. That's the trade-off between risk and reward. The choice is yours. To make the best choice, you must learn how to invest money.

Some employees don't think they should take *any* risk with their benefits money. It's their right to choose. Others are willing to take some risk for better yields and benefits growth. (Check out your risk tolerance in chapter 6.)

## *PYRAMID CLIMBING: BEWARE OF HEIGHTS*

The risk triangle shows how risk and reward are related and illustrates the trade-offs among YIELD, GROWTH, and SAFETY. You have to consider these relationships to get the most out of your benefits dollars.

Some benefit plans, like most 401(k) and 403(b) plans, give you limited choices as to where your share of the money is invested. That means you have to consider specific options like investment instruments and vehicles.

The risk pyramid that follows, like the risk triangle, portrays the risks and rewards of investing. It shows specific types of investments according to their riskiness.

The safest vehicles you can invest your money in are at the bottom. As you move up the pyramid your potential rewards grow. But so does the risk of loss of the money you've put in. In some situations, like a bankrupt company that goes down the tubes, you can lose every penny.

Commodity
Futures Contracts

Collectibles,
Start-up Companies' Stocks

Limited Partnerships, Real Estate,
Put and Call Options

Blue-Chip Stocks, Growth Mutual Funds

Balanced Mutual Funds, Preferred Stocks,
Convertible Securities

Municipal Bonds, Corporate Bonds, Money-Market Funds,
Pension Funds, Guaranteed Investment Contracts

Insured Bank Accounts, U.S. Treasury Securities,
U.S. Savings Bonds, Bank CDs, Insurance Cash Values

If you're not familiar with all these kinds of investment instruments or vehicles, you'll find descriptions in Chapters 7, 8, and 9.

## LAYING LOTS OF EGGS IN THE NEST

"Don't put all your eggs in one basket" may be a tired old saying. But it's very useful when you're investing your benefits money. The money experts say it another way. They say: "Diversify."

Suppose you need to make decisions on how to invest some benefits money. You lessen your risks when you spread the money over a number of different types of investments. That's one reason you're given several choices of where to put your money by plans like 401(k), 403(b), and some profit sharing plans.

Your goals, what you want your investments to do for you and when, should be a guide to diversifying. The resulting mix may look like minestrone soup. But the idea is to make these neat nest eggs safer.

Direct some of your money in these plans to very safe and stable options like insured bank savings accounts. They don't turn up much income, but your capital will always be there. Put some other portion of your money into investments that are less safe but reward you with greater income or growth.

## PLAY LIKE A PRO: HEDGE YOUR BENEFITS BETS

Say you have available to invest on the first day of each quarter the sum of $900. This could happen, for instance, if you had to make choices of how to invest a 401(k) contribution, or if you retired and had a big chunk of money coming from a pension plan, or if you were laid off and had a large sum of money coming from severance pay or from your interests in various benefit plans. You know you should take some steps to make this money work harder for you, but how can you do so without taking too much risk?

One way is through dollar-cost averaging. It's a catchy name that investment experts invented for a simple investing technique that gives the most bang for the buck. The technique can be used when buying almost anything, but stocks are used here to make the system easier to explain. Dollar-cost averaging takes a long-range view of investing, which is the view you should always take when selecting investments.

Here are some assumptions for the following table, which compares investing a fixed dollar sum with dollar-cost averaging, versus buying a fixed number of shares without dollar-cost averaging:

You select a stock or mutual fund to invest in. Its price fluctuates between $3 and $15 over a time period of five calendar quarters in this example, though you can invest for as long a time as you like and get the same results.

| Investing a fixed dollar sum with dollar cost averaging | | | vs. | Purchasing a fixed number of shares without $ cost averaging | | |
|---|---|---|---|---|---|---|
| Cost per share | Number shares purchased | Amount invested | | Cost per share | Number Shares purchased | Amount invested |
| $6 | 150 | $900 | | $6 | 100 | $600 |
| 3 | 300 | 900 | | 3 | 100 | 300 |
| 9 | 100 | 900 | | 9 | 100 | 900 |
| 15 | 60 | 900 | | 15 | 100 | 1,500 |
| 12 | 75 | 900 | | 12 | 100 | 1,200 |
| Totals | 685 | $4,500 | | | 500 | $4,500 |

*Table adapted from Oppenheimer Management Fund, Inc. material which appeared in a PaineWebber Inc. brochure.*

You can see how much better the results are when you invest a fixed amount of money (third column) at specific periods of time rather than buying a fixed number of shares (fifth column) at the same times. When you dollar-cost average a total of $4,500 at the fixed rate of $900 each quarter, you acquire 685 shares at an average cost of $6.57 per share ($4,500 divided by 685 shares = $6.57 per share).

If you use the same total of $4,500 to buy 100 shares at a time, you buy only 500 shares at an average cost of $9 per share ($4,500 divided by 500 shares = $9 per share). Now, assume that the stock goes up to $10 per share. The 685 shares bought by dollar-cost averaging are now worth $6,850. But the 500 shares bought under the other method of buying a fixed number of shares at a time are worth only $5,000—that's $1,850 *less!*

There's a safety factor in dollar-cost averaging, too. Suppose the price of the stock drops way down to $5 per share. Your 685 shares are now worth only $3,425—trouble! You lose $1,075 ($4,500 invested minus current value of $3,425 = $1,075). But with the other method the value would be only $2,500 (500 shares times $5 = $2,500). That's a loss of $2,000 ($4,500 invested minus current value of $2,500 = $2,000).

Of course, the loss is on paper unless for some reason you have to cash in the stocks. As this example shows, prices of stocks go way up as well as way down. That's true of most investments, even the house or apartment you live in.

Dollar-cost averaging helps you jump over the hurdle of deciding exactly when to put your money into any investment. When you dollar-cost average, you don't have that decision. The right time to begin the steady flow of dollars, but not all of them, is right now.

---

### ACTION IDEA

There's another way to hedge your bets when you've received a large chunk of benefits money that you have to put to use either in an IRA in which you make the investing decisons yourself, or in your personal investing. It's called a stop-loss order. It's a device to prevent a large loss in any stock you may buy, or to preserve a gain should the price of the stock head south.

The stop-loss order tells your broker that when a stock reaches a certain price, he or she should sell it at once. You set that price when you buy the stock, and the level you set it at depends on how much risk you're willing to take.

Point is, there'll be times when you have to make decisions regarding the investment of some benefits money. Dollar-cost averaging and stop-loss orders give you two ways to protect yourself from big losses. Use them.

---

*So Bill Ticknor found out that the mystery of investing wasn't so mysterious after all. He's a little clearer on where he's going and how his financial benefits are going to carry him there. You should be feeling the same way.*

# 6

▼

# INVESTMENT ADVICE

## *Judging Your Personal Position on Risk Versus Reward*

B ill Ticknor is no expert yet. He's only scratched the surface of what he needs to know to get the most from investments involving his employee benefits. He's not sure how much risk he wants to assume, or which investment vehicles he wants to put his benefits faith in.

He's eager to learn more.

Two main occasions call for investment savvy to hook up with benefits. One occurs when a worker changes jobs and has a chunk of cash dropped on his or her plate. The other happens when an employer offers employees a menu of investing options through plans like a 401(k) or other savings vehicles for them to contribute to, as in Bill Ticknor's situation.

In the first case, when you've had serious money plunked down in front of you, why get mixed up in the whole confusing matter of stocks, bonds, markets, mutual funds, and all that stuff? Why not put your money in a bank savings account, where it'll earn interest and grow?

There's a very good reason: inflation, and what it does to the cost of living. America's inflation rate has never been lower than 2% in the last twenty-five to thirty years, and it's been six or seven times that high from time to time. That means you've got to fight back somehow. Or you'll find, ten or fifteen years down the pike, that the bucks you stashed away in a savings account buy only fifty cents' worth of food and other things you need, even though they've earned some interest.

Keep in mind, too, that taxes are going to take a bite out of the interest you're earned in your savings account.

So there's no getting around it: You've really got to learn something about investing, or you'll fall behind getting the max out of many of your best benefits. You not only have the problem of figuring out how to manage serious money when it gets tossed your way. You also should be saving *something* on your own, outside your benefit funds, each year. No matter how small that savings is, you must protect it against inflation and taxes. Investing is really your only defense against those twin thieves.

That doesn't mean you're going to drop everything, pick up the stock market tables, and jump headlong into buying stocks. You can't make smart investment decisions either for investments in your benefits packages or in your personal savings until you know how you really feel about money at risk. You need to take your personal "risk pulse" to find out what your risk tolerance is.

## STEPS TO ASSESS YOUR PERSONAL RISK TOLERANCE

Are you so concerned about losing a single dime of benefits money that you'll take a white-knuckle flight in your dreams every night if you have any part of it or your savings at risk? How much is your peace of mind worth? You may think it's worth a lot. But you don't want to trade entirely inflation-reduced values in your benefit monies for total peace of mind.

You'll have to answer the white-knuckle question and other similar ones to determine your risk tolerance, or just how shy of risk you are. It would be nice if some neat formula would do that job for you, but there's no such thing. Moreover, how you feel about risk doesn't stand still. It changes as you grow older, as your financial resources get better or worse, with the number of dependents you have, and with the ups and downs of your income.

The first thing you can do to take your risk pulse is to consider the following categories or general descriptions of mental approaches to risk that all people have, to one degree or another. Later, after you've had a chance to zero in a little more specifically on which category you fit into at present, you'll see better how to shape investment decisions for your benefits packages.

- **Category 1**—You don't like sudden ups and downs in value—that's called volatility by investment experts. You like stability and expect to get back every penny of the money you put up. On top of that, you like a guaranteed rate of return so you can easily figure out how much you're going to earn. You want to be able to get your cash out without any delay.
- **Category 2**—You want to get a good income from your investments. But you're willing to see a small portion of it invested in vehicles that may go up and down in price because you know that over a long period of time you'll need to see the money you invest appreciate—that is, to go up in value to combat inflation.
- **Category 3**—You're willing to take a little risk by investing in bonds or other instruments which may not have a top rating but pay higher interest because of that. These aren't the "junk bonds" of ill repute. They may be longer-term bonds which pay higher rates, and you're willing to put your money out for a longer period of time before cashing out. You will consider putting as much as half your investment into stocks, though you'll want to stick to the "blue chips": stock offered by big companies with records of paying hefty dividends over many years.
- **Category 4**—You'll look at more aggressive growth stocks for your investments. You may keep some of your money, say 20%, in bonds, but you'll seek higher interest payers even

though you know they'll fluctuate in value when overall interest rates change. Being able to cash out quickly isn't as important to you as being able to cash in on high run-ups in the prices of the stocks and bonds in which you invest.

- **Category 5**—You're not interested in having any money in fixed-income investments like bonds. You're aggressively seeking growth and don't mind being fully invested in stocks. You know that the stock markets, as measured by various averages such as the Dow Jones Industrial Average and Standard & Poor's 500 Average, do go up and down. Still, you're willing to have the prices of many of your investments move around even more than the averages. You do, of course, expect over the years to have a much higher investment return than you can get in any other category.

## QUESTIONS TO ASK YOURSELF ABOUT RISK

To draw another bead on your own attitudes toward risk, ask yourself how you feel about these questions, and place a check mark under the appropriate heading of "Fully Agree," "Partly Agree," or "Strongly Disagree":

|  | Fully agree | Partly agree | Strongly disagree |
|---|---|---|---|
| 1. I am very concerned that my income will not keep up with inflation. | — | — | — |
| 2. I want maximum total return right now. | — | — | — |
| 3. I want to be able to get out of any investments quickly even if I have to get less money now. | — | — | — |
| 4. I want maximum growth of my savings from now until I start drawing the money out. | — | — | — |
| 5. I don't want all my nest eggs in one basket. | — | — | — |
| 6. I want my savings invested so I cannot lose any of the money I've put in. | — | — | — |
| 7. I want my investments to go up more than the market averages, and if they go down more than the averages I won't worry. | — | — | — |

Here's what your check marks say about how you feel about risk taking: If you fully agree with questions 1, 2, 4, 5, and 7, you have quite a high tolerance for risk. You may even go in for bungee jumping or rock climbing. Because you're a risk taker, though, doesn't mean that you shouldn't hedge your bets and invest intelligently.

If you agree partly with those same questions, you're willing to take some risks. You may be the type who'll play games like ice hockey, but only with full safety regalia on.

If you disagree strongly with these questions and agree fully with questions 3 and 6, then you want safety above all else. You're like the person who never leaves the house without wearing a belt *and* suspenders! That's not necessarily a bad attitude toward risk. It severely limits, though, how you'll invest your money. Still, even when you're worried almost totally about safety, when you carefully monitor and move your money around in the safe places, you'll get far better results than someone who rummages around money matters like an absent-minded professor. You've got to get involved, or your benefits money will go down the tubes.

## A THIRD CHECK ON YOUR FEELINGS ABOUT RISK

If you're sure about your risk IQ, you can skip this next quiz. But it may help you refine your own opinions of how you feel about risk.

1. How do you feel about the liquidity of
   your investments? Should it be
   _____ High (1)
   _____ Medium (7)
   _____ Low (12)                    _____ Score
2. Although investment returns can't be
   guaranteed, do you have a figure in mind
   you'd like to get?
   _____ Yes (1)
   _____ No, I want the max (10)     _____ Score

3. Total return from investments is the sum of
   dividends, interest, and capital appreciation
   Generally, the more emphasis you place on
   high income (dividends and interest only), the
   less potential for capital appreciation. Do
   you have any specific figure for annual income
   to be earned from your investments?

   _____    Yes (1)

   _____    No, I want a very high total
   return on my investments (10)     _____     Score

4. How much time you're willing to take to reach
   your investment objectives has a big impact
   on the ability to get there. The longer you're
   willing to take, the more likely that the ups
   and downs of the markets will average out,
   giving you a better chance to make it big. What
   is the approximate length of time you're
   willing to keep your money invested?

   _____    1 to 3 years (3)

   _____    3 to 5 years (7)

   _____    More than 5 years (12)     _____     Score

5. How much and how often you decide to take
   money out of your investments has a lot to
   do with what kinds of risks you may take.
   Which of the following situations do you
   think fits your investments best?

   _____    No substantial withdrawals in next
   five years (10)

   _____    Fewer withdrawals than additions
   during the next five years (5)

   _____    More withdrawals than
   contributions during next five years (0)     _____     Score

6. Check the one statement below that
   best fits your investment objectives in general.

   _____    Growth: emphasis on greater capital
   appreciation with no immediate income
   consideration (18)

   _____    Growth with income: both
   equally important (12)

_____ Income: emphasis on dividends
and interest with some capital appreciation (6)
_____ Preservation of capital: emphasis
on protection of principal with income (1)

_____ Score

7. Which category best matches your attitude
toward investment risk? (choose one)
_____ Aggressive: willing to make high-risk
investments (18)
_____ Moderate: willing to take some
risks (10)
_____ Conservative: basically risk-
averse (4)                                    _____ Score

Now total up your scores. They can range from a low of 11 to
a high of 90. Most likely your score is somewhere in between.
Keep in mind that no score is "good" or "bad." It's just another
way to check on how you feel about risk. And that's very important for you to get the max out of your benefits.

In general, though, if you scored between 11 and 22, you fit
into Category 1 of the categories listed earlier in this chapter.
Scores from 23 to 44 fit into Category 2; scores from 45 to 66 fit
into Category 3; scores from 67 to 82 fit into Category 4; scores
of 83 and over fit into Category 5.

Take all these measures of your risk tolerance. They'll help
you know yourself better and help you make more intelligent
investment decisions for your benefits. Keep in mind, too, that
you should check up on your risk tolerance about once a year.
Your scores will change with changes in your age, income and
financial resources, number of dependents, and upcoming
heavy expenses like college for your kids. As your feelings
about risk become different, alter your investment strategies
for your benefits packages to suit.

## *THE RETURNS THAT VARIOUS INVESTMENTS GET*

Past returns of various types of investments are never a guarantee of future results. Still, studies over long periods of time do give some clues to the kinds of returns that various investment vehicles get. Keep in mind, though, that you're trying to keep the values of your benefits ahead of inflation, as well as trying to maximize the income to live on after you retire.

A study of investment returns over a long period of time—since 1926—by Ibbotson Associates, Inc. of Chicago, showed these results:

| | Since Jan. 1 1926 | Best Year | Worst Year |
|---|---|---|---|
| Stocks (S&P 500) | 10.3% | 53.9% in 1933 | -43.3% in 1931 |
| Long-Term Treasury Bonds | 4.8% | 40.4% in 1982 | -9.2% in 1967 |
| Treasury Bills | 3.7% | 14.7% in 1981 | 0% in 1938 |
| Inflation | 3.1% | | |

This study assumes that *all* dividends and interest were reinvested. This is the usual case with investments in your 401(k) and other benefits.

Stocks, however, don't give you as much immediate cash in dividends as does interest from bonds. They give about half the yield of bonds in immediate cash, but you get a much bigger increase in value, called appreciation or capital gains. Add the appreciation return to the interest or dividend return and you get total return. You can't spend increases from appreciation until you sell the stocks. So, from a practical standpoint, you shouldn't direct everything in your benefits packages into stocks. You need to strike a balance between bonds, which give you fixed income, and other vehicles like stocks, which may give differing returns each year. By investing in both kinds you add the safety factor of diversification.

Many companies increase their stock dividends over time. Some even have records of increasing dividends every year. That's a plus for stocks. Bond interest, though, is fixed for the life of the bond. Higher dividend income combined with the growth in the prices of stocks helps offset the loss in buying power caused by inflation. That loss is NOT offset with the fixed interest of bonds.

## ACTION IDEAS

How should you decide how much of your assets should be invested for safety, for income, and for growth?

Surveys have shown that investing habits change as people grow older because their goals and needs change. As you might expect, these priorities differ among age groups like this:

Individuals Aged 25–34
1. Overall security
2. Children's education
3. Home buying
    Individuals Aged 35–44
1. Retirement
2. Children's education
3. Overall security
    Individuals Aged 45–64
1. Retirement
2. Overall security
3. Emergencies

Keeping the above results in mind, take these factors about yourself into account:
- your age and state of health;
- how much risk you're willing *and able* to take;
- how much money you have to back you up;
- how much you must rely on income from your investments;
- what you think inflation will be;
- how much you want to leave to your heirs.

## *HOW TO BE A CONSERVATIVE INVESTOR*

Now that you have some clues about how you personally feel about risking the hard-earned money that resides in your benefits, here's a caution: Even if you're willing to take fairly big risks—that is, if you've a high risk tolerance—don't take high risks with money you're really going to need to live on during retirement. Retirement money must supplement your other income when your wage or salary is no longer a major factor in your livelihood and you're depending on pension, Social Security, and savings.

---

### ACTION IDEA

If you really crave to take a flier in the stock market, fine. Just do it with fun money, money you can get along without. Even then, take only calculated risks. Just because a "friend" gives you a hot tip—say, inside news that silver is going to double in price because Uncle Sam is buying it to make future coins out of sterling—don't take the tip.

Instead, make a real study of investing. Your library is full of books on the subject. Read several of them. Pick up *The Wall Street Journal* each day and *Business Week* regularly. Learn what's going on in business, finance, and the markets. Take an adult-education course in investing at your local high school or at a college night school.

Do this for a minimum of three months before you risk a penny in high fliers in the stock or other markets.

As for commodity markets, don't even use fun money for a flier in them. The only people who make money in commodities are the brokers or salespeople who sell the options to buy.

---

The object of conservative stock investing is to get some growth of capital without going through the nightmare of extreme ups and downs in prices. Rapid fluctuations in prices of stocks often cause investors to cash out at just the wrong time. What a blow to the values in your 401(k) or other benefits should you switch from a good investment to cash at just the wrong time!

Conservative investing usually concentrates on buying stocks in well-established companies which pay above-average dividends and regularly increase them. Dividends are the proverbial "bird in the hand" because they guarantee that one of the two parts of your investment return will be positive. The other part, changes in stocks' prices, can be positive or negative.

For example, suppose you buy a stock for $20 a share which pays an annual dividend of $1. That's a 5% annual return ($1 divided by 20 = 5%). If the stock rises 10% or $2 during the first year you own it, the addition of the $1 dividend ups your total return to $3, or 15%. If the share price falls 10%, the dividend offsets half the decline, cutting the loss to 5%. This illustration applies equally well to prices of mutual funds which are more likely to be bought with your benefits money than are individual stocks.

## *TAKING THE LONG-TERM VIEW*

Dividend-paying stocks have two other important advantages:

1. They can play a big role in helping you build capital if you reinvest them. When mutual funds are in one of your benefits, the reinvestment is automatic. Dividend reinvestments generate the same power of compounding you hear about with interest-paying savings accounts, only the returns are normally much higher.
2. Cash dividends and dividend increases are the most obvious indications of the company's profit-making powers and tell you that management has a positive opinion about the company's future. That's the kind of investment you want to select for your benefits package. Some mutual funds concentrate on buying good dividend-paying stocks to achieve their objectives of paying high dividends to their shareholders.

Avoid the common mistakes many investors make as outlined in figure 12. They're more applicable to you when investing your own savings outside of your benefits, but they can help you, too, when you're directing the investment of funds in your 401(k) or other benefits.

*Figure 12. Pitfalls you can avoid in investing*

## MISTAKES THAT INVESTORS COMMONLY MAKE

- They fail to set goals. Without goals, investors can't intelligently pick investment vehicles. They lack incentives to invest.
- They don't find an investing strategy they can live with and instead skip around with different kinds. That never pans out.
- They hand over all responsibility for investment decisions to advisors. No one can win that way, as no one knows as much about an investor's finances and goals as the investor does.
- They don't diversify their investments. When a big single investment goes sour, they are losers.
- They keep too little cash ready for emergencies. When a financial problem arises, they are forced to sell investments at just the wrong time. That's quite a common mistake when investing personal savings.
- They look only at the immediate return of an investment and as a result never get in on really big capital appreciation.
- They don't understand the real costs of investing, such as fees, expenses, commissions, and the like. As a result they overestimate the return and underestimate the costs of getting into and out of an investment.
- They pick investments based only on past performance. That's no guarantee of future results and keeps investors from taking a look at promising new ways to make more money.
- They worry too much about paying taxes. It gets them to buy or sell for tax reasons rather than for solid financial ones.
- They try to decide when to get into or out of the market by timing its ups and downs. Not even the super-pros in investing can catch the market turns precisely.
- They fail to use tax-deferred investment vehicles, like IRAs, 401(k)s, Keoghs, and the like, when they're readily available. (Not applicable to investing for qualified benefits plans, of course, since they're already tax-deferred.)
- They fall for "hot tips" and do no personal research.
- They fail to keep good records, a sure way to get an invitation for a visit to the IRS.

Don't hesitate to question the benefits person in your company about investment methods. Use the list of "common mistakes" as a backup for your questioning.

## KEEPING TRACK OF YOUR INVESTMENTS

When you've reached the point where you're thinking like an investor, you should jump right into making important investment decisions. Your first ones may concern a 401(k) or similar tax-deferred benefit plan. You'll decide between putting all your eggs in a fast-growth basket (surely not a wise thing to do, as you know by now; always diversify) and putting some eggs in that basket, others in a fixed-income fund, and still others in a balanced mutual fund.

Beyond the danger of getting invited to an unpleasant session with an IRS agent over taxes you may (or may not) owe, there are other reasons for keeping good records of investments. To be sure, some of the record keeping for investments in your benefits packages will be done by your company, with reports given to you. Part of your record keeping is to set up separate files for each one of the benefits reports you get. You'll find that a semiannual review of them will trigger questions for you to ask your benefits person. And the review will give you ideas on how to improve the performance of your benefits money.

Even more important, though, are the records for your personal investments, the ones outside any benefits package. Suppose, for instance, you leave your company and you're entitled to get a big chunk of change from its 401(k) plan. You decide to get the company to roll it over into an IRA you've set up for that purpose. Now, an IRA is simply an "envelope" to stash money away in. It's not an investment vehicle itself. Once the money is inside the IRA you need to decide what kinds of investments to make, how to diversify them, and so on. For these purposes you must keep good records.

One of the top reasons for keeping good records is that they help you make more money. When you track carefully how your investments are doing, you can weed out the poor performers and replace them with potentially better ones. When you track and record the performance of, say, a mutual fund in your 401(k), you can decide whether to leave it alone or direct that the money be placed elsewhere.

Another good reason for record-keeping is to allow you to meet your financial goals more closely. Good records help you keep tabs on how well you're doing to meet your financial objectives.

Figure 13 gives you a kind of scorecard for keeping records of your personal investments. Photocopy and enlarge it to 8" x 11", make a dozen copies, and set up a three-ring notebook to keep your records handy.

*Figure 13. Record of securities transactions*

## SECURITIES BOUGHT AND SOLD

Company name _____

Type of security: Common stock _____ Preferred stock _____

Secured bond _____ Debenture _____ Other _____

Brokerage firm _____

Account executive's name _____

Telephone number (    ) _____

### PURCHASES

| Date | No. of shares | Certificate number | Unit price | Commis-sion | Tax | Cost | Total investment |
|------|-----|-----|-----|-----|-----|-----|-----|
|      |     |     |     |     |     |     |     |
|      |     |     |     |     |     |     |     |
|      |     |     |     |     |     |     |     |
|      |     |     |     |     |     |     |     |
|      |     |     |     |     |     |     |     |
|      |     |     |     |     |     |     |     |

**SALES**

| Date | No. of shares | Certificate number | Unit price | Gross price | Expense | Amt. rec'd | Gain/ (loss) |
|------|------|------|------|------|------|------|------|
|  |  |  |  |  |  |  |  |
|  |  |  |  |  |  |  |  |
|  |  |  |  |  |  |  |  |
|  |  |  |  |  |  |  |  |
|  |  |  |  |  |  |  |  |

*It doesn't take a financial genius to ascertain risk, plan invest-ment strategy, and keep an effective scorecard. It does take planning and perseverance. Bill Ticknor is hanging tough as he learns the tricks of the trade. So should you.*

# 7
▼

# 401(K) PLANS

## *Latest Hot Rod Leading the Employee Benefits Pack*

**B**ill *Ticknor is still worried about the salary reduction aspect of the new company benefits plan. At first glance, it seems like he's cutting a hole in his own pocket. But he needs to take a second glance at what's being offered as an investment vehicle.*

Two of the sweetest benefits ever concocted to help employees build up retirement money are called by a now well-known combination of numerals and letters: 401(k) and 403(b) plans.

For many people, the 401(k) presents big problems as well as big opportunities. It's made more than a few people rich. But most employers fail to provide education or training in how to invest this benefits money. How it's invested has a huge impact on how much retirement money you accumulate over the years.

Most 401(k) plans offer at least three options for investment, though there's a trend to offer more. Since most such plans are provided to companies by organizations which specialize in them, it doesn't cost your company anything to offer many more options for investment. So, with other people in the plan, encourage your top executives to increase the number of options. One company offers its employees thirty-six choices! (Check out figure 14 for examples of what three companies are offering.)

*Figure 14. What three companies offer in 401(k) plans*

---

### COMPARE AND CONTRAST: 401(k)s
**If you want to see how your company's 401(k) plan stacks up against some biggies, take a gander at these facts:**

1. Auto company . . . matches 50% of employee contributions up to 5% of salary . . . catch: match is in company stock . . . other investment options are GICs, common stock, and current-interest fund . . . employee can change dollar amount of investment monthly and can alter investment selections once a month . . . performance reports and personal statements come twice a year.
2. Computer company . . . matches 30% up to 5% of employee salary, in cash . . . offers six investment choices including company stock, large- and small-company equity funds, money market, and government securities . . . employees can change contribution amounts four times a year and alter selections twenty-four times . . . they can get monthly updates on performance via their PCs, as well as automated voice-response programs for personal account updates.
3. Consumer products company . . . matches 75% of employee contributions but only up to 2% of salary . . . match comes in form of cash (2/3) and company stock (1/3) . . . three choices besides company stock: GICs, diversified equity, and government securities . . . employees can change amount of contributions at any time, investment selections twice a year, and allocation of existing balances twice yearly in increments of 5% . . . plan participants get monthly reports on all funds and quarterly personal statements.

---

Bear in mind that the company is helping *you* build up retirement monies with a 401(k). Unlike many regular pension plans, where the company contributes all or most of the money to fund them and you're automatically included when you meet its terms, the 401(k) requires you to:

- decide to sign up for the plan;
- set aside part of your salary to go into the plan's fund.

All 401(k) plans are for profitmaking companies; 403(b) plans are for not-for-profits, government agencies, educational institutions, and the like. They're similar, but not the same:

|  | 401(k) | 403(b) |
| --- | --- | --- |
| Money you put in | Usually 10% to 15% of salary to allow for employer's contribution; annual cap on how much you can put in which rises each year to account for inflation | Usually 25% of salary due to lack of employer's contribution; annual cap on how much you can put in which rises year to year to account for inflation and is greater than 401(k) |
| Matching company money | Usual for company to match from a few cents for each dollar you put in, to dollar-for-dollar | Not customary for employer to match any of money |
| Vesting | Immediate for your money; 5 to 7 years for matching money | Immediate; usually no matching money |
| Taxes | Forward averaging allowed to reduce taxes | Forward averaging not allowed |
| Investment advice | Usually available from benefits | Usually not available from provider |

## THE NUTS AND BOLTS
## OF 401(K)S

To save further tongue twisting, the 401(k) will be the main subject here. It goes by other names too, including:

- pension plan;
- thrift plan;
- profit sharing plan;
- salary reduction plan.

It has characteristics of all. These plans have become popular for a variety of reasons:
- personal income tax savings;
- sheltering from tax the earnings in the plan's fund;
- matching contributions from employers as sweeteners;
- a source to borrow from for "hardships," which may include medical and educational expenses.

These good deals are not without some price and some interesting wrinkles. But the pluses overwhelmingly favor your blasting full bore into a 401(k) if your company offers one.

Some individuals—like Bill Ticknor—are reluctant to set aside even a small part of their salaries or wages to get into the plan. They point out that:

1. their money will be locked up in the plan's fund for many years and they won't be able to use it;
2. they can't afford to set aside any money at all, what with the high cost of living these days, aggravated by prices rising faster than their pay;
3. they have little control over how the funds in the plan are invested;
4. they don't like this shift of responsibility for accumulating retirement money from the company to them;
5. they fear that reducing their salary might have some effect on the size of their Social Security benefit when they retire.

There's some merit to some of these complaints. However, the pluses still outweigh the minuses:

1. All 401(k) plans have ways that you can borrow money from them, though they are limited as to how much you can borrow and for what reasons. You'll pay interest on the amount you borrow, but since the money is yours, you're paying interest to yourself.
2. Most companies sweeten the deal. They contribute to the plan anywhere from a few cents for each dollar you put up,

to a full dollar for each dollar you put in. Furthermore, you don't pay any income tax, federal or state, on the dollars you contribute.

| | |
|---|---:|
| Say your annual taxable income is | $30,000 |
| You contribute in a year to the fund | $ 2,000 |
| You'll be taxed by federal and state on | $28,000 |
| Your combined federal and state tax rate | 30% |
| Your tax savings are (30% x $2,000) | $600 |
| Your net out-of-pocket cost is | $1,400 |

Now, suppose your company matches your contribution dollar for dollar. It contributes $2,000 to the 401(k) fund as you did. You now have $4,000 working for you in the fund. After the company's contribution becomes fully vested, it all belongs to you. You can borrow against it. You'll be able to take it out when you retire, or when you leave the company.

Both yours and the company's contributions may then be taxable. And if you're under age 59 ½, there's that 10% penalty to pay, unless you take steps to postpone the tax and avoid the penalty by rolling all the money over into another plan or an IRA.

3. It's true that many organizations are trying to shift some of the costs and responsibilities for retirement income, and some other benefits, too, from the company to the individual employee. But many of them still provide the regular, noncontributory type of pension plan on top of the 401(k).

4. Your Social Security benefits won't be affected at all by your signing up for a 401(k) plan and having your salary reduced by contributions to the plan's fund. Uncle Sam gets a double dose of money because the company is paying the same amount of its money into Social Security as it deducts from your pay. If your salary is $35,000 a year and you contribute $2,000 from it to the 401(k), you and the company will pay Social Security on the full $35,000, not the reduced amount of $33,000.

You'll get annual statements from the 401(k) plan administrator showing how much money you have credited to you (money you put in, and money the company put in), how much of the company's money is currently vested, and how much the money has earned for your account. (Check out figure 15 for one company's report.) When you do retire, you'll have some options on how to take the money, which are usually quite similar to your options in a regular retirement plan.

*Figure 15. Sample 401(k) annual report*

---

### ACME SERVICES CORPORATION
#### To: All 401(k) plan participants
#### Subject: Annual report for the year ending (date)

Enclosed you will find a statement of your individual account balances in the Plan for the plan year ending (date).

The Acme Services Corporation matching contribution this year is at the rate of 50% of your required contributions ($50 for every $100 you contributed).

We are pleased to report a profit for both your Participant Contribution Account, the account where your money or contributions are invested, and in the Acme Services Contribution Account, the account where the matching Acme Services contributions are invested.

The actual earnings this year are as follows:

Participant Contribution Account _____

Acme Services Account  _____

As a reminder, your Participant Contribution Account is invested in certificates of deposit, obligations of the U.S. Government, and Guaranteed Investment Contracts. Your Acme Services Account is also invested primarily in fixed-income obligations, provided, however, that up to 50% of your Acme Services Account may be invested in stock and/or debentures of Acme Services Corporation.

If you have any questions with respect to the above or to your individual statement of contributions and earnings for the current plan year, please call (name and phone extension).

[*This company attaches a memorandum to the Annual Report to participants, which is reproduced below.*]

---

## ACME SERVICES CORPORATION MEMORANDUM

**To:** _____ **Social Security No.** _____

### Re: 401(k) Plan

The balances and contributions made to your accounts in the Plan are
as follows:

Account balances as of (date) _____

*PARTICIPANT CONTRIBUTION ACCOUNT*

| | |
|---|---|
| Required contributions from you | $_____ |
| Previous amounts withdrawn | ($ ——————— ) |
| Investment earnings on your contributions | $_____ |
| Total value of your Participant Contribution Account (100% vested) | $ _____ |
| Amounts available for withdrawal subject to applicable footnotes | $ _____ * |

*ACME SERVICES CONTRIBUTION ACCOUNT*

| | |
|---|---|
| Acme Services contributions | $ _____ |
| Investment earnings on Acme Services contributions | $ _____ |
| Total value of your Acme Services Contribution Account | $ _____ ** |
| Your current vested interest in Acme Services Contribution Account | _____ % |
| Total value of your Participant Contribution Account and Acme Services Contribution Account | $ _____ |

\* May be withdrawn, if not previously withdrawn, without
showing hardship.

\*\* May not be withdrawn prior to termination of employment.

## GICS: MAYBE HEAVEN, MAYBE HELL

When guaranteed investment contracts (GICs) were invented
some years ago, shouts of "hallelujah" burst from the mouths of
tens of thousands of individuals who had interests in 401(k)
benefit plans. They were in seventh heaven with GICs. And

why not? Where else could you get a high, fixed rate of return guaranteed for two to eight years from some of the biggest and strongest insurance companies in the world?

The stampede was on, and before you could whistle "Dixie" well over half the money in 401(k)s was invested in GICs. Afraid to be shut out from offering a runaway best seller, big banks came up with their own version, called bank investment contracts (BICs).

So, are GICs a sure thing? No. It turns out that not only are they not a sure thing, they're not always the real thing. For safety, for example, they're only as good as the credit of the insurance company that issued them. True, many GICs are backed in states that have guaranty insurance plans to cover them as they do regular insurance policies. But that guaranty is only as good as the credit of the organization that makes it. It's not "safe, safe" like the federal deposit insurance you're used to at most banks, which covers deposits of up to $100,000.

Moreover, when interest rates leap, the value of GICs drops fast. Manna from heaven? Hardly.

Then, too, a lot of large insurance companies and banks have fallen from grace over the years. That's made it difficult, and sometimes impossible, for them to pay the interest rates they "guaranteed." Some insurance companies became so pressed they couldn't even cash out those contracts held by 401(k)s that wanted to get their money out. So certain insurance companies froze their GICs, stopped redeeming them. And in some cases they resorted to the fine print in the contract, which allowed them in tough times to renegotiate the guaranteed rate.

On the plus side, though, most 401(k) plans hold enough different GICs so that one failure won't pull down the whole house of cards. There have been some failures to keep the contract guarantees, but no wholesale defaults.

---

**Benefits alert:** If you've directed a big chunk of your benefits money into a GIC portfolio (take care—some of the GIC funds have names that don't indicate they're invested in guaranteed investment contracts), here are some things you should do:

1. Ask the plan administrator which insurance companies or banks are behind the GICs or BICs in the plan.
2. Check these issuers out for financial soundness using ratings from

Standard & Poor's, Moody's, and A. M. Best Company. If you're reading any financial news, you may spot trouble with the issuers in the press.

3. Consider shifting some of your money that's in GICs to another fund or option offered by the plan. Keep down the percentage of new money going into GICs.

4. Put pressure on your management to move the 401(k)'s investments from weak issuers of GICs to stronger ones. ▼

## THE 401(K): GET RICH QUICKER

Many working people think it's silly to start saving for the "golden years," especially when they're still in the early stages of their careers. They don't grab opportunities their employers give them to get rich quicker.

Well, if you're in the group that thinks this way, turn your skeptical eyes on the following table. It assumes that you contribute $600 a year, only $50 a month, to the 401(k) plan and your employer matches half of that, or $300 a year.

| | Your annual payment | Your co's. payment to your acct. | Rate of rtrn | Your total payments | Value of your account |
|---|---|---|---|---|---|
| After 10 years | $600 | $300 | 6% | $ 6,000 | $ 11,862 |
| | $600 | $300 | 8% | $ 6,000 | $ 13,041 |
| | $600 | $300 | 10% | $ 6,000 | $ 14,346 |
| After 20 years | $600 | $300 | 6% | $ 12,000 | $ 33,111 |
| | $600 | $300 | 8% | $ 12,000 | $ 41,184 |
| | $600 | $300 | 10% | $ 12,000 | $ 51,543 |
| After 30 years | $600 | $300 | 6% | $ 18,000 | $ 71,154 |
| | $600 | $300 | 8% | $ 18,000 | $ 101,952 |
| | $600 | $300 | 10% | $ 18,000 | $ 148,041 |

Look at the way your money grows. It grows much faster than other kinds of savings because it's tax deferred. You don't need to take some of the earnings out of the plan to pay taxes.

What's wrong with this table? The main thing is its assumption that over a period of thirty years you'd contribute only $50 a month. Surely as your income went up you'd add more to the pot, and your employer would, too. You'd end up with a much bigger nest egg after ten, twenty, or thirty years or at any time in between. You can't, though, contribute an unlimited amount to a 401(k) plan. There's an annual limit. It's indexed for inflation and goes up modestly each year. Check with your benefits person for the maximum amount each year, and ratchet up your contribution if you can.

The table may not be realistic in another way. It shows your company contributing 50 cents for each dollar you put in. That's known as the company's matching contribution. The more you put in, the more the company has to put in.

However, not all companies match 50 cents to the dollar. Some give less. Others base it on a formula. One company slides its matching contribution from 50 cents to $1.50 for each buck you put in, depending on its profits. Look at it this way: If you put in a dollar and your company adds 50 cents, that's like getting 50% interest the first year—hey, compare that with the 5% (at times even less!) interest rate of a savings account. And, if your company went up to $1.50 for each dollar you put into your 401(k) account, that would be a 150% interest rate.

Is there any more doubt in your mind that 401(k)s will make you get rich quicker?

## SIGN UP TO GET INTO THE 401(K) ACT

You're not automatically covered when you meet certain age and service requirements by a typical 401(k) plan as you normally are with a regular defined-benefit pension plan. Each company can set its own eligibility requirements, though they can't be discriminatory. Generally, though, your employer will set a certain date, like July 1 of each year, for employees to join the plan.

*Figure 16. A 401(k) participation form*

---

## A 401(K) THRIFT PLAN FOR EMPLOYEES OF
## ACME SERVICES CORPORATION
### ACKNOWLEDGEMENT OF PARTICIPATION AND
### SALARY REDUCTION AGREEMENT
#### To: The Administrative Committee*

I hereby acknowledge receipt of notice that I will be eligible to contribute to the Acme Services 401(k) Thrift Plan as of July 1, and that I am subject to all the provisions and terms of the Plan. My election of Beneficiary or Beneficiaries is indicated on the attached form.

My date of birth is _____My Social Security number is _____

☐ I hereby agree to make Required Matching Contributions to the Plan through a salary reduction by payroll deduction in the amount of——% (either 1%, 2%, 3%, or 4%) of my monthly compensation beginning July 1 until further notice (highly compensated employees are limited to a maximum of 3%).

☐ I hereby agree to make Voluntary Contributions to the Plan through a salary reduction by payroll deductions in the amount of —— (1% to 15% in multiples of 1%, but only if the maximum amount for my Required Matching Contributions has been elected above) of my monthly compensation beginning July 1 until further notice (highly compensated employees are limited to a voluntary maximum of 5% of compensation).

I understand that I may withdraw any or all of the above contributions to the Plan for "hardship" on any October 1, January 1, April 1, or July 1, subject to the limitations and penalties set forth in the Plan provided notice is properly given and approved by the Committee prior to those dates. I further understand that if I withdraw any or all of the above Required Matching Contribution for "hardship," I will not be entitled to any matching Acme Services contributions for the then-current plan year. I also understand that no earnings on my contributions may be withdrawn and that no earnings will be credited for the current plan year (the year in which the withdrawal is effective) on any amounts withdrawn.

This salary reduction agreement will remain in force until either modified or discontinued by me or the terms of the Plan.

---

Date                     Participant

*Return this form to Employee Benefits department on or before July 1.

When you do sign up, you'll be asked to fill out and sign a form called something like "Acknowledgement of participation and salary reduction agreement." Figure 16 is an actual example of one company's form.

You'll also be asked to sign another agreement covering the payment of the money in the plan in case you die before you've drawn out all of the money you're entitled to. Figure 17 is a copy of this form, usually called the "Beneficiary Form."

## BETTER TO SWITCH THAN FIGHT

Say you're salting dollars away to the max in your 401(k). Say your company's plan offers you four choices to sock your dough into. Which ones should you choose? What percentage of your money should go into each option? When and why should you change?

Your decisions depend largely on three things:

1. your risk tolerance (check out chapter 6);
2. your age;
3. your willingness to think and act like an investor.

Risk tolerance is kind of like a gambling quotient. Some people are so cautious when it comes to money that they can't stand the idea of losing a penny. They would literally bury their cash in a tin can in their backyards if it weren't for the greater convenience of bank savings accounts insured for up to $100,000 by the Federal Deposit Insurance Corporation.

At the other extreme are real gamblers. They'd bet their whole 401(k) on a hundred-to-one shot in the Kentucky Derby if it were allowed.

*Figure 17. Typical beneficiary form for 401(k) plans*

---

## BENEFICIARY FORM
### To: The Administration Committee

---

In accordance with the provisions of the above Plan, I select the following Beneficiary(ies) to receive the balance in my account at the time of my death, and I select the following manner of payment to such Beneficiary(ies). Such selections are subject to (a) my right to revoke, amend, or change them by notifying you in writing to that effect and (b) to all terms of the Plan. These selections revoke any prior selections by me.

*Note: Under the terms of the Retirement Equity Act of 1984, your spouse is automatically your primary beneficiary unless you elect otherwise and obtain his/her written consent.*

1. Primary Beneficiary(ies)                Relationship

_____            _____

_____            _____

2. Contingent Beneficiary(ies)           Relationship

_____            _____

_____            _____

3. Request for Payment _____    (a)LUMP SUM; or

   (b)____Payment over:          (i)_____(number of years) or

                                 (ii)_____per month until acct. is
                                      fully distributed.

If a child or children of mine shall be named as Beneficiary(ies) to share equally under 1 or 2 above (but not when a child or children of mine shall be named under both), any other child or children hereafter born to or legally adopted by me shall share equally in the benefits payable to the named child or children, unless otherwise indicated herein. If more than one Beneficiary is named under 1 or 2 above, the Beneficiaries shall receive the benefits, if living, in equal shares unless otherwise indicated herein.

_____            _____
Date                           Signature of Participant

CONSENT OF SPOUSE (if not named as Primary Beneficiary; if no spouse, write N/A below):

Date:_____Signature of spouse: _____
Spouse's signature notarized by: _____

---

The problem for individuals at both of these extremes of risk tolerance is that they're both going to be losers. The ones who scurry for the shelter of insured savings accounts normally see the buying power of their safe accounts severely eroded by inflation. Inflation rates have been all over the map over the years, and there's nothing on the horizon to suggest that they won't jump up and down in the future. During only the last two decades they've reached nearly 16% and have been down as low as 3%—but not for long.

The point is, whether inflation is 16% or 3%, the "take no losses" savers do, in fact, lose. Sure, they get their deposits back in full, but what's their buying power? When inflation is low, banks cut interest rates, so the "take no losses" players are still behind the eight ball with lower buying power.

At the other end of the spectrum, the gamblers bet on things like commodity options. When the price of soybeans doesn't hit the right level, they don't get back even the money they put into the option. They lose it all.

After finding your risk tolerance, the next influence on your decisions for your 401(k) cash is your age. Generally, the younger you are, the more risk you can take. You may not have the stomach to take it, but you can and should because you can make up losses more easily than older people. Also, you're at greater risk because you have more years for inflation to cut down the value of your savings. So you should take more chances to get a higher return than interest-bearing investments normally give you. Conversely, the older you are, the more cautious you should be.

## YOU BE THE JUDGE

Say your 401(k) offers you four ways to invest your money. Usually each option consists of a mutual fund or some other type of professionally managed fund.

Fund #1—A fund invested in federally guaranteed securities like U.S. Treasury bills, notes, and bonds or federally guaranteed mortgages known as GNMAs (Ginnie Maes).

Fund #2—A fund of common and preferred stocks issued by large, well-established corporations. The values are supposed to grow at least as fast as the economy and possibly much faster. Over a period of many decades they've grown faster than the economy has.

Fund #3—A fund made up of guaranteed investment contracts (GICs) designed to produce greater income than savings accounts or CDs.

Fund #4—A balanced fund, one that mixes blue-chip stocks with bonds issued by well-financed corporations to give you income and a shot at some growth in value.

Here's a chart for spreading around, or allocating by percentage, the money going into your 401(k) account.

| Your age | Fund #1 Gov't bonds | Fund #2 Stocks | Fund #3 GICs | Fund #4 Stock/bond |
|----------|---------------------|----------------|--------------|--------------------|
| 20–34 | 0 | 50% | 20% | 30% |
| 35–44 | 10% | 50% | 20% | 20% |
| 45–54 | 15% | 45% | 20% | 20% |
| 55–64 | 20% | 30% | 30% | 20% |
| 65–70 | 60% | 10% | 20% | 10% |

You can see from the table that the younger you are, the more you should invest in funds that provide growth. That's not just because you want to make a big score. It's also because inflation is a bigger enemy of yours when you have twenty or more years to go to retirement than it is when you have only ten or fewer years.

Moreover, over the last sixty years or so common stocks have given greater returns than any other kind of security, an average of just over 10%. During the decade from 1982 to 1992 the return from stocks was about 18%. Take any ten-year period over the last sixty years, and stocks have outperformed corporate bonds and treasury securities.

More risk? To be sure, over a few years. Greater reward is a near certainty over ten or more years. Question: Why not put *all* your money into common stock funds? Answer: You need to diversify for safety in the short run, in case you need to make sudden withdrawals for emergencies.

Why fear inflation? Because it hurts your buying power more than it helps investments' returns. Take a look at the next table, which shows how radically inflation lessens the value of your savings.

| In this number of years | the buying power of $100,000 sinks to this amount at these rates of inflation: | | | | |
|---|---|---|---|---|---|
| | **4%** | **5%** | **6%** | **7%** | **8%** |
| 5 | $82,190 | $78,350 | $74,730 | $71,300 | $68,060 |
| 10 | $67,560 | $61,390 | $55,840 | $50,830 | $46,320 |
| 15 | $55,530 | $48,100 | $41,730 | $36,240 | $31,520 |

Even older people need to invest some money to protect themselves against inflation. Run your finger along the fifteen-year line in the above table and see how drastically people aged 65 can be hurt by inflation during the rest of their lives.

You may find that your risk tolerance changes as you become more familiar with investing. You may put a little higher percentage of your cash into stocks when this happens than the table on the preceding page suggests. When you start thinking and acting like an investor, that, too, may influence you to change the percentages for each kind of investment fund.

### ACTION IDEA

When you move from one age group to the next, don't make quick changes in the allocation of your 401(k) assets from one fund to another. Instead, direct your new monthly additions of cash into the funds where you want an increased percentage of your assets. Of course, at some point you may have to switch more money out of a fund to push it down to 10%.

This strategy may take a year or two to get the allocations adjusted in each fund, but it's a more profitable way to make the changes.

---

Surveys have shown that on average, individuals who receive pensions from regular defined benefit plans and Social Security get only about two-thirds of their retirement income from these two sources. That's tough to live on, especially since most people retire on only about 70% of their final pay—quite a comedown.

Most retirees supplement their pensions and Social Security with earnings from investments, withdrawals from their nest-egg savings, and part-time work. Retirement experts estimate that 401(k) plans will provide up to half the retirement income for the baby-boomer generation as it starts to retire.

That source of income is going to become even more important as companies and other organizations move away from defined benefit pension plans that provide a steady income for life. More and more organizations are moving toward contribution plans such as 401(k)s, profit sharing, ESOPs, and others. This shift puts much more responsibility on employees to prepare financially for their retirement years.

---

**Benefits alert:** Experts say that the biggest mistake employees make when choosing how to invest their 401(k) plan money is being too conservative. That's borne out by the fact that nearly 90% of the money in 401(k)s is invested in interest-paying vehicles like GICs, CDs, U.S. Treasury securities, and savings accounts. That's true whether employees are 28 or 58.

Nearly everyone below the age of 60 should be putting more money into common stock funds and into balanced funds of stocks and bonds than they're currently doing. Grab the brass ring before it's too late, and see that your money is invested in instruments that have some opportunity to GROW. ▼

## MORE WAYS TO MAKE AND MOVE
## YOUR MONEY

You ought to salt away cash in your 401(k) to the max to get advantage of the tax savings. Contrast that tax situation with putting money in a savings account, a CD, or most any other investment outside the 401(k). The IRS will tap you on the shoulder each year for its cut of your profits in such cases.

That's a real argument for contributing the maximum amount to shelter it from taxation. And anything your employer chips in to match your contribution grows tax deferred, too. Moreover, what your employer kicks in doesn't count against the legal limitations on the amount you can contribute each year.

But, you argue, what if you sock away all that cash, which you can't touch until you retire without heavy penalties, and you suddenly need it? That's a bitter pill to swallow.

Fortunately, most 401(k) plans let you borrow funds from your own account in certain hardship situations, such as:

- medical expense emergencies;
- college education for the kids;
- a down payment on a new home;
- avoiding eviction or foreclosure on a mortgage;
- some other purposes specified in the plan.

You'll have to pay interest on the loan, but that's not all that bad because you're paying the interest to your own account, so you're paying interest to yourself. Usually the interest rate is tied to some base; for instance, it may be a couple of percentage points above the rate banks charge to their best customers. Not a bad deal.

Generally you'll have to repay the loan within five years, though loans to buy a home are usually stretched out to ten or fifteen years. You can't borrow all the cash in your account, normally only one-half, and a maximum dollar limit is imposed.

**Benefits alert:** Borrowing against your 401(k) sounds like a good idea. But is it? Depends.

1. You may be jeopardizing your only retirement fund other than Social Security.
2 If you leave the company, your employer may demand immediate repayment of the loan in full.
3. You may create a tax problem if you don't pay back the loan right away. The IRS will claim you've drawn down your 401(k), unless you've used the cash for catastrophic medical expenses, and will slap you with a 10% tax penalty if you're under age 59½. You'll also owe regular income tax on what you've borrowed and not repaid.▼

## *YOUR RETIREMENT MONEY: A TAXING PROBLEM*

You can come into tax problems with retirement money long before you actually retire. They can hit you when you change jobs, for example. Or when your company downsizes and dumps you out on the street, as one poor soul put it, "like the rest of the garbage." In such circumstances you could have substantial chunks of money coming your way from your participation in qualified pension plans, profit sharing, or other thrift plans.

Trouble is, you can easily bump into huge taxes on these wads of money if you don't do things right. What a way to ruin your biggest benefits.

Unfortunately, when it comes to taxes you can't fully trust the advice of—well, anyone. Uncle Sam admits that its people at the Internal Revenue Service who answer tax questions are right only 80% to 85% of the time. And you're stuck with the bill for more taxes even if an IRS employee gives you wrong advice!

The problem with giving tax advice in a book, though, is that Congress has gotten into the nasty habit of changing the tax laws almost every year. To make matters worse, new rulings and court cases often change the opinions of even the best tax experts, like CPAs and tax attorneys. So the following tax information on retirement benefits was right when it was written. But parts of it may have changed. Always check it out.

When your employer pays you what's called a "distribution" (which can be all the money allocated to your account) from a "qualified" retirement plan ("qualified" means that the plan was looked over by the Treasury Department, which said it met all the rules), you have some choices to make:

- Roll the money over to an Individual Retirement Account (IRA). (A rollover is just what it sounds like: You move the money—roll it over—from one kind of retirement plan to another.) Beware: there are potential tax problems doing this relatively simple task. Check them out.
- Keep the money, and pay taxes and maybe a penalty on it.
- Leave the money, if you can, in the employer's plan.

Your age comes also into the tax picture: under 55, over 59½, and between 55 and 59½.

- Under 55: Let the money stay in your employer's plan, if possible—and it may or may not be—but you don't pay tax. A rollover into an IRA is possible, though it has its own taxing problems which can be solved.
- Over 59½: Roll over the money into an IRA or take special tax treatments such as five- or ten-year forward averaging— certain rules apply, but they lower the tax bite.
- Between 55 and 59½: If you were born before 1936, you have the same choices as if you're over 59½. If you were born on or after January 1, 1936, you'll pay an early-withdrawal penalty unless you've left your job.

The following table shows your choices and tax situation.

You can see how you can temporarily make a great escape from paying any tax by taking the cash and rolling it over into a new qualified plan or an IRA within sixty days after you've received it. You can roll over part of the cash and use the rest for whatever you want. The earnings of the partial rollover will be tax deferred, if you do it right, until you're age 70½ or start pulling cash out. You'll pay tax on the part you didn't roll over, though, and that cash is *NOT* eligible for forward averaging.

| | Rollover | Lump-sum | Leave with employer |
|---|---|---|---|
| **What you do** | Roll over the money into IRA | Keep the money | Leave your money where it is |
| **Tax effect** | None | Taxed as current income | None, unless you take out periodic payments |
| **Things to think about** | • You have to roll over within 60 days after you get the money or you'll get stuck with tax<br>• You won't get stuck with a penalty<br>• The IRA grows with no current tax<br>• You can take payments out at any time<br>• You can put this money into a future employer's plan | • If you're under 59½ you may have to pay a penalty<br>• If born before 1936, eligible for 20% capital gains tax<br>• You can't put this money into another employer's plan | • No tax to pay now as account grows<br>• You can take periodic payments taxed as income without penalty if you get payments over 5 years or until age 59½, whichever is longer<br>• No control over how your money is invested other than plan allows<br>• Can only get money as plan allows |

Table adapted from "Deciding What to Do with Your Company Retirement Money" by T. Rowe Price Investment Services, Inc.

## *401(K)S: THE MORE THINGS CHANGE...*

You've been advised frequently in this book that when it comes to taxes, check them out. While this book was being written, Congress came up with a new wrinkle, to make money for the government, of course, with regard to rollovers of cash you have in your company 401(k), profit sharing, or other thrift plans.

The table above shows that the "tax effect" under "rollover" is "none." That can still be true, but you have to work a little harder to make the tax effect "none."

Say, for example, that you have $30,000 in your retirement account, such as a 401(k), when you leave the company. The new law requires your company to deduct 20% of that money, that's $6,000, when it issues you the check. To avoid this deduction, you must now set up an IRA, then ask your company to *roll the money directly into it*. Actually, your company must let you choose whether to collect the cash, leave the money in its plan, or have it transferred to your IRA or another pension plan, such as one your new employer may have.

If you don't go that route and take the money less the $6,000 deduction, you can still get a refund of it when you file your tax return. But you can't just roll over the $24,000 net you received. You must get another $6,000 and make your rollover the total of $30,000. Then you can claim a refund of the $6,000 withheld when you file your tax return. As before these changes, your rollover must be done within sixty days.

That's the bad news. The good news is that the law was also changed to allow you, assuming you stay on the job, to roll over portions of your 401(k) or other tax deferred savings plan (at least 50% of it) into an IRA and still retain its tax deferred status. That requires, of course, that the plan you're in allows such withdrawals. START LOBBYING NOW FOR THAT WITHDRAWAL BENEFIT IF YOUR COMPANY'S PLAN DOESN'T ALREADY ALLOW IT.

This is an excellent opportunity for you to diversify your investments outside the several choices you may have in your company's plan. It gives you much greater control of exactly how your money is invested. And the earnings on it are still tax deferred—you don't pay tax until you take cash out.

## *HEY, IT'S YOUR MONEY*

The Department of Labor has issued rules (effective January 1994) that can have an impact on your 401(k) plan if your company chooses to play by them. They give rights like these:

1. You get options to choose among three or more kinds of investments.
2. You can switch among those investments each quarter.
3. You can ask for information about these various investments so you can choose the ones best for you.

These rules, unfortunately, don't touch on another important area—how much of the costs of the plan are being dumped on you and other plan members. These costs are administrative, investment management, and loads, or in the case of insurance products, surrender charges.

Ask your benefits contact which charges the company absorbs and which ones are paid out of the 401(k). If you're lucky, the company pays them all. But if all or some of these costs are being sloughed off on the plan, you'll have slower growth and less money to retire on.

In the latter case, squawk loudly. Urge company management to find no-load providers and no-cost 401(k) administrators—or to let the company pick up these costs. Bosses and managers in the plan will benefit, too, when the company, not the plan, pays.

## *TROUBLE AHEAD?*

401(k) plans have been around only since 1978. So the crowds of takers from these plans haven't yet started drawing on their accounts for retirement income. Big question: Will there be enough money in the pot?

Some ominous signs of trouble are looming. Part of the half-empty-money-pot problem results from the vicious swings in interest rates that have occurred since many 401(k)s were set up. They've pulled the rug out from under optimistic projections of the sizes of participants' nest eggs.

Think about it. You could buy a three-year CD in the early '80s with an interest rate of 16% to 17%. Later on you could direct your 401(k) money into a GIC that brought in a certain 10% to 12%. That lulled to sleep many plan participants, as well as "expert" financial planners. They thought earnings were sure things. Many of them projected earnings in their accounts at what they thought was a conservative 8%, which would seat them in Fat City by retirement time. So they didn't sock away as much in the plan as they could. Worse, they failed to learn how to think like investors to generate more earnings.

Then the bottom fell out of interest rates, as it always does over time. CDs began paying 3%. GICs couldn't meet their guarantees. High-interest-rate bonds were called. New ones paid hardly any more interest than CDs. Result: For many 401(k) plan participants, there's just not going to be enough money in their accounts when they reach retirement age.

Solution? Make sure that some of your money is invested for total return. That's the current yield plus growth of the principal amount. Don't poke around looking only for the best current interest rates and total safety. Make sure that you direct some of your 401(k) cash into growth investments.

*Our friend Bill Ticknor is a lot more sanguine now about the money that's being siphoned out of his paycheck every week. In fact, he's beginning to relish reading about the financial ups and downs of the companies covered in the business sections of his papers. He realizes it's his money on the line in some instances. It could be yours too.*

# 8

▼

# OTHER INVESTMENT DEVICES

## *Sizing Up Mutual Funds, ESOPs, and More*

**B**ill Ticknor is beginning to get the hang of this financial stuff. He's taken his own risk pulse and started crystallizing his options in the new 401(k) plan his company is offering. He's still a little hazy on the main choices in mutual funds, and he hasn't yet looked into his own company's stock option plans.

Many of your benefits are aimed at different targets. All of them help you make or save money, but they do it in different ways. You can control how much you can make or save in some of them. In others you can't.

To help you focus more clearly on your chances to improve each type of benefit, take a look at the following chart, which breaks them down into broad general types. Since we're on the topic of financial benefits and investments, numbers 6 and 7 are the pertinent categories.

| BENEFIT TYPE | USUALLY PROVIDED BY |
|---|---|
| 1. Health and medical cost protection | Health and medical insurance, HMOs, PPOs |

| | |
|---|---|
| 2. Protection for your family | Group life insurance |
| 3. Loss of current wages | Disability insurance |
| 4. Building savings | Payroll deduction plans for U.S. Savings Bonds, other thrift plans |
| 5. Funds for retirement | Defined benefit pension plans |
| 6. Deferring current income to supplement retirement income or for other uses | 401(k) and 403(b) plans, SEPs, SERPs, SARSEPs, IRAs |
| 7. Investments to build current and future wealth | Employee stock ownership plans (ESOPs), stock option plans, stock purchase plans, restricted stock awards, mutual funds, profit sharing |

You can make a difference in the amount of money you'll get out of those items. They give you a chance to substantially boost your future income and wealth.

## PICKING PROFITABLE MUTUAL FUNDS FOR YOUR BENEFITS INVESTMENTS

Mutual funds are likely to play a big part in your benefits investments. At present, many organizations offer several choices of mutual funds for participants to choose from. They all possess certain overall characteristics with differing objectives, such as aggressive growth, high yield, balance, safety, etc. The company, or the organization hired to do the grunt work with its benefits plans, picks the mutual funds for the plan. You don't have any say, in most plans, about which funds they're going to offer.

That's the situation now. Government prodding, though, is likely to revise present and future plans to leave the choice of funds, many choices, up to you. So you should learn something about how to pick mutual funds, how you can get best results, things that can go wrong, and mistakes you can make. How well you understand mutual funds will have a big impact on the growth and values of your 401(k) and other benefits.

Basically, a mutual fund is simply an investment company that buys stocks, stocks and bonds, or bonds alone, which some investment management expert has recommended, in order to achieve the fund's objective of growth, high income, safety, or whatever.

Some funds charge a commission, known as a load, when you buy them. The commission rates run from 2% to 8.5% but have been trending down in recent years. Other funds, no-load funds, don't charge a commission when you buy. Some funds don't make you pay a commission when you buy but do charge one when you sell. That's called a back-load. Still others charge certain expenses to the fund itself, not directly to you. But you're really paying for it in fees to cover advertising and marketing expenses. Some investors call them 12b-1 funds after the section of investment law that permits this kind of fee. All funds pay management fees to the experts who pick the securities to be bought or sold for the fund. Other expenses for handling the administration of the fund are also taken out of the money in the fund.

## GETTING STARTED IN MUTUAL FUNDS

If it sounds to you like a lot of money is being made off mutual funds, you're right. On the other hand, mutual funds have been nearly runaway best sellers at times for the funds' shareholders because they've often achieved their money-making objectives. Mutual funds also give the average person on your block a chance to participate in the financial markets without putting up huge sums of money to start investing. The risk is less, too. Most funds give employees a safer and sounder way to generate more income in their 401(k)s or other benefits than they can get from bank savings accounts, CDs, and other fixed-income investments.

You can, for instance, get started buying a mutual fund with an investment of as little as $100. You can keep contributing when you want to put in more money for as little as an additional $25. More typical of initial purchases are $2,000 to start and additions of $100 monthly or whenever you want to make them. Of course, when your company buys mutual funds to go into one or more of its benefits, it contributes much larger sums and may pay lower commission rates.

When you choose a mutual fund in your benefits package, the dividends paid by the fund are automatically invested in additional shares of the fund. That's an excellent strategy because it gives you a much faster buildup of the value of your benefit. Also, by reinvesting the dividends, you escape the taxes you'd have to pay if the dividends were paid out to you.

When you buy a mutual fund as part of your personal financial planning rather than as part of a company benefit, the fund will give you a choice of reinvesting the dividends or taking them in cash. Your decision should be guided by whether you need the cash right now or whether you can let it buy additional shares in the fund to get the advantages of compounding. With either choice, however, you'll be liable for income taxes on dividends paid unless the fund is made up of tax-exempt securities.

**A cautionary note:** Most mutual funds let you reinvest the dividends without paying any commission. A few mutual funds do charge a commission on reinvested dividends, however. Since the commission reduces the amount of money that's working for you, you should make sure that the fund with a sales charge for reinvested dividends does extremely well, better than average, for its shareholders. Otherwise the commission will eat too heavily into your profits.

**A second cautionary note:** Before you embark on any mutual fund voyage, make sure you've got all your oars in the water. Review the common mistakes outlined in figure 18 that fund investors like yourself could make. Then brief yourself in figure 19 on the Glossary of Mutual Fund Terms you're likely to encounter on your journey.

## BRICKS TO BUILD YOUR WEALTH: EMPLOYEE STOCK PURCHASE PLANS

Stock purchase or stock option plans are potentially one of the best money-making benefits you can get. When you hold stock in your company, you're a part owner. The more shares of stock you have, the larger portion of the corporation you own.

*Figure 18. Traps to beware of in mutual fund investing*

---

## SEVEN COMMON MISTAKES IN MUTUAL FUND INVESTING

1. Falling for advertising that emphasizes high yield. You ought to look for total return as well as a fund that meets your objectives.
2. Buying a fund without checking into all the fees, commissions, and expenses. A load fund is not necessarily more expensive over a period of years than a no-load. Other charges can significantly affect how well the fund pays its shareholders.
3. Not reinvesting all dividends paid to get the advantages of faster growth through compounding.
4. Failing to consider a fund that's in a family of funds that lets you shift to another fund in the family, without charge, when your objectives change or you're not satisfied with the performance of the fund you bought.
5. Not checking the fund's application form to take advantage of the many privileges that most funds offer, such as preauthorized purchases, telephone transactions, wire transfers, and the like.
6. Not doing some library research through various mutual fund reviewers before making a decision to buy.
7. Choosing a fund based on its latest yield or ranking rather than looking back over its performance for the last five and ten years.

---

*Figure 19. The language of mutual funds*

---

## A GLOSSARY OF MUTUAL FUND TERMS

**Automatic investment plans**—You specify to your mutual fund how much you want to invest each month or each quarter. Then you give your bank written instructions (funds usually provide you with the forms for the bank) to allow the fund to draw the amount from your checking account until you instruct it to stop.

**Back-load**—A fee charged by some funds when you sell all or some of the shares you hold in it.

**Check-writing service**—Some funds offer you the privilege of writing checks against the money represented by shares in your account in the fund. When the fund gets the check, it sells shares in your account for cash to cover the check. Some funds do not charge for this service. Most funds have a minimum limit on the size of the check you can write, which is often $500. When you do write a check, you have to remember that you may be liable for taxes if the shares sold cost less than their value when you wrote the check. You then have a capital gain, which is taxable. (This check-writing service is not available, of course, from funds in a benefit plan.)

**Diversification**—Most funds invest in fifty to one hundred or more securities at any time. This lessens your risk of loss.

**Dividend reinvestment**—An option for you to tell the fund whether you want dividends paid to be reinvested in additional shares of the fund or paid in cash to you. (Dividend reinvestment is automatic for fund shares in benefits plans.)

**Excessive trading**—Most mutual funds limit the number of times in a year that you can buy or sell your shares in the fund or exchange them for shares in other funds in the same family.

**Exchange privilege**—As your goals change, you may exchange all or part of your shares in one fund to another fund at low or no cost.

**Family of funds**—A single organization that offers a number of mutual funds (some go as high as twenty-five to thirty) to investors to meet differing objectives. You can often switch from one fund in the family to another at no or low charge.

**Fund-to-fund dividends**—You can add a new account in the family of funds by automatically investing your dividends from your dividend-paying fund into shares of another fund in the same family.

**Load**—The commission charged by some funds when you purchase shares. Some funds also charge a load, or commission, for reinvesting dividends.

**Objectives**—The fund spells out for you its objectives, whether they are growth, income, exemption from taxes, etc.

**No-load fund**—A fund in which no commission is charged for the purchase of shares.

**NAV—Net Asset Value**—The price per share for the fund normally calculated daily as of the close of the New York Stock Exchange. The price is determined by subtracting the liabilities of the fund from its assets and dividing the result by the number of shares outstanding.

**POP—Public Offering Price**—The price at which fund shares are offered to the public. It's normally the same price as the NAV for no-load funds. For load funds, the commission is added to the NAV to determine the price to the public.

**Prospectus**—A document that spells out a lot of information about objectives, actual results of the fund over periods of years, fees, expenses, sales charges, etc. It tells you about the risk level of the fund, its policies and management, and the background of persons advising the fund on investments. Government rules *require* that you be given a copy of the prospectus for a mutual fund *before* you invest.

**Toll-free access**—Most funds have a toll-free 800 number you can call for assistance or service. Many of these toll-free lines operate twenty-four hours a day, seven days a week. Within specified limits, you can telephone a fund to sell shares you own and have the cash delivered to you.

---

## ACTION IDEA

Go to your public library and ask the librarian at the reference desk for reading material on mutual funds. Ask if the library has one of the services, such as Morningstar or Wiesenberger, that discuss the performance and rate the quality of mutual funds.

After you've studied this material, pick a fund that meets some objective of yours—safety, income, growth—and that has a very low initial investment amount, like $100 or $250. Call the fund's 800 number—one will usually be provided—and ask for a prospectus.

When you get it, read it carefully. When you understand the information given, *and only when you understand it*, fill out the application and send it to the fund with the minimum initial investment. Keep in mind that you can always get out of a fund, usually with only a telephone call, if you get worried that you've made a mistake.

Why go through this exercise? You'll learn more about mutual fund investing by being an active participant than in any other way. You'll be far better able to make good decisions on investments that are in your benefits package and boost up their return, too.

Owning stock means you're entitled to have some say in how the corporation is run. You exercise your say by voting for the board of directors, which oversees the company. At times you'll be asked to approve or disapprove of some of their actions. Your vote may not be a very strong one, but directors must pay attention to what stockholders want or risk getting voted out.

The value of your stocks can increase and decrease. If the price goes up, you make a profit when you sell. If the price goes down, you lose when you sell. Keep in mind, though, that stock prices go up and down, and you don't have to sell unless you want to.

Here's how a typical employee stock purchase plan works:

- You'll be given a prospectus, which gives all the details about the stock purchase plan, how much of it you can buy, how its price is set, and many other particulars.
- You'll be told that there is an "option period" of a specific length, say twelve months; at the beginning of the period the company will give you options to purchase a certain amount of stock, with the purchase to be made at the end of the option period.
- The corporation sets a certain date for you to enroll, such as September 1.
- You'll be given a form to enroll in the plan and to designate how you'll pay for the stock, how much you want to buy, and how much you're permitted to buy.
- The prospectus will tell you how the price of the stock is calculated and what kind of discount, if any, from the market value you'll get. Many companies let you buy the stock under option at 85% of its market value.
- You'll be told about the tax situation when you're given the option, when you buy, and when you sell the stock.

To illustrate the workings of a stock purchase or option plan, here are Questions and Answers based upon one company's actual plan. The company helps employees pay for their stock through monthly payroll deductions.

*Q. How do I enroll?*

**A.** If you've been continuously employed by the company for two years before September 1, you're eligible to participate in the twelve-month option period which begins on that date. Enter the amount of your monthly investment on the enrollment form. The amount must be at least $5 but no more than 15% of your base pay (base pay does not include overtime or special bonuses).

*Q. How much should I invest?*

**A.** That's up to you. The plan guarantees you'll pay less than market value for your stock, though only you can decide how much you can afford to set aside each month. Once you do decide, you cannot increase your monthly investment. (**ADVICE: Sign up for as big a payroll deduction as you can.**)

*Q. How do I invest?*

**A.** Your monthly investment will be deducted from your midmonth pay and automatically deposited in a special savings account in your name.

*Q. What happens to my money during the option period?*

**A.** It earns passbook interest while you're in the plan. You may withdraw the money, with interest, at any time up to August 16 next year. However, if you remain in the plan after August 16, your option will be exercised and your investments will be used to purchase our company's common stock. (**ADVICE: This is a win-win deal—your contributions are earning interest even if you don't buy the stock.**)

*Q. How many shares can I buy?*

**A.** The number of shares you buy is determined by the amount of money you invest divided by 85% of the fair market value of our stock on the opening day of the option period. For example, if you decide to invest $50 a month (a total of $600 during the option period), and 85% of the fair market value of our stock is $25 a share on the first day of the option period, you would buy twenty-four shares. You may not buy more than five hundred shares during the option period. Also, you may not purchase shares to exceed $25,000 in fair market value determined at the beginning of the option period.

*Q. How is the price I pay for my stock determined?*

A. It will be 85% of the fair market value at the beginning of the option period or 85% of its fair market value at the end of the option period—whichever is lower. (**ADVICE: In this case you're guaranteed a profit the day you exercise the option.**)

*Q. Can I lower or discontinue my monthly pay deduction during the option period and still buy some shares?*

A. Yes. You may do that one time during the option period, but you'll buy fewer shares.

*Q. If I stop working for the company during the option period, can I still stay in the plan?*

A. No. You must be an active employee as of August 31 to get the stock optioned to you. If you leave the company, your money and interest earned will be returned to you. (**ADVICE: Hang onto your job until after you've exercised your option— this is one benefit you *can* take with you.**)

*Q. Can I lose money participating in the plan?*

A. You can't lose money before the stock is purchased and transferred to your name. Once it's yours, you can lose money if the price goes down and you sell your shares at a lower price than the price you paid.

*Q. What happens if I die during the option period?*

A. The money in your account plus interest will be turned over to the beneficiary named on your enrollment form. Neither your estate nor your beneficiary can exercise your option.

*Q. How do I get my stock, and what do I do with it?*

A. You'll get a stock certificate shortly after the end of the option period. Keep it in a safe place. If you want to sell or transfer it, review carefully the information on selling and re-registering, which will be given to you with the certificate.

*Q. Do I have to pay any brokerage fees?*

A. Not when you buy the shares, but you may have to pay a broker when you sell them.

*Q. What's the effect of my being in the plan on my income taxes?*

A. This is a complicated question, and some of the simple answers appear in the following table. For the hard ones, **CALL IN THE TAX EXPERTS.**

| When this happens | The Federal tax impact is | In this year |
|---|---|---|
| You're granted an option to buy | INCOME NOT AFFECTED | — |
| Interest is credited to your account | ORDINARY INCOME: you must pay tax on the interest | The year it's added |
| Stock is bought and put in your name | INCOME NOT AFFECTED | — |
| You get dividends on your stock | ORDINARY INCOME: you must add them to other income | The year they are paid |
| You sell your stock within one year of the end of the option period | CALL IN THE TAX EXPERTS | |
| You sell your stock more than one year after the option period ends or you die owning the stock | CALL IN THE TAX EXPERTS | |

Some companies will help you with the last two circumstances. The best advice, though, if you're in any of these situations, is to see a tax expert.

Don't, however, let possible tax complications deter you from investing in stock options if you really believe your company is going places. Think about those hardy souls who worked for Coca-Cola when it started up. They invested in Coke's stock and ended up with more money than they could easily spend. Or, more recently, read the stories of Microsoft Corp., which has made at least two billionaires and quite a few millionaires through the benefit of ownership of stock.

The stock purchase plan described above is only one kind.

There are many variations of this type of benefit. Some give employees the right to buy over a number of years at a fixed price rather than just a one-year option period. Some don't offer the immediate profit of letting you buy at 85% of the market price. Some option plans offer stock at 100% of the market price on the date the option is exercised, though participants can wait for the market price to go down before they buy the optioned stock.

Are stock purchase or option plans another way to get rich quicker? If you've done some homework about your company's finances and future outlook and know the risks and potential rewards, they sure can be. Not quite as good a deal as the 401(k)s, but well worth socking money into whenever you can. There's a trend toward greater employee ownership, and stock purchase and option plans are one part of the movement. (**ADVICE: Get in on the action. This is a benefit that gives you some control over how to turn it into more money.**)

---

**Benefits alert:** Some employees think that if they don't buy company stock through the stock purchase plan they'll be considered disloyal. That's nonsense.

In any event, always keep in mind that your first loyalty is to yourself and your family. Unless you're positive that your company's stock is a blockbuster and that you'll make a bundle by buying as much of it as you can, don't put *all* your money into this benefit. Keep some of that income you can currently get along without and put it directly into mutual funds and even into common stocks. You'll learn much more about investing when you do some of it on your own without your company's involvement. You'll make more money, too.▼

---

## THE TRUE STORY ON PROFIT SHARING

Profit sharing has a nice sound to it. Some companies label nearly every fringe benefit "profit sharing." No doubt management thinks participants will appreciate their benefits more if they think they're getting a share of the profits.

Some 401(k) plans are labelled profit sharing benefits because the companies contribute some of their cash to them. Others call stock purchase or stock option plans profit sharing. Neither is wholly accurate, since many such plans, like 401(k)s, get cash from the company even during down years when it makes no profit.

True profit sharing plans have been around for years, though they currently seem to be an endangered species. Possibly they're disappearing under the weight of many new types of benefits that are springing up and displacing them.

A real profit sharing plan looks something like this:

- The plan is drawn up and submitted to the U.S. Treasury Department to be "qualified." That doesn't mean that Uncle Sam approves it. "Qualified" just means that the plan meets government rules and therefore the company can take the cash it puts into the plan as a tax deduction. The earnings of the cash in the profit sharing fund are not taxed until they're distributed to the plan's participants, who must count the cash as part of their incomes and pay tax on it.
- Typical plans set aside a certain percentage of the profit, perhaps 10% to 20%, to be paid to shareholders in cash dividends or added to the earnings the firm keeps, known as retained earnings.
- After this percentage is set aside, as much as 20% to 25% is put into a fund or trust for the members of the profit sharing plan. The remaining profits after that deduction are usually held by the company as additions to retained earnings.
- The most common approaches to distributing the cash in the fund or trust are these:

    1. It's distributed shortly after the end of the year to eligible employees in proportion to their base pay. They pay income tax due for the year in which they get the cash.

    2. It's accumulated in interest-paying investments over a period of, say, ten years. Each year's profit is allocated to each employee in proportion to his or her base pay. At the end of ten years, one-tenth of the employee's account is distributed to him/her. Tax is due in the year the cash is received.

3. When an employee leaves the company for another job, he or she is entitled to all or part of the share of profits in his or her account. How much and when the cash will be paid out depends upon the terms of the plan.

4. When an employees dies, the amount in his/her account in the profit sharing trust is distributed immediately to beneficiary(ies). It's part of the employee's estate.

5. When an employee retires, the amount in his/her account in the profit sharing trust is distributed to the employee in a lump sum or spread out over years to supplement retirement pay. Income tax is due in the year the cash is received.

## YOUR COMPANY'S ESOP: FABLE OR EXCELLENT BENEFIT?

ESOP stands for Employees' Stock Ownership Plan (note that the "O" is for ownership, not option). An ESOP has one thing going for it that neither the 401(k) nor the stock purchase plans do: You don't have to put up a dime of your own cash to buy it.

It's true that you're really getting the stock as part of your compensation, and there are some strings attached. But you put up no cash. In fact you may get some cash back in dividends each year. Moreover, you get a healthy feeling that you're one of the owners of the corporation.

To be qualified by Uncle Sam, an ESOP must deal primarily in the corporation's own stock. An ESOP operates something like this:

Each year the company's board of directors votes a certain amount of cash for the use of the ESOP's trustees. They, in turn, pay that cash back to the company's treasury to purchase shares of stock at the current market value per share. (If your company's stock is not traded, management will bring in an outside appraiser who will determine the stock's fair market value.)

The trustees then allocate all the shares purchased to the participants in the plan. The shares are apportioned to each person by a ratio of each individual's salary to the total salaries of the participants in the ESOP.

When the company pays a dividend, the cash is normally passed through the ESOP to each individual according to the number of shares allocated to him or her (check out figures 4 and 5 in chapter 2).

The actual shares of the stock are not issued to you until you leave the company, either for another job or to retire. Normally you have to be in the ESOP for a number of years before you have a right to take the shares with you or to sell them. Most plans give the company the right to buy back your stock for its then market value. That means that if you want to sell your stock for cash, you have to offer it first to the company, which has what's called the right of first refusal.

When you reach normal retirement age, if the company refuses to buy your stock, you can either hold onto the shares or sell them through the stock market or to anyone interested in buying them.

When you leave the company before retirement age, the company can delay buying back the shares, usually until you're age 55.

You don't have to sign up for the ESOP. Normally you're covered by the plan automatically as soon as you become eligible. It's possible that the value of the shares allocated to you can go down, but since you've paid nothing in cash for them, it's hard to see how you can lose.

**A cautionary note:** ESOPs are often classified as retirement plans. If your company's ESOP is the *only* retirement plan covering you, be wary. Because the ESOP invests in one stock, your company's, the risk is much greater than is true with other retirement plans like regular defined benefit plans and 401(k)s.

### ACTION IDEAS

If your company doesn't have an Employee Stock Ownership Plan, now might be just the right time to start the ball rolling with your fellow employees to get the company to set one up. You can point out that there are many advantages to the company. They include:

1. Motivation of employees that comes with ownership.
2. Tax advantages to the company including deductions for dividends paid, deductions for repayment of money borrowed to buy shares for the ESOP, and others.

3. A means for the owners of a closely held corporation with no market for their shares to sell their stock, or part of it, to the ESOP at a fair market price.
4. A means for owners to defer paying capital gains taxes on shares they sell to the ESOP.
5. A way to create new capital for the corporation by substituting a benefit paid for in stock rather than in cash.

---

*Numbers and figures are hard to digest in large quantities, and Bill Ticknor is beginning to feel a little financial-frenetic. But he knows he can come back to these chapters when he has a specific question about an investment choice or an ESOP strategy. What he doesn't have yet is the last piece of the financial puzzle, where personal investing fits into his corporate benefits picture. He's ready to tackle that aspect of his money game plan. So are you.*

# 9
▼

# PERSONAL INVESTMENT INSTRUMENTS

## *Meshing IRAs and Annuities with Company Benefits*

**M**r. Ticknor is in the home stretch of his race to bring home a winner when it comes to the financial aspects of employee benefits. The last leg: learning how personal investments fit into the employee benefits financial picture. He's heard about annuities and IRAs but wants a firm grasp of them before he commits to his overall strategy.

Bill Ticknor is not alone. You've undoubtedly heard about annuities, too. What are they, anyway? They're contracts usually issued by insurance companies that pay back the buyers' money plus a certain amount of interest. The key factor, of course, is that the buyers can elect to get payments for the rest of their lives, even if they live to be 100!

That last factor makes annuities a favorite investment vehicle for many defined benefit pension plans. The plan administrator takes the cash the company contributes and uses it to buy annuities to cover each participant in the plan. When individuals retire, they can choose to take monthly payments immediately or let the annuity keep building up, tax deferred, until they decide it's time to draw out the cash.

Annuities can be used inside benefits plans and outside of them, too. You can use them to fund an IRA. Indeed, one kind of IRA is called by the Internal Revenue Service an "Individual Retirement Annuity," though you're limited to putting in $2,000 a year. You should know all about annuities to help you with your personal investing as well as for your decisions on benefits plans.

---

### ACTION IDEA

If your company has a supplementary employee retirement program (SERP), the cash in it is usually only as good as the credit of your employer. If it gets into financial trouble, you can bet the ranch that management will grab the cash in the SERP to keep itself alive and the company from going down the tubes. As a result, your supplementary retirement income will be blown away.

To lessen that risk, try to get management to buy individual annuities with the cash in the SERP to cover each participant. Ask for delivery of the annuity contract to you. That'll give you some control over money that's been set aside for your retirement while you're employed.

---

## ANNUITIES CAN BE GOOD, BAD, AND BEAUTIFUL

If you think you're going to need the money you're saving in your personal investments before you're age 59½, don't buy annuities with it. If you think there's any chance you'll have to tap into those savings before about ten years have gone by, don't buy annuities no matter what your age.

Ask yourself these two key questions before considering buying annuities outside of a benefits plan:

1. Will you be at least 59½ before you start making withdrawals from savings invested in annuities? If you're not that age, you'll be slapped by the IRS with a 10% penalty on cash withdrawn, and you'll pay income tax on the interest earned in the annuity, too. (There's an exception to the 10% penalty, if not the income tax. If you choose to have the money in

the annuity paid out to you monthly for the rest of your life, the IRS waives the 10%.)
2. Can you lock up the money you put into an annuity for ten years? Just about every company that sells annuities will charge you a fee for withdrawing cash before seven to ten years—it varies from company to company. And the fee for withdrawal can be steep, 7% or more, though the percentage usually declines by a point each year until it reaches zero. Because these contract charges on withdrawals are so steep, generally you'll lose whatever your gain from tax deferment should you withdraw cash in fewer than ten years.

Having listed some of the bad things about annuities, what's good about them?

If you're financially able to start setting money aside to give you a supplement to your income during the later years of your life, annuities are one of the best ideas around. Generally they're safe, pay a reasonable rate of interest, and grow rapidly in value thanks to compounding and tax deferral. You can often get an above-average guaranteed interest rate for the first few years, and a lower rate in later years. Of course these guarantees are bait to get you in, and they're only as good as the insurer that offers them.

Moreover, unlike other kinds of investment vehicles, you can buy an annuity that'll outlive you and your spouse or other named beneficiary. It'll keep paying you for the rest of your lives. You'll never have to worry about outliving this particular financial resource, at least not if you buy the right kind.

Yes, it's true that your age comes into play when considering buying annuities. You can, of course, buy them at any age, though buying them after age 75 calls for judgment as sharp as that of a house poker dealer operating behind the curtains of a high-stakes game.

At the other end of the age spectrum, you should most likely avoid buying annuities as a personal investment when you're under age 49, though most insurance agents who sell them would scream bloody murder at that assertion. But you don't want to start cashing them in before age 59½ because of the

10% penalty. You don't want to cash them in in less than ten years or you'll also get clobbered with fees by the company that sold you the annuity. So keep in mind that the time for buying annuities for retirement is during middle age.

## BUT THEY CAN BE BEAUTIFUL

So what's beautiful about them? Annuities are ideal for deferring taxes on their earnings. And should you receive a substantial sum of money all at once—an inheritance, a large bonus, or big severance pay, you can sock the whole amount into annuities, rather than be limited.

You may think of plunking any sizable sum into an IRA. But what if your bonus comes to $7,500? Or you receive an inheritance from your Aunt Minnie of $5,000? Or you move to another company and your thrift plan dumps $10,000 into your lap? When you buy an annuity from an insurance company, you're not restricted to a maximum that you can put in, as you are with an IRA. Generally, you need fork over only a minimum of $2,500.

You can buy annuities of several types: deferred, immediate, fixed, or variable.

A deferred annuity starts paying you at some specified age, though you can start payments earlier if you wish. You can buy it with one lump sum, known as a single premium, or in installments.

An immediate annuity starts paying you right away and, of course, requires you to pay its premium up front.

A fixed annuity guarantees to pay you a fixed amount each month for your life, and you can arrange to have payments continued for the life of your spouse, too. The monthly amount you get depends on your age, when the payments are to start, and other factors.

A variable annuity does not guarantee you return of principal (the amount you put in), interest, or other income. The insurance company invests in groups of securities like corporate bonds, various mutual funds, and even some stocks. Its aim is to provide you with a higher return than you'd get with the other types of annuities.

## BENEFITS CHECKOFF: *PUTTING ANNUITIES UNDER THE MICROSCOPE*

In thinking about annuities, you have two main decisions. The first involves how to buy them, either by making one big lump-sum payment or by accumulating them over a number of years on some kind of an installment plan.

The second decision to think about involves withdrawing the money. You'll have many choices of how to take the money out, ranging from all at once to monthly payments for the rest of your life, with many choices in between.

Here's a roundup of some of the many types of payout plans and what insurers call them:

- ✔ *Life only:* This option provides you with income for life. Payments may be monthly, quarterly, semiannual, or annual.
- ✔ *Life with term certain:* You get payments for life, with payments to continue to your beneficiary if you die before the number of years you pick, usually five, ten, fifteen, or twenty years.
- ✔ *Joint and survivor life option:* You get income for your life, and when you die another person—your spouse, for instance—will get the payments, or a portion of them, for life.
- ✔ *Installment refund life option:* You get payments for your life, but if you die before you've taken out the amount you put into the annuity, your beneficiary gets the balance.
- ✔ *Unit refund life option:* Your beneficiary gets the refund in a lump sum rather than in installments.
- ✔ *Payments for a specified period:* You may get payments for a specified period of time, usually one to thirty years. The payments continue to your beneficiary if you die before the specified years are up.

**Benefits alert:** You've reached age 50. Each year you get a bonus that nets you, after taxes, about $6,000. You think about socking away the $6,000 in bank CDs maturing when you are age 60, to build up a nice nest egg for your retirement. The CDs are safe, and the ones that stretch out longer pay a pretty good rate of interest.

You then hear about annuities. You check them out and find that you can invest the $6,000 each year in separate single-premium annuities for ten years each. By age 60, you'll have invested $60,000, the same amount as you'd have invested in CDs.

Of course, you can always get at the cash with either CDs or annuities. You'd pay the bank a penalty on early withdrawal of the CDS, though, and you'd also lose some of the cash to insurance company fees if you withdrew from the annuities. Worse, from the standpoint of annuities, Uncle Sam would sock a 10% penalty on your annuity withdrawal because the interest it's been generating is tax deferred.

But tax deferral may be the key to your decision on whether or not to buy annuities. Assuming the CDs and annuities earn the same rate of interest, you'd have to pay income tax *each year* on the CDs' interest, while the earnings in the annuities would NOT be taxed until you start taking out the money. So with the CDs you'd lose the use of the money you shell out for taxes, whereas with the annuity you would have *more* money to put aside if you want to.

Some people don't mind paying taxes to support Uncle Sam's bad habit of buying $600 toilet seats. But others find that's about as much fun as getting mugged on payday.

The choice between a taxable and tax-deferred investment for your retirement years is yours.▼

---

The second decision to think about involves taking your money out of the annuity. Fortunately, you can change your decision up to the time you start taking cash out. How you take the money out, though, has a great deal to do with how much money you get—either in a big chunk or each month (when you ask for monthly payments, you're "annuitizing" in insurance jargon). Your selection also affects how long you'll get payments, how long your spouse will get them, how much and when you'll pay taxes, and how much may or may not go to your heirs. (You won't pay taxes on the money you've contributed—that's yours—only on the earnings in the annuity.) Be careful interpreting sellers' "tax-free" claims. Some portion of each payment you withdraw will not be taxable, but some portion will be. While many states have certain rules about how much insurance companies must pay out, other states don't.

The scariest horror story is the one about the guy who'd put many thousands of dollars into an immediate annuity. He chose the "for life only" option, which would pay only for as long as he lived, and he died driving home from the insurance agent's office. Examine every option carefully and get full explanations of what happens to payments with each.

## ACTION IDEAS

Keep in mind that annuities are sold, not bought. So take the sales agent's enthusiasm with a grain of salt. Remember that projections of the increasing value of the annuity are just projections and may not actually result.

You may be reassured that your money is completely safe. It's true that during the time before you draw the money out, it's backed up by special reserves in some states. But after you start to draw it out, it goes into the insurer's general investment funds. Make sure you pick out the insurance company carefully. Lots of them have gotten into trouble in recent years. Check out their ratings with A. M. Best & Co., Moody's Investors Service, and Standard & Poor's. Buy annuities only from companies with the highest ratings, no matter how attractive the bait to buy may be.

Take special care when buying variable annuities. You must want to be involved in investment decisions to take the additional risk. Though the risk may be small, it's worthwhile, because you have a handle on when and where part of your money is invested and so can increase your control, as opposed to what you may have with other types of annuities. Remember, with variable annuities, insurance companies don't guarantee interest or return of principal or the amount of payments.

## ALL ABOUT IRAS

A lot of people think that IRAs are dead in the water. Newspaper publicity given to congressional tinkering with taxes gave the impression that when the solons on Capitol Hill severely limited tax deductions for IRA contributions, it was no longer a good idea to tuck money into the IRA envelope. Putting it bluntly, that's wrong.

Some other people think that they can't contribute to an IRA because they can't cough up $2,000 at one time. Wrong again. It doesn't take a $2,000 investment. That's the max you can put in, in any one year. There is no minimum.

Why do you need to know something about IRAs? For one thing, an IRA gives you a vehicle into which you can pour money and have it earn interest on which you'll pay no taxes until you start drawing it out. Make no mistake about it, all the pension plans you'll ever have plus Social Security won't make you as comfortable as you'll want to be in retirement. You need to save to provide yourself with a supplementary source of income. An IRA lets you earn more on your savings.

A second reason for learning all you can about IRAs is that you may suddenly come into a big distribution from one or more of your benefit plans due to your changing jobs or becoming a victim of a corporate downsizing. When that happens, an IRA gives you a perfect vehicle for rolling over the cash you'll get and avoiding taxes on it, if you do it the right way (see chapter 7). You can roll over any amount you get from a qualified plan. There's no limit. When you get such a distribution, you're not going to be seeing chump change. It's going to be serious money.

## SO WHAT'S THE REAL SCOOP ON IRAS?

Actually, IRS Publication 590 says that "IRA" stands for Individual Retirement Arrangement, though the more popular term you see is Individual Retirement Account. There are several types of IRAs:

- Individual Retirement Account
- Individual Retirement Annuity
- Simplified Employee Pension—a SEP-IRA
- Employer and Employee Association Trust Account—a trust for you in the form of an IRA

An IRA is a personal savings plan that offers you tax incentives to set aside money for your retirement. In some cases, you can deduct your contributions to an IRA in whole or in part. Further, any gains or earnings in the account are not taxed until they are distributed to you.

You have to set up an IRA with a qualified institution such as a commercial or savings bank, a stock brokerage firm, or a life insurance company.

You can set up an IRA if you have taxable compensation— wages, salaries, tips, commissions, fees, bonuses, or taxable alimony—during the year and haven't yet tipped the age scale at 70½. You can contribute up to $2,000 or 100% of your taxable compensation, whichever is less, to your IRA each year. But you have to have taxable compensation. If you just have interest, rent receipts, or dividends, you can't use that income to contribute to an IRA. You have to get a wage, salary, commission, or fees in exchange for work, or receive taxable alimony. You're not limited to any percentage of salary for your annual contribution. If you earned only $1,100 in a year, you can contribute the whole $1,100 if you wish.

All of the hullabaloo about the elimination of deductibility of contributions under certain circumstances muddied the water about whether or how much can be deducted to reduce your annual April 15 bout with income taxes. Be certain to talk with your accountant to get the official word on this issue.

## ABOUT DEDUCTIONS AND CONTRIBUTIONS

Suppose you fall into the "no deduction" or "partial deduction" category. Is it worthwhile to contribute to an IRA? The answer, generally, is a loud "yes." Look at it this way: There aren't many ways you can escape taxes on any kind of earnings you generate. But taxes on earnings in an IRA are tax deferred. You don't escape them forever, but you don't have to pay tax on the earnings in the IRA next April 15. So it almost always pays to contribute to an IRA to the extent allowed.

One more thing about nondeductible contributions: When you do start drawing the money out, the nondeductible amounts you put in come out tax free, of course. You'll have to include the earnings of the IRA in your income, but not the principal.

The maximum amount you can contribute to an IRA, whether it's deductible or nondeductible, is $2,000. If your spouse doesn't work and has no earned income, you can set up a separate spousal IRA and contribute $250 a year to it. In fact, when you have IRAs for both yourself and your spouse, you can split the contribution between the two accounts any way you want to—$2,000 to yours and $250 to your spouse's, $250 to yours and $2,000 to your spouse's, or any other split—though you can't exceed the $2,250 limit for both. If your spouse works, though, he or she can set up a separate IRA with his/her own earned income and contribute $2,000 a year to it, too. That means you can contribute $2,000 a year to an IRA, your spouse can contribute $2,000, for a total of $4,000 a year for the two of you.

---

**Benefits alert:** Suppose you're in an income category of $25,000 to $35,000 if you're single, or $40,000 to $50,000 if you're married and filing income tax returns jointly. You're entitled to a partial deduction for your contribution to an IRA. Here's how to calculate the amount:

- First, determine your excess income. That's the amount your income exceeds $25,000 if you're single or $40,000 if you're married, filing jointly.
- Then, use this formula:

$$\frac{\$10,000 - excess}{10,000} \times \$2,000 = \text{maximum deduction for IRA contribution}$$

---

If you want to roll over your IRA assets into another IRA, you can. If you get a payment from another qualified retirement plan that you want to roll over into your IRA, you can, though you'll have to get the other retirement plan to roll the money over directly to your IRA rather than putting the cash into your hands first. If you get the funds first, the company has to withhold 20% of the amount for the IRS. You can roll over the money you received; but you must add to that sum the amount witheld, and then make a claim for a refund of the money withheld when you file your income tax return. That's a chore and best to avoid.

## ACTION IDEAS

The federal government gives, and it takes away. Not long ago a change in tax law allowed still-employed participants in qualified pension and profit sharing plans to take part of their vested interests in the plans and roll them over into their own IRAs without any taxes payable. Formerly only employees who left the company were able to roll over their pension benefits into IRAs.

The change caused a rush by employees to their benefits administrators asking for the cash to roll over. Many of them were unhappy with the way the money in their benefits plans was being invested and felt they could do a better job managing the money in their own IRAs. Others, no doubt, just wanted to play "investment manager."

Alas—most pension and profit sharing plans do not allow such withdrawals, called "in-service transfers," and permit participants to borrow from 401(k) plans only for hardships. That possible "escape hatch" is really slammed shut by the fact that no hardship exists if an employee just wants to tuck the money away in an IRA.

Chances are you'll have to leave the money in the plan. In the long run that's probably advantageous to you. Build up and manage your IRA with other earnings.

Okay. So you've got an IRA already, or intend to start one up. What do you do with the $2,000, and maybe another $250 for your spouse, that you tuck away in the IRA envelope each year? Statistics show that about two-thirds of all the money in IRAs is invested in fixed-income instruments. They include CDs from banks, savings accounts, some bond mutual funds, and money-market mutual funds. Maybe that made sense in the early '80s, when CDs and some money-market funds paid as high as 17%! But that was only a short-term blip as investing goes.

It makes much more sense to sock at least a good part of the money into something that grows. You can set up an IRA with most mutual funds for much less than $2,000. There are many choices, of course. If you go into a family of no-load funds, you can diversify among aggressive-growth, big-dividend, and balanced funds. Review the earlier chapters on directing the investment of cash going into a 401(k), and you'll be able to transfer that strategy to suit your needs for your current age, income, financial resources, and number of dependents.

## HOMING IN ON IRA INVESTMENT PERCENTAGES

It's sensible to think about your IRA as a growth vehicle rather than an income provider. Until you're within five or six years of retirement, here's a recommendation for what to do with your IRA money:

- stash away about 50% of your IRA money in aggressive-growth equity mutual funds;
- put 40% in either balanced or bond funds;
- keep about 10% in cash equivalents like money-market mutual funds, savings accounts, or CDs.

---

### ACTION IDEA

Say you already have an IRA. When was the last time you really reviewed what's in it? Many individuals start an IRA with a bank or other financial institution and leave all the decisions on what to do with the money to the person who's handling the account.

Make no mistake about it. Your IRA is much too small to get more than just a quick brush-over by the person who's managing your money.

Point is, you should take charge of your IRA yourself. That's called a self-directed IRA. You can set one up with, say, a discount stock broker, get the current IRA funds transferred directly to the new institution, and with the help of this book make your own decisions on what should be done with the money in it.

It's time to stop letting some disinterested person make the decisions on investing the money in your IRA. Take that job over yourself, today.

---

Generally you can start withdrawing from your IRA without any penalty after you reach age 59½, though you'll have to include what you withdraw in your taxable income for the year. You must start drawing your IRA assets by April 1 of the year you reach age 70½ whether you've stopped working or not. The amount you must withdraw each year depends on the life expectancy of you and your IRA beneficiary. The IRS provides a convenient table showing required minimum withdrawals by life expectancies. You can take all the money in your account or more than the required amount in any year, of course.

The amounts withdrawn each year are taxed at ordinary income tax rates. Of course, as mentioned before, your nondeductible contributions are not taxed when you take them out of your IRA.

These are the current rules for IRAs. Congress is tinkering with them and making proposals to again make all IRA contributions tax deductible. Also, some senators and representatives have drafted bills to allow withdrawals from IRAs before age 59½ for certain purposes, such as buying a first home, college education, etc. As has been written before, always check out the current status before making any moves.

*It's time to take our leave of Bill Ticknor. He's plumb tuckered out now anyway. But he's quite pleased with all his newfound knowledge on the financial and investment aspects of his benefits. He needed that knowledge to tap his benefits to the fullest. So do you.*

# 10

▼

# INSURANCE
# BENEFITS

*Protecting Yourself with Personal and
Corporate Coverage*

### THE CASE OF THE CRITICAL COVERAGE

Maureen O'Reilly had never really thought about life insurance for herself. Her husband, Norm, had coverage from his job, and she was sure she had seen something about life insurance for herself in the benefits booklet she had gotten when she started back at work after her Kevin was in school full time.

That complacent attitude toward life insurance was shattered when her best friend, Chris, lost her husband in a car accident. After the funeral expenses and other problems were taken care of, Chris told Maureen that she and the kids were moving back in with her parents. They just couldn't afford to live as they had been on her dead husband's life insurance proceeds.

Maureen still wasn't too worried, but she prodded Norm into checking on his policy. She was startled to learn that he had less than $60,000 worth of coverage, a number she knew stacked up poorly in terms of their living expenses.

She was even more aghast when she checked on her own "worth." Norm and the kids would be in serious shape if they *depended on her company-paid life insurance policy to be of any help if she were to meet an untimely demise.*

*Maureen faced a quandary. She knew Norm would brush aside her concerns with his usual "Don't worry, I'm busy" excuse. And she was wary of the reputation of insurance salespeople. So she went to her company's benefits consultant. His expertise, and her investigations, combined to give her new peace of mind when it came to her family's security.*

"P-s-s-s-t. Wanna put your money into a perfect investment? You get safety . . . liquidity . . . high income . . . good growth . . . and tax advantages. And don't sneeze at this: It doesn't take a lot of your time and energy to manage it."

Maybe you'll never have that kind of message whispered in your ear. But maybe you've been so turned off over the years by jabbering salespeople that you haven't really heard the story of all these neat features that are actually wrapped up in tidy packages.

And who's gift-wrapping the packages? Hold onto your hat. It's the life insurance industry!

## PLUGGING UP THE INSURANCE GAPS

If your company is like most, it offers many kinds of insurance benefits to you, ranging from life to accident to disability to medical to dental. When you look at these benefits, though, you'll likely discover that you need to buy some of these same types on a personal basis to plug up gaps in your corporate benefits plan or to supplement it.

To maximize your insurance benefits, you should first investigate what you've got. Then figure out what additional coverage you need so you can put together the best combination of personally bought insurance with your corporate benefits coverages.

## BACK TO THE BASICS OF LIFE INSURANCE

The life insurance benefit that most employers cover you with is called term insurance. It pays your survivors cash if you die. That's a good benefit, though term insurance builds no other value.

The death benefit is typically related to your annual salary. If you're making $30,000 a year and the coverage is one times your salary, your survivors will get $30,000 if you die; if it's one and a half times salary, the death benefit will be $45,000, and so on.

Many companies put an upper limit on the amount they'll cover you with, and that's something you should check out right now with your benefits person. You may find the upper limit is so woefully short of what you think your survivors will need that you'll want to take out more life insurance on your own—either directly or by buying supplements through your company.

Figure 20 gives you a look at some of the features one company offers its employees in terms of supplemental insurance.

A lot of so-called experts will tell you that the only kind of insurance to buy is term. But there are a number of things to think about before you blindly take such advice. Not the least important of these is that personal term insurance is usually sold for a one-year term, and then it must be renewed.

You can get what's called "guaranteed renewable" term insurance so you don't have to worry that you'll lose it. Or you can buy up to ten years of term at one time for a higher premium. But a most important point to keep in mind is that as you get older, the term insurance premium gets larger, and it becomes quite large when you get up into your 50s and 60s. That's not the case with permanent whole life insurance policies where you can get a premium with a maximum rate fixed for your life.

*Figure 20. Details for buying supplemental life insurance*

## Supplemental Group Life Insurance

*Choosing coverage*

Amounts of insurance range from $10,000 to $100,000 in increments of $10,000.

*Who is eligible?*

You are eligible to apply for insurance under this program if you are a permanent, full-time employee working 20 or more hours per week.

If you apply for coverage during your initial eligibility period, your application will be approved regardless of your medical history. If you apply after your initial eligibility period, only a brief health statement will be needed to establish your insurability.

Insurance is effective on the first day of the month following approval by our carrier, provided you are actively working on that date. If not, insurance begins on the second day you return to full-time active employment.

*Disability factor*

If, prior to age 65, you become totally disabled for six consecutive months, our insurer will continue your insurance without further payment of premiums as long as total disability continues and proof of disability is provided.

*Convertibility*

Upon termination of employment you may apply for an individual permanent policy up to the same amount submitting evidence of insurability. Application for conversion must be made within 31 days of termination.

*Payroll deductions*                    Premiums are paid through easy, man-
                                        ageable and convenient deductions
from                                    your paycheck.

*Cost of premiums*

| $10,000 | $20,000 | $30,000 | $40,000 | $50,000 |
|---------|---------|---------|---------|---------|
| $2.20   | $4.40   | $6.60   | $8.80   | $11.00  |

| $60,000 | $70,000 | $80,000 | $90,000 | $100,000 |
|---------|---------|---------|---------|----------|
| $13.20  | $15.40  | $17.60  | $19.80  | $22.00   |

### A New Wrinkle in Term Insurance
**A few insurance companies have come up with a group insurance policy that can pay you benefits while you're still alive.**

Generally you can choose to collect this benefit if you're terminally ill or injured, or if you have a life expectancy of twelve months or less. If you need a major organ transplant such as heart, lung, liver, or bone marrow to help you live longer than twelve months, you may also be able to collect.

Usually only a percentage of the face value of the policy can be paid to you. Some states regulate that amount, which may be as low as 50%. Still, in dire circumstances the money could be very important to your financial security.

Such group policies are not approved for sale in all states. Stir up your benefits department to get further details.

## OLD BUSINESS BECOMES BOLD BUSINESS

Many years ago insurance companies offered only one type of insurance other than term. It's called whole life or guaranteed permanent life insurance, and it is still sold. Unlike term, which pays off only in case of death, whole life includes a whole bunch of sweeteners like cash values and savings elements that grow more quickly than bank savings accounts. If the insurance company makes money, it pays you dividends, which you can take in cash or use to buy more insurance. You can borrow against a whole life policy or turn its value into lifetime retirement income.

Not too long ago, insurance companies climbed out of their ruts and began to create a lot of new kinds of policies. They're still at it. The new ones are fundamentally combinations of term life and guaranteed permanent life, though they're often dolled up with fancy names to make them more salable.

The newest kinds of policies combine savings benefits with death benefits and give you some flexibility in deciding which type you attach the most importance to. Usually an insurance agent will ask how much of a death benefit you want and how much money you want to spend, and will crank those and other data into a computer program which spits out a combination of the two types of insurance that matches the data given. As you grow older and your finances change, you can make changes in the policies' payoffs to suit your new circumstances.

Take a look at the table on the next page. It gives you an overview of some common present-day insurance products such as universal life, variable life, and universal/variable life policies, as well as whole life.

Then review figure 21, which gives you a good idea of what a whole life annual benefit statement will look like.

## A QUICK LOOK AT THE NEW LOOKS IN LIFE INSURANCE

*Universal life* rolls together features of term life, whole life, and savings. Its term life feature provides low-cost death benefits. Whole life features are cash values and low-interest loans. The savings feature lets the insurance company invest in corporate bonds, T-bills, and some equities to provide growth and returns that are competitive with other investments.

When you buy a universal life policy you can change the mix of death and savings benefits to meet your new needs. For instance, when you're young, you may want to emphasize a high

| | | | |
|---|---|---|---|
| *Whole life* | • Fixed premium payment but can borrow on policy to pay premiums<br>• Provides protection<br>• Cash values build steadily | • Interest paid guaranteed<br>• Policyholder can borrow against<br>• Dividends can be taken in cash or used to buy more insurance | • Fixed death benefit which can be built up by paid-up additions |
| *Universal life* | • Policyholder can alter premium amount paid or omit payment<br>• Cash values vary with fund performance<br>• Provides protection | • Insurance company invests cash values for guaranteed minimum interest but may earn larger returns<br>• Policyholder may borrow or take partial payments | • Death benefit can be varied by policyholder |
| *Variable life* | • Fixed premium payment but can borrow on policy to pay premium<br>• Cash values vary with fund perfor-mance with risk to policyholder<br>• Provides protection | • Policyholder chooses mutual fund to invest cash values<br>• Policyholder can borrow against<br>• Generally no interest rate guarantees | • Variable death benefit but not lower than face amount of policy |
| *Variable/ universal* | • Can vary or omit premium payment<br>• Cash values | • Policyholder chooses mutual fund to invest cash values | • Variable death benefit with initial guaranteed amount |

| • Provides protection | • Policyholder can borrow against | • Holder can vary death benefit which |
|---|---|---|
| | • Interest varies | may also vary with value of mutual fund. |

*Figure 21. Sample whole life annual benefit statement*

## ANNUAL BENEFIT STATEMENT
## AS OF (DATE)

POLICY NUMBER: 0000000                    PLAN: WHOLE LIFE
POLICY DATE: 00/00/00
PREMIUM: $000.00
PAYABLE: MONTHLY

### SUMMARY OF POLICY BENEFITS

|  | *DEATH BENEFIT* | *CASH VALUE* |
|---|---|---|
| BASIC POLICY | $ 334,021.00 | $ 5,073.78 |
| DIVIDEND ADDITIONS | $ 1,712.00 | $ 558.76 |
| PAID-UP ADDITIONS RIDER | $ 12,145.00 | $ 3,964.24 |
| TOTAL | $ 347,878.00 | $ 9,596.83 |

This year's increase in your basic policy guaranteed cash value, plus your current dividend, provided a sum of $ 5,632.54.

Your policy also included the following riders and benefits:

Waiver of premium benefit

ADDITIONAL FACTS ABOUT YOUR POLICY BENEFITS

Note: Amounts shown in this section are included in the summary of benefits.

- Your dividend option is: dividend additions
- Your current annual dividend of $558.76 was applied to purchase $1,712 of dividend additions.

BENEFICIARY INFORMATION:

ABOUT YOUR ANNUAL BENEFIT STATEMENT

1. At the top of your statement, you'll find basic information about your policy. It includes the type of plan you purchased and the date your insurance protection began. If you have an outstanding loan, the amount of loan and loan interest are shown, along with the applicable interest rate. This section includes the amount of your premium and how often payments are due.

2. The summary section of your statement highlights how much your policy has grown in value this year. It shows the amount of your basic policy, any riders you purchased, and any dividends you have left at interest or applied to buy additional insurance. (These values assume that premiums are paid through the statement date, and have not been adjusted for any outstanding loans and loan interest.)

3. The additional section shows your current dividend option, the amount of your dividend, and how it was applied to meet your needs. It may also contain other details about the coverage on your policy.

---

death benefit. Later you may want to build up earnings for more retirement income and accept smaller death benefits.

As the chart on page 163 shows, you can jack up the premium payment, lower it, or even omit paying it entirely. Of course, any of these moves will change what you'll get out of the policy. If you omit premium payments, the insurance company will dip into the cash reserves to continue the death benefit. If there aren't enough reserves, the death benefit goes down or the policy can even lapse.

*Variable life* policies shift some risk to you. Instead of the company picking out what to invest your premiums in, you select them, usually from a list of various kinds of mutual funds. As the chapters on investing show, you can lose as well as win with mutual funds.

The big kicker in this kind of policy is that you can jump into a raging bull market and win big by changing the investments in your policy from those that are lagging to those that are roaring ahead. If the mutual funds you pick do well, your cash values and death benefits will increase. If they do poorly, they'll decrease.

*Variable/universal* policies combine what are thought to be the best features and advantages of both types.

## BORROWING AND TAX ADVANTAGES OF PERMANENT LIFE INSURANCE

As you pay premiums to the life insurance company, and as it invests your money, the cash values and savings increase. Part of the increase comes from guaranteed rates of interest. Another part may come about because the insurance companies typically earn interest greater than the guarantee.

The insurers credit dividends (in the case of mutual insurance companies) or excess interest (in the case of stock companies) on the cash values. Neither the guaranteed nor the excess interest is taxable when credited. It accumulates tax free. That's why it grows more quickly than bank savings-account interest, on which you must pay tax each year.

You can choose what to do with the dividends paid by mutual companies. Take them in cash, use them in some policies to make future premiums vanish, or buy additional paid-up life insurance. Over a long time, say fifteen years, dividends can buy enough additional life insurance to double (or more) the face value of the original policy. Similarly, excess interest credited by stock companies can multiply the policy's investment values and death benefit over time. These cash values can be turned into retirement income, and at that time the interest accumulated does become taxable.

Another nice feature: If you bought your policy before June 21, 1988, you can borrow from it tax free. If you bought after that date, loans you take *may* be taxed. You'll have to ask your insurance company to advise you on that.

## HOW MUCH LIFE INSURANCE DO YOU NEED?

You'll never get a perfect fix on how much life insurance you need. It changes nearly every day because the answer involves so many variables. There are about as many formulas, charts, worksheets, and computer programs available to help you come up with a figure as there are pages in this book. It's here, though, that well-trained salespeople can help. You have to find ones who'll put reality ahead of commissions.

Before you start collecting specific numbers, ask yourself these foundation questions:

(a) How long do you want those who depend on you to depend on your insurance proceeds for security?
(b) Do you want your insurance to immediately wipe out major expenses, like a home mortgage?
(c) How much can your survivors depend on receiving from other sources, like a spouse's job or pension/government income?
(d) Would a reduction in lifestyle for those you leave behind be acceptable?
(e) What future major financial hits, like college expenses, could impact what your family will need?

## BENEFITS CHECKOFF: FIVE IMPORTANT FACTORS IN ESTIMATING LIFE INSURANCE NEEDS

You'll need the following data at the very minimum to estimate your life insurance needs, whether you do it yourself or give the problem to someone else:

✔ the death benefits from your current employer's plan;
✔ death benefits from any personally owned policies;
✔ Social Security benefits for your spouse and children (check out chapter 11);
✔ any other income from savings and investments;
✔ earnings of your spouse if employed.

The information you collect will give you the best reading on how much income your survivors will have. The next step in determining how much additional insurance you may need is to estimate all family living expenses—food, clothing, housing, etc.

1. If you have a monthly budget, that'll be your best source of information on current living expenses. If not, take a look at your checkbook for a couple of months and see what kinds of expenses you've been paying. Your latest income tax return may also help you figure out your current living expenses.
2. Reduce your current living expenses by about 20% to 30%. That's a reasonable amount to allow for your own spending, though you may adjust it a little depending on the size of your family. Don't reduce the expense by half—things just don't work out that way.

Now translate the cash your survivors will get in a lump sum from your insurance to the annual income that it will produce when carefully invested. Five percent is a good figure to work from. At times it may be higher and at other times, lower. Add to that total all other income, and that'll be the amount your survivors can count on.

Compare that figure to the living-expense total. Say there's a gap of $10,000 a year. How much additional life insurance would you need to plug up this gap? That depends on what kind of yield you'll get from the insurance proceeds. If you use five percent as the return, then you'll need $200,000 of additional insurance to provide that kind of income.

**ADVICE:** You can also use a "spend down" strategy in this calculation. This means that your survivors will not just spend the income from the insurance money they invest but will also spend part of the principal. As they spend the principal, of course, the income from the portion spent disappears. There are formulas, though, that will allow them to determine how many years it will take to spend all the principal at different rates. If they use a "spend down" strategy, you'll need to buy *less* additional insurance.

For example, suppose your survivors have a nest egg from your insurance benefit of $100,000, and they invest it to yield

8% a year. Here's how much they can withdraw from the $100,000 investment each month under the number of years the nest egg will last:

| 15 years | 25 years | 35 years |
|---|---|---|
| Withdraw per month $956 | $772 | $710 |

The nest egg will run out in twenty-five years if your survivors "spend down" $772 each month. Alternatively, if they spend $667 a month, the $100,000 nest egg will remain intact.

---

**Benefits alert:** A key factor in your personal insurance needs is how much coverage you're getting from your company. The more it provides, the less you have to buy on your own. Check with your boss to see what the chances are that your company can be persuaded to increase everyone's group life insurance coverage. Company coverages save you a bunch of money.▼

---

## A QUICK AND EASY ROUTE TO MORE LIFE INSURANCE

If you're covered by a group term life insurance policy when your employment ends, most policies give you a chance to convert the group term life to an individual life insurance policy. You'll also be given a chance to convert to an individual policy if you move to a job classification in the company that the company does *not* cover with a life insurance benefit.

All policies have conditions for conversions that may be regulated by state law. So it pays to read your own policy carefully to find out what conditions apply to you.

Generally, to convert your group life insurance to an individual policy you'll have to meet these conditions:

1. Make a written application to the insurance company for a policy and pay the first premium within thirty-one days of the date on which your coverage under the group policy ends.

2. Convert to a policy *other* than term life. You can, of course, buy a term insurance policy from the same company rather than converting. However, you'll have to have a physical exam to determine your insurability if you buy term. If you convert to another kind of life insurance from the company's group policy, you *do not* have to take a physical exam.

3. You may have to be covered under the group life insurance policy for a number of years before you can convert to an individual policy.

4. The amount of coverage will most likely be restricted to less than your coverage under the group policy.

5. If you miss making an application within thirty-one days, you won't be able to convert.

## READ IT AND WEEP: RED FLAGS IN INSURANCE POLICIES

When you sign up for your company's life insurance benefit, you're agreeing to all the terms of the master policy that your company has agreed to with the insurance company. There's not really anything you can do to change them. But you should look for the red flags in the copy of the policy prepared for you and other participants so you'll know where you stand.

## SEVEN RED FLAGS IN LIFE INSURANCE POLICIES

✔ Red flag #1: "The amount of life insurance shall be 65% of the benefit smount for any person who is 65 years of age or older." *Caution*: If you work past 65, your coverage will drop, and that fact should be considered in your planning.

✔ Red flag #2: "The benefits and amounts may be terminated or changed in accordance with the provisions of the Policy either as a result of a change in the Employee's status, or amendment or termination of the Policy." *Caution*: When you're transferred or promoted, check to see if your coverage has changed.

✔ Red flag #3: "All statements made by the Employer or by

any person insured shall be deemed representations and not warranties." *Caution*: It's not what they say or even the way that they say it. What counts is what you get in writing.

✔ Red flag #4: "The Policy may change at any time by written agreement between Employer and the Insurance Company without the consent of the Employees insured or of their beneficiaries." *Caution*: You don't have any say over the insurance, though you should be told of any changes.

✔ Red flag #5: "If the Employee applies after thirty days from the date he first became eligible, or he previously elected to end his insurance, he must then furnish evidence of his insurability before he may be considered for insurance." *Caution*: Apply on time, or you'll have to take a physical exam.

✔ Red flag #6: "Cessation of active work by the Employee shall be deemed end of employment if the cessation of active work is on account of the following: sickness or injury, being temporarily laid off, having been granted a leave of absence." *Caution*: Your coverage may end without your being aware of it.

✔ Red flag #7: "Any increases or decreases in amount of insurance due to a change in class shall become effective on the Premium Due Date coincident with or next following the date of change in class." *Caution*: A raise in pay doesn't mean your insurance goes up that same day. Check it out with your benefits person for the exact date.

## BUYING STRATEGIES

You don't have anything to say about the cost of your corporate life insurance, though you may be able to get your employer to pick up more of any part of the premium that is deducted from your pay. This kind of insurance is cheap, so normally you've got a bargain in your pocket.

That's not always the case with personal insurance, though, and it pays to shop around. A word of caution: The least expensive won't be the best if the insurer is on thin ice and may fold up like a cheap suitcase during hard times. You could have your protection cut off and lose your savings in a worst-case scenario.

## GETTING RATINGS ON INSURANCE COMPANIES

There are more than 2,500 insurance companies, and any of them will be happy to sell you the kind of insurance you want. But buying insurance is often a long-term investment, so you should use some care in selecting the right company. You want to be sure that the insurance company survives you.

The best-known company that rates insurance companies is A. M. Best Company, which publishes Best's Insurance Reports. Best's top rating is A++, then A+, then A. Many libraries have the Best publication in their reference section. If it's not there, try a general insurance agency.

Two other companies also rate insurance agencies, and when you're investing a lot of money in insurance, check out their opinions, too. They are Standard & Poor's, and Moody's. You'll probably find them in your public library, too, or in a local college or university library.

When you do shop around, one of the first problems you'll run into is the sales agent's rosy projections of the buildup of the cash values—the investment portion of your policy. Each state requires that the agent show you what future values will be, based on the company's guaranteed interest rate. And they usually show a buildup of cash values based on the current interest rate being paid.

The fly in the ointment, though, is the projection of future interest rates the insurance company may pay. Nothing currently stops an agent from showing you what the buildup will be at, say, 13% interest even though his company has never paid out that much. Or the agent may project the cash values at the best rate ever credited to policyholders and try to convince you that "with the change in the political situation, you can bet that interest rates are going sky high."

What to do? Just keep in mind that the illustrations you're given are neither totally valid predictions nor accurate track records. Take what you're told with a shaker of salt, even if it is printed out impressively by a computer!

## BUYING INSURANCE LESS EXPENSIVELY

Some insurance companies allow and encourage their client companies to let employees supplement the amount of their insurance coverage by buying additional insurance through the employer. If you're eligible for, say, $60,000 of coverage under the company plan, you usually can buy an additional $20,000 of term life insurance from the same company through your employer.

Most companies will deduct the premium payments for this supplemental insurance from your pay. It's less expensive to buy this way (after all, the insurance company's marketing and sales costs are near zero, so it can keep premiums low), and it's convenient. Your benefits package may include information on supplemental insurance. If not, check it out with the benefits department.

Another type of personal life insurance to look into is no-load or low-load life insurance. It's typically sold by telephone. There's been some shift toward this kind of life insurance, just as there was some twenty years ago to no-load mutual funds.

The big money-maker here is not lower premiums. Rather, it's a more rapid buildup of cash values. The cash values of the traditional whole life policy are hammered down by agents' commissions and other up-front expenses. The up-front costs, or loads, are so heavy that at the end of the first year the cash value may be zip, zero, *nada*, nothing. And even after the first year, these hefty expenses may skim off 5% or 8% from the premium.

Think of it from this angle: You pay a first-year premium of, say, $2,000. For some reason you have to drop the policy at the end of the year. You would walk away with nothing, or maybe a pittance like $100.

With no-load or low-load insurance, the first-year commission may be 10%. But your first-year premium earns interest. So if you cancel at the end of the year, you would be able to walk away with 90% to 95% of the $2,000 you paid in. Maybe not a great investment, but you're not sandbagged either.

What's the catch? None of the top-notch, major insurance companies sell no-load insurance. They claim that over the long term they'll outperform the no-load players (they're prob-ably right) and you'll earn more money over ten years or more. Also, the no-load or low-load companies aren't as safe as the top insurers. You're taking on a greater risk for the greater reward of faster cash value buildup.

## FIRST-TO-DIE AND SECOND-TO-DIE LIFE INSURANCE

Some spouses who both work are opting for what's called "first-to-die" insurance coverage rather than separate policies. Under first-to-die insurance, both spouses are covered for the same amount of insurance. But the policy pays off only for one—the first to die. The idea is that the survivor needs the money to take care of the kids and other expenses when the family in-come is drastically reduced.

The premiums for this kind of policy are typically 25% less than if each spouse takes out a separate policy. The catch: If one partner is much older or in poor health, the premiums may be set so high as to offset any cost advantages.

The second-to-die policies cost even less. They're usually geared to pay estate taxes. If you can forecast that you or your survivor will have an estate that'll be clobbered with estate tax-es, take a look at second-to-die insurance.

---

### INSURANCE SHOPPING MADE EASY

It pays to shop for life insurance, but it can be a real drag fighting off all those hungry insurance salespeople. Assuming you've made some deci-sions about how much and what kinds of life insurance fit you best, you may want to try one or more of the "telebrokerages." These are ser-vices that provide quotes from a number of companies. They don't work for just one insurer as many agents do.

SelectQuote (800-343-1985) is described as a "full-service term life insurance broker, dedicated to helping clients purchase the insurance coverage they need, at a price they can afford." SelectQuote claims that it quotes for companies that have never "failed to pay a valid life insur-ance claim" for as long as they've been in business.

After you call, you'll get quotes from five companies and some writ-ten information to help you understand what they've given you.

Some catches: They quote companies with ratings lower than the best. They won't quote companies that don't sell through independent agents. Some policies quoted may not be available in all states. The small-est policy offered is $50,000. The quotes are for term insurance only.

InsuranceQuote (800-972-1104) is another telebrokerage. It claims to put more emphasis on safety. It says the companies it quotes must have top ratings from the three major rating agencies. You'll get five quotes from InsuranceQuote too.

---

## RETIREMENT INCOME FROM LIFE INSURANCE

With almost all life insurance policies other than term, you can use the built-up values in the policies to give yourself retire-ment income for the rest of your life. Many kinds of options are available, and they usually include all those given for pension plans in chapter 12.

As you'll read, government regulations now require that you take a joint and survivor option from a qualified defined benefit plan. That's one that makes sure your spouse gets at least 50% of your pension after you die, unless he or she consents in writ-ing to give up that right.

The problem that raises is that your monthly check will be less under a joint and survivor option than if you took straight monthly payments for yourself alone for the rest of your life. The insurance companies have jumped into the breach by of-fering to sell you a policy on your life. They sell the idea that the extra cash you get each month on the unreduced annuity will more than pay for the life insurance. Whether it will or not depends on many factors. Here are some you must consider.

1. If your spouse is in poor health, the joint and survivor annu-ity from your pension plan makes less sense. If you're in poor health, the joint and survivor annuity makes more sense, and you may not be insurable at any reasonable rate.

2. If you're female, your life expectancy is longer, and you can buy life insurance more cheaply than a male.
3. If your pension plan has a cost-of-living adjustment (a COLA), taking the joint and survivor annuity is likely to be more attractive than buying insurance.
4. Life insurance benefits are tax exempt when taken in a lump sum, whereas pension plan payments are taxable.
5. Will the additional cash from an unreduced pension benefit really pay for the life insurance? The odds: It's unlikely for males, because of life expectancy and higher premiums; it takes time for females, often as long as five years.

*Maureen O'Reilly is now armed with some of the information she needs to discuss her (and her family's) life insurance needs with her spouse and her boss. You should be too. So do it.*

# 11
▼

# GOVERNMENT BENEFITS

## Getting All That's Coming to You

### THE CASE OF THE INJURED EMPLOYEE

Henry Carter was mad as hell. He'd mangled his hand in a machine at work. He'd needed two operations to fix it; had spent nearly a month in the hospital and then three more months getting well at home. Now, his first hour back on the job, his supervisor called him into his glassed-in cubicle to tell him he was fired for violating a safety rule. That violation, the supervisor said, had been the cause of the accident.

"Not so fast," Carter said. "Why didn't you can me right after the accident investigation if the safety violation was the real reason? Hey, wait a minute, I know what you're doing. You're getting back at me because of the Workers' Compensation claim, which will cost big bucks. That's a helluva way to run a business. You waited 'til I got back so you could twist the knife in me."

"Not true," shot back the boss. "Yeah, we're upset—because you were careless. You broke one of our safety rules, and that's why you got hurt. We don't care a bit about the comp claim. It's the safety rule you broke, and you were told right from the beginning that breaking any of those rules would result in immediate discharge."

*"We'll see about that," yelled Carter as he backed out the door. "You can't take that long after the accident to fire me. I'm gonna get a lawyer, and we'll see you in court."*

*They did, and the judge agreed with Carter that because the company took so long to fire him, that was circumstantial evidence that retaliation for the Workers' Compensation claim was a significant factor in a wrongful discharge. The court awarded Carter big bucks in damages, legal expenses, and attorney's fees.*

Normally, Workers' Compensation (WC) laws operate to settle claims of disabled workers, like Henry Carter, short of the courthouse. That's what they were originally designed for and in most cases do.

In recent years, though, exceptions to WC laws have cropped up. You should keep your eyes peeled, if you're hurt at work, to see if you're entitled to a fairer deal than you get through Workers' Compensation. Retaliation for making a claim, as in Henry Carter's case, is considered against public policy, though not all states allow employees to sue for retaliation in their courts. Another exception: In some states, workers are allowed to sue outside the WC system when their employers know they're exposing employees to risks like asbestos or poisonous chemicals.

That doesn't mean you should go into a "sue the SOBs" frenzy when you're injured on the job. It just means that you should know and fight for your rights should you ever become disabled by a work-related accident or by a disease resulting from your occupation.

WC is just one of the benefits you need to know about that are provided or mandated by the government rather than by your employer. Your employer gets involved, of course, with paperwork and cash.

Among such government-sponsored, -mandated, or -provided benefits beyond Workers' Compensation are:

1. unemployment benefits;
2. Social Security disability payments;
3. Social Security retirement benefits;

4. Social Security survivors' benefits;
5. Supplemental Security Income (SSI);
6. Medicare and Medicaid;
7. state disability payments;
8. death benefits from WC programs.

The point is that you need to know about *all* your current and potential benefits—not only in case of need, but also for the influence they may have on your decisions about buying such things as additional life insurance, supplemental health insurance, long-term care, disability policies, and the like. You want to take care of yourself and your family, for sure. But when you know what government benefits are out there for you and your family members to use, you won't drive yourself to drink or to the poorhouse trying to cover every potential expense.

Government benefits, which you've contributed cold, hard cash to, through taxes, work hand in hand with those your employer provides to take a big load off your shoulders.

## *WHAT YOU SHOULD KNOW ABOUT WORKERS' COMPENSATION*

Each state, as well as the District of Columbia, Puerto Rico, and U.S. territories like the Virgin Islands and Guam, has its own Workers' Compensation laws. There's also a law to cover federal employees, and the Longshoreman's Act to cover maritime, shipbuilding, and ship-repair workers. Interstate railway employees are covered by the Federal Employers' Liability Act.

WC laws meet a number of objectives. The ones you should be most interested in are quick replacement of lost income due to injuries on the job, and payment of medical benefits no matter who's at fault. For the most part, too, WC laws let you skip going to court over a personal injury, with all the delays and expenses that route entails. You shouldn't be hit so hard in the wallet due to an injury that you have to step down from Big Macs to rice patties.

Some attempts have been made to replace the many WC programs with a single federal one. That's unlikely to happen, though periodically some person in Congress throws a bill into the legislative hopper that would set minimum WC standards for all states to meet.

## WHAT'S IN WC FOR YOU

If you're a full- or part-time employee, odds are ten to one that you're covered by a state WC law. Three states—New Jersey, Texas, and South Carolina—let companies elect whether or not to come under the law, but if they don't, they're open to big risks of lawsuits. Most employers in those states elect to come under the law. Also, some states let companies self-insure rather than pay premiums to an insurance carrier for WC coverage. Some big employers do self-insure. But they're still governed by WC laws.

If you're classified an independent contractor, your situation in regard to WC may be iffy. Some companies have attempted to save employment costs by calling certain of their people independent contractors, who are not normally covered by WC.

---

### ACTION IDEA

If you have any question in your mind at all regarding whether your company classifies you as an employee or an independent contractor, simply ask. There's potentially a lot of big benefit bucks riding on the answer.

Usually, though, you can tell by your compensation check or pay envelope. If nothing is taken out of your pay for withholding tax, Social Security, and other deductions, the company may be classifying you as an independent contractor.

Get your status clarified before putting in any substantial length of time on the job. That's especially important if you're running any risk of getting hurt or sick from some occupational hazard. You may be cut out of a lot of money-saving benefits like health insurance, Workers' Compensation, disability pay, and the like.

If you're being paid "off the books," you're not covered. When any benefit like WC is available, make sure you're covered by it. Working "off the books" to avoid taxes and other deductions is penny-wise and pound-foolish.

---

The major benefit of WC is that you're covered for any injury that arises "out of and in the course of employment." That means the injury must be on-the-job and work-related. If you break a finger while arm wrestling in the company cafeteria, you won't get WC benefits. If you're hurt while driving to work, you're not covered unless you have a job with duties similar to those of a traveling salesman. If someone runs into you in the company parking lot, though, you're covered, as you are when driving a company vehicle on business.

If you're hurt at home while doing work ordered by the company, you may be compensated for an injury. That may be true, too, when you're hurt heading for the company rest room, during recreational or social activities on company grounds, if you're an uninvolved victim of a fight at the company, and in some other circumstances. You'll find gray areas of WC coverage that only WC experts can interpret.

---

### ACTION IDEA

Say you're minding your own business on the job when another employee playfully tosses a giant ball of tinfoil at a worker next to you. The tinfoil bounces into your workspace and gashes your arm badly enough to make it unsafe for you to operate your equipment for two weeks.

Go to your boss, after getting first aid, and make the following suggestion: Rather than filing a WC claim that'll pay for doctors' visits, a tetanus shot, and disability pay for two weeks, ask the company to pay these costs directly to you. Suggest that you be paid your full wage, rather than the disability pay rate, because the company stands to benefit from lower WC premiums.

For the company, paying small claims is like paying a deductible on a car insurance policy. The company is self-insuring for small costs to make big savings on WC premium costs.

You can't—and shouldn't—get rich from Workers' Comp. But you can up your take-home pay with this kind of strategy.

## CASH ON THE BARRELHEAD

The idea of Workers' Compensation is to pay you enough to cover your losses. That includes your earnings and medical expenses, like doctors' fees and hospital costs. If you're severely hurt, WC pays for medication and vocational rehabilitation.

WC laws classify disabilities as:

1. temporary total;
2. permanent total;
3. temporary partial;
4. permanent partial.

Most cases are temporary total disability. You're not able to work on your job at all, but you're expected to recover and go back to work.

The amount of money you get depends in part on your weekly pay. It differs from state to state, and the max you'll get ranges from 60% of wages in Idaho and $198 a week in Mississippi to 80% of spendable earnings up to a max of $700 a week in Alaska. Among all states, the most common fraction of earnings paid to WC claimants is two-thirds. These numbers change from time to time. WC is no get-rich-quick scheme, but the benefits come in handy when you need them most.

Income payments in most states usually continue for the length of time you're disabled. Some states, however, have a limit on the number of weeks they'll pay and also on the total amount. The limit on weeks of WC income replacement range up to five hundred; the total amounts go well up into six figures. It's a good idea to check these numbers out with your local WC office, because they change periodically.

**Benefits alert:** Because you're not going to get your total income replaced, negotiating with your company to pay you direct, as suggested in the previous Action Idea, might result in the company continuing your pay in full for a short disability—a better deal than getting 60% to 80% from WC. And when your employer continues to pay you, you won't lose any pay for any waiting period that WC laws may impose.▼

If you lose a hand, foot, finger, or other member in an accident, you'll be entitled to a specific sum of money set by law, called a "scheduled" benefit. That payment may or may not be in addition to any other money coming your way, depending on state law.

If you die in an on-the-job accident, your spouse and children get paid specified amounts over a period of time.

Payments for medical and hospital care are provided immediately. Income payments are delayed by waiting periods of three to seven days, depending on state WC laws. In some instances you don't get paid at all for the waiting period. In others you can recapture the disability pay for the three or seven days.

---

### ACTION IDEAS

You're entitled to rehabilitation pay when rehab is needed to get you in shape to do your normal work. Suggest to your boss that you be given appropriate work to do away from the workplace while you're still recovering. Studies have shown that people who get involved in productive work at home, rather than sitting on their duffs all day in front of a TV set, recover more quickly.

Suggest, too, that the company call you back as soon as you're able to do some kind of work that is less physically demanding than your regular job, something that won't hurt your rehab efforts. Let management know about companies like Chrysler which design special jobs for injured workers. Raytheon Corp., famous for its Patriot antimissile missiles, actually has physical therapists visit recovering workers on the job to help them get better sooner.

Getting back on the job sooner rather than later is a good deal for both you and the company. You get back to full pay sooner. Your company's loss experience, which affects the WC insurance premium it pays, is lower so it saves money. The company also saves money on overtime or part-time workers who fill in to get your duties done. And, another plus, you're more productive than any person filling in for you.

---

Social Security has a disability program that pays benefits to disabled workers if they're under 65 and the disability is expected to last a year or more (check out chapter 4). If you're eligible for the Social Security benefit, though, you may find that you don't get much greater income. The states work with the Social Security Administration to see that WC payments plus Social Security disability payments don't exceed 80% of your average annual pay. This kind of coordination of benefits is covered more fully later in this chapter.

Some states also permit injured employees to get both WC and unemployment insurance benefits, though generally the unemployment benefit will be deducted from what's paid under Workers' Compensation programs.

## UNEMPLOYMENT BENEFITS

You may not want to think about the dreaded condition of unemployment. But unemployment insurance is a benefit that'll make your day when it's needed. While Workers' Compensation is based on state laws, the Federal Unemployment Tax Act really governs the unemployment insurance laws of the fifty states and U.S. possessions.

Though the feds control the taxes collected for unemployment compensation and set minimum standards for eligibility, benefit amount, and how long benefits are paid, the law lets the states set their own standards within the federal guidelines on eligibility, how much to pay, and for how long.

Your employer pays all the taxes, both federal and state, to cover this potentially valuable benefit—except in two states, where employees are also taxed. They are New Jersey and Alaska. Two other states may also require employee payments for unemployment insurance under certain conditions. They are Pennsylvania and West Virginia.

All states pay weekly benefits for at least twenty-six weeks of unemployment, though this duration is extended from time to time during periods of high unemployment.

The amount of payment is aimed at providing about 35% of your weekly pay with a max that depends on the state's average weekly wage. The payment amounts vary quite a bit among states. The idea is to pay enough to keep you and your family eating, but not in your town's finest restaurant. Unemployment benefits aren't enough to keep you from actively seeking work long before they run out.

Keep in mind that benefits are payable only for *involuntary* unemployment that is not a result of misconduct. Just because you quit when you're tired of working doesn't mean that you can sit on your fanny and collect cash from the state unemployment fund. Your former employer can make a case against your getting any money at all if you've quit on your own or without good cause rather than being fired or laid off due to economic conditions.

## *BENEFITS CHECKOFF: UNEMPLOYMENT ELIGIBILITY*

Here are six rules to think about if you're faced with unemployment:

- ✔ You can draw on unemployment even if you were a part-time worker.
- ✔ If you take a leave of absence or go on strike, you can't put in for UI.
- ✔ You can draw unemployment when you retire.
- ✔ Your best bet for pulling in UI benefits occurs if you're terminated due to lack of work, as evidenced by a plant closure or the elimination of a position.
- ✔ If you're fired for misconduct, like breaking company policy, you can be denied UI.
- ✔ If you voluntarily quit, you disqualify yourself from UI unless you have a strong reason, such as sexual harassment.

---

### ACTION IDEA

Most states interpret unemployment compensation laws in a way that's favorable to employees whenever possible. Employers, however, often contest unemployment claims—they have a financial interest in having as few claims as possible, as the rates they are charged can depend on having few claims.

That's why you should be very careful during interviews that you may have with your boss or the personnel department after you've been told you're being laid off. Don't give any interviewers anything they can use to deprive you of your benefit.

That's especially true if you've quit due to harassment, intolerable working conditions, etc. They may try to get you to admit to some kind of "misconduct" that could be used to make you ineligible for benefits. It's best to say nothing at all and reserve your good reasons for a hearing on your claim should one be called due to a contest by your former employer.

One employee quit his job and then filed for unemployment benefits. His former employer said he should be disqualified for benefits because he quit "without good cause." At the hearing on his case, though, the employee pointed out that he'd been employed for ten years in a white-collar, supervisory job. Two months before he quit, the company had suddenly given him a mop and broom, and he was ordered to sweep and mop a warehouse floor every day whether or not there had been any traffic in it. The employee claimed that anyone put in such a position would feel compelled to quit. The hearing officer reinstated his claim for benefits.

For help, go to or call the nearest unemployment office and ask for any literature it may have that explains your rights and gives examples of cases that support claims for benefits.

---

## GETTING YOUR DUE FROM SOCIAL SECURITY

You may think that collecting anything from Social Security is a long time off. But the truth is that the system offers some benefits that you may be eligible to collect for yourself or your family right now.

Part of the Social Security (SS) taxes you and your employers have paid is used to finance the benefits of Social Security's disability program. Go to a Social Security office or call the 800 number listed in most phone books under Social Security Administration or U.S. Government (currently the number is 800-772-1213), and ask for a booklet on the disability program. The booklet gives many details, including:

- what is meant by "disability";
- who can get Social Security disability benefits;
- disability benefits for people with HIV infection;
- disability benefits for children;
- how much work you need for SS benefits;
- how to apply;
- who decides if you are disabled;
- how disability is determined;
- rules for blind people;
- what to do if your claim is denied;
- your first check;
- how much you will get;
- how other payments affect benefits;
- when benefits may be taxed;
- how you can get Medicare if you're disabled;
- reviewing your disability;
- what can cause benefits to stop;
- benefits while you work;
- supplemental security income.

Generally, if you're covered by Social Security, you're covered by its disability program. You have to be under 65, of course, or else you'd draw SS retirement payments. You may even be eligible for payments if you're getting a pension from work *not* covered by SS and you become disabled. Some individuals who have worked for nonprofit organizations have never been covered by Social Security, but they can still qualify for SS disability.

There's even better news. Your coverage includes certain members of your family, including:

- your unmarried son or daughter (including stepchild, adopted child, and, in some cases, grandchild) who is under age 18 or under 19 if in elementary or secondary school full time;
- your unmarried son or daughter disabled before age 22— benefits may start as early as 18;
- your spouse caring for your child who is under 16 or disabled and is also receiving checks;
- your spouse who is age 62 or older;

- your disabled widow or widower—benefits are payable at age 50. The disability must have started before your death or within seven years after death;
- your disabled surviving divorced wife or husband. If the marriage lasted ten years or longer, benefits are payable at age 50 on the same basis as to a disabled widow or widower.

As you read in chapter 4, you can't start getting disability benefits from SSA before five months have gone by. Furthermore, your disability must prevent you from doing any substantial gainful work, and that condition must be expected to last for at least a year or result in death. Naturally you're going to have to show medical evidence about your condition and how it prevents you from working.

If you're getting WC benefits for your disability, the SS disability payments for you and your family may be affected. You generally can't get from all programs combined more than 80% of your average weekly earnings for a period of up to a year before becoming disabled. If you're getting a government pension, that may reduce your SS disability payments. You'll find some sticky wrinkles in the program. You can easily iron them out by asking about them at your SS office.

---

### ACTION IDEA

Supplemental Security Income (SSI) is a federal program run by the Social Security Administration. But the money for SSI checks comes from income taxes, not from Social Security taxes. SSI is not just for adults. Monthly checks can be paid to disabled and blind children, too.

SSI is for people who don't own much or don't have a lot of income. It pays monthly checks to people who are 65 or older, or are blind, or have a disability. "Blind" can mean either totally blind, or having very poor eyesight. "Disabled" refers to people who have physical or mental problems that keep them from working and are expected to last at least a year or to result in death.

If you feel that you or someone in your family may qualify for Supplemental Security Income, call your SS office and ask for a booklet called "SSI." After reading that, call SS with any further questions you may have.

## SOCIAL SECURITY RETIREMENT BENEFITS— THEY'RE THE REAL THING

Most employees now realize that Social Security will *not* be the only source of their retirement income. It's just one part of a three-part source from which you'll draw money to support you when you start taking your "longest vacation." The other parts: private pensions which include 401(k)s, defined benefit plans, and profit sharing; and your own personal savings in IRAs, mutual funds, bank accounts, CDs, and the like.

Social Security, it's true, puts a firm foundation under your retirement income. But like any building, the foundation is normally smaller than the rest of the structure. It's a base to build on.

SS is not a bank, a savings account, or a checking account. It's a pipeline. What you and other workers are putting into that pipeline right now is flowing out the other end to the people who are drawing benefits today, though currently some surplus is stashed away.

Some gloom-and-doomers say that the SS system can't make it. They say that at some time the number of people paying in will get fed up with the costs and knock off the whole system. Some of them even say that if they personally invested the money they put into SS they could take more out than they'll ever get from SS. Don't you believe it. Few people have the perseverance and money-making know-how to invest the money over their lifetimes to accomplish that goal. What's more, Social Security covers vastly more than simply retirement income.

Don't worry about the gloomy predictions of the end of Social Security programs. Some 50 million people are currently getting benefits while at this point more than 135 million are paying into the system with the expectation of getting benefits later on. Those people have such a huge interest in getting their own SS benefits that they'll guarantee that the system continues.

### WHAT SS IS COSTING YOU

You see the deductions in your checks or on your pay envelopes. The SS deduction should be labelled FICA for Federal

Insurance Contributions Act, though some employers still use the abbreviation OAB (Old Age Benefit).

You and your employer each contribute a certain percentage of your pay into the Social Security trust fund up to certain limits. Check with your employer for the current percentage and at what pay limit the deductions cut out. Your local Social Security office can give you that information, too.

---

### IS YOUR SOCIAL SECURITY MONEY SAFE?

Don't let anyone tell you that the money being paid into the SS trust fund is being spent on whatever Congress decides it should be spent on—from $600 Air Force toilet seats to $100 The Allen Wrench People for the space program. It's not.

By law the money is invested in U.S.-backed securities, special-issue bonds that pay interest. It's the safest investment in the world today, backed by the full faith and credit of the United States of America.

It's true that these bonds will have to be paid off in the future. But that's no different from the government having to pay you off when you buy Treasury bonds, notes, and bills.

---

Not all of the SS deduction goes for retirement, disability, and survivors' benefits. Some of it is going for hospital insurance.

The whole percentage is paid on wages up to a certain annual limit. A smaller percentage is paid until you earn somewhere up in six figures. The way the law reads now, the percentage of tax is scheduled to remain the same. The amount of your pay the tax is based on can change each year.

### HOW MUCH WILL YOU GET WHEN YOU RETIRE?

Don't bother guessing. The Social Security Administration will give you its best estimate. Call 800-772-1213, or go to your local SS office, and ask for the form "Request for Earnings and Benefits Estimate Statement" (form SSA-7004). You'll see a reproduction of this form in figure 22 on page 194. It requires a few minutes of work on your part. Use figure 22 to help you get started collecting the data the form asks for before you pick it up or your copy arrives in the mail.

---

**Benefits alert:** Some people who claim to be retirement or financial planners are offering a service to find out your estimated retirement pension amount for you—*for a fee*. But you can get it for yourself direct from the Social Security Administration, and the information is *free.*▼

---

You'll note on form SSA-7004 that you're asked to make an estimate of your future average yearly earnings. Not easy. Even if you expect to earn substantially more than you do now, don't take inflation into account, and don't put in a wishful figure. Your best bet is to simply list your current year's earnings as your future average earnings estimate. The SSA is going to adjust them upward to account for an average wage increase anyway. Furthermore, you should keep tabs on your estimated retirement benefit. Make a new request for it every two or three years. That'll eliminate the need for accurately estimating future pay.

## GETTING YOUR PIECE OF THE SOCIAL SECURITY PIE

It doesn't take much to become eligible for Social Security. Generally you need only forty quarters of coverage (that translates into ten years of work) in which you earned certain minimum amounts. Those amounts are a pittance; you can't live on them, and they change year to year. Check with Social Security if it's important to you to find out.

---

### ACTION IDEA

Eligibility requirements for becoming fully insured under Social Security are very easy to meet. You might, therefore, want to urge a spouse who chooses to be a homemaker, rather than an employee, to consider becoming self-employed and earning money from a home-based business. Some spouses set themselves up as free-lance writers or editors. Others have taken in clerical jobs like typing or addressing envelopes. Still others have turned their kitchens into a kind of bakery and sold their special recipes by mail.

It takes very little cash income, currently something under $600, to earn a "quarter of coverage." It takes only about a year and a half to get into the SS system, and ten years makes sure your spouse is fully covered for life. Neither task is hard to do over thirty-five to forty years of marriage.

The payoff: When you reach retirement age, you'll have a choice of the always available spousal pension, which is roughly one-half of yours. Or your spouse can take her or his own retirement benefit, which may, in fact, be much greater than the one provided under SS's usual spousal coverage.

---

## ANOTHER BENEFIT OF SS: SURVIVORS' BENEFITS

Survivors' benefits are another insurancelike coverage you get from Social Security. You'd be hard pressed financially to buy enough life insurance to equal the replacement income that your survivors may get should you die. It's all part of the SS program. You pay nothing extra for it.

SS survivors' benefits can be paid to your:

- Widow or widower, with full benefits at 65 or older or reduced benefits as early as age 60. A disabled widow or widower can get benefits at 50.
- Widow or widower at any age if she or he takes care of your child who is under 16 or disabled and receiving benefits.
- Unmarried children under 18 (up to age 19 if they are attending elementary or secondary school full time). Your child can get benefits at any age if he or she was disabled before 22 and remains disabled. Under certain circumstances, benefits can also be paid to your stepchildren or granchildren.
- Dependent parents at 62 or older.
- Divorced wife or husband under certain circumstances.

There's also a special one-time payment of $255 at death that can be made only to certain family members. These survivors' benefits make up quite an "insurance" policy. They're potentially worth a great deal of money. Keep this in mind when you're shopping for life insurance. Once you've taken into account the money SS will pay to your survivors, you may want to cut down on the amount of insurance you buy, in order to save the premium costs.

Like many other benefits, these age and money amounts change. So pick up the phone and check them out.

## MEDICARE: SPEARHEAD OF HEALTH AND MEDICAL BENEFITS

You can't sign up for Medicare before age 65, unless you've been getting SS disability benefits for twenty-four months or you have kidney failure. Medicare is a two-part program of health insurance. Part A is the hospital insurance plan, and you're in it without cost when you sign up. It covers most hospital costs, but you're responsible for the cost of a semiprivate room for the first day.

Part B is optional and costs money. If you take it, the premium, which varies but is currently about $40 per month, will be taken out of your monthly Social Security check. Part B pays 80% of most doctor's bills, medical equipment, and certain outpatient services to doctors who accept it to pay their bills in full. Doctors who don't take Medicare as full payment (known as accepting assignment) are forbidden by law to charge you more than 15% over the approved Medicare benefit.

If your physician doesn't accept assignment, you'll pay the doctor, who will send a claim to Medicare, which will send you a check for 80% of its approved amount. As noted before, the approved amount may be less than the doc charges. Part B has an annual deductible which is modest (currently $100) but which has been increased from time to time.

Because neither Part A nor Part B of Medicare covers everything, private insurers have leapt into the breach and offered Medigap policies (check out chapter 4). When the time comes

*Figure 22. Request for Earnings and Benefit Estimate Statement*

## SOCIAL SECURITY ADMINISTRATION

## Request for Earnings and Benefit Estimate Statement

To receive a free statement of your earnings covered by Social Security and your estimated future benefits, all you need to do is fill out this form. Please print or type your answers. When you have completed the form, fold it and mail it to us.

1. Name shown on your Social Security card:

First    Middle Initial    Last

2. Your Social Security number as shown on your card:

3. Your date of birth:    Month    Day    Year

4. Other Social Security numbers you may have used:

5. Your Sex:  ☐ Male  ☐ Female

6. Other names you have used (including a maiden name):

7. Show your actual earnings for last year and your estimated earnings for this year. Include only wages and/or net self-employment income subject to Social Security tax.

   A. Last year's actual earnings:
   $ _____ . 0 0
   Dollars only

   B. This year's estimated earnings:
   $ _____ . 0 0
   Dollars only

8. Show the age at which you plan to retire:

9. Below, show an amount which you think best represents your future average yearly earnings between now and when you plan to retire. The amount should be a yearly average, not your total future lifetime earnings. Only show earnings subject to Social Security tax.

   **Most people should enter the same amount as this year's estimated earnings (the amount shown in 7B).** The reason for this is that we will show your retirement benefit estimate in today's dollars, but adjusted to account for average wage growth in the national economy.

   However, if you expect to earn significantly more or less in the future than what you currently earn because of promotions, a job change, part-time work, or an absence from the work force, enter the amount in today's dollars that will most closely reflect your future average yearly earnings. Do not add in cost-of-living, performance, or scheduled pay increases or bonuses.

   Your future average yearly earnings:
   $ _____ . 0 0
   Dollars only

10. Address where you want us to send the statement:

Name

Street Address (Include Apt. No., P.O. Box, or Rural Route)

City    State    Zip Cod

I am asking for information about my own Social Security record or the record of a person I am authorized to represent. I understand that if I deliberately request information under false pretenses I may be guilty of a federal crime and could be fined and/or imprisoned. I authorize you to send the statement of my earnings and benefit estimates to me or my representative through a contractor.

Please sign your name (Do not print)

Date    (Area Code)  Daytime Telephone No.

ABOUT THE PRIVACY ACT
Social Security is allowed to collect the facts on this form under Section 205 of the Social Security Act. We need them to quickly identify your record and prepare the earnings statement you asked us for. Giving us these facts is voluntary. However, without them we may not be able to give you an earnings and benefit estimate statement. Neither the Social Security Administration nor its contractor will use the information for any other purpose.

SP

Form SSA-7004-PC-OPI (6/88) DESTROY PRIOR EDITIONS

for you to consider them, take as much care with the insurance agent as you would with a used-car dealer. There's been some settling down of rates and coverages, but the main thing to be careful about is not to become overinsured. You may pay a lot of premiums only to discover that duplicate coverages are "coordinated." That is, if one policy pays for a claim, another policy won't kick in for the *same* claim. Too much Medigap insurance is a waste of money, not a maker of money.

Health Maintenance Organizations (HMOs) and some other medical plans are known as "prepayment plans." That's because you pay for medical care before you actually get it. These plans are like a combination of an insurance company and a doctor/hospital. Like an insurance company they take care of health care costs in return for a premium. Like a doctor/hospital they give actual health care.

Some such plans have government contracts to provide services to Medicare beneficiaries. If they do, they must provide all the services covered by Medicare. If you sign up for a prepayment plan, Medicare pays the plan an amount for the costs of covered services less deductibles and what you'd normally pay—called coinsurance. So a prepayment plan may require you to pay a monthly premium to it.

*Henry Carter went to a lawyer, so he didn't need the information in this chapter. But you do. It's important to coordinate the benefits you are due from the government with those due from private sources. It's just another way to save your hard-earned dollars and to spend them where they do the most good.*

# 12

▼

# RETIREMENT PENSIONS

*Preparing for Your Longest Vacation*

### THE CASE OF THE RESTRICTED RELATIVES

I t hadn't ever happened to him, at least not directly. Ryan Baerga was cruising through the Christmas holidays, not a care in the world. He liked his job, made decent money, had a more than passable social life for a 26-year-old. Yeah, life was okay.

In fact, Ryan was really looking forward to New Year's, when the entire family including his grandparents planned to journey to California. They were his favorites, and he theirs. They used to shower him with so many gifts that his sisters claimed it made him a spoiled brat. He grinned at the memory.

But the gifts were few and far between lately. Probably, he thought, because he was older now. So he was stunned to hear that his grandparents had decided not to make the West Coast trip. And even more startled to learn the reason: They couldn't afford it.

The idea that people who were retired—especially his family—had any problems at all had never crossed his mind. And money problems? How could that be?

*He got a Christmas present for them: two tickets to join everyone in California. And he spent a lot of time listening to them talk about their current lifestyle. It got him thinking. And acting, as soon as he got back to work.*

Hey, what could be more fun than planning for the longest vacation of your life—retirement! No matter what your age, now's the time to plan.

---

### WHY SAVING SOONER FOR RETIREMENT IS BETTER

Say you want to accumulate a quarter-million bucks to put you on Easy Street when you retire. Say also that you're cagey enough to be able to average 10% a year on your investments. Here's how much you'd have to sock away *each* month to end up with $250,000 in your stash:

| Years to retirement | Your monthly investment |
|---|---|
| 40 | $   40 |
| 30 | 120 |
| 20 | 326 |
| 10 | 1,211 |

---

Make no mistake about it—you'll be ready to take a seat on the bench after thirty-five to forty years on the business playing field. At least you'll be ready mentally; you can take that to the bank.

But what about financially? Are you going to be able to shift into your "longest vacation" as smoothly as your car shifts down from overdrive? Or will you look like a person fighting off Maine black flies when you're battling with the people you owe money to?

Maybe you think that a company pension plus Social Security will let you lead the comfortable life of Reilly. Will it? Hey, you never know.

## A PRIMER ON PENSION PLANS

Most private pension plans today are "qualified." The U.S. Treasury Department hasn't exactly stamped them with a kind of "Good Housekeeping Seal of Approval." But it's looked them over and said they're okay according to the rules of the Internal Revenue Service.

If the plan you're in is qualified, that makes Uncle Sam your partner. Should you need any help standing up for your pension rights, that tall, bewhiskered guy in the blue, white, and red striped suit will go to bat for you.

Benefits experts have dreamed up a bewildering array of retirement plans. Most of them, though, are simply variations of one or more of these seven types:

1. defined benefit plan;
2. defined contribution plan;
3. profit sharing pension plan;
4. money purchase pension plan;
5. 401(k) plan;
6. Simplified Employee Pension (SEP);
7. target benefit plan.

None of them may fit your plan exactly because names like "cash balance plan" or "tax effective retirement account" or others are often used as synonyms for one of the seven listed. When in doubt about the type of plan or plans your company may have you in, ask your benefits person to explain. If that person doesn't know, hang in there until you get an answer.

Don't hesitate to ask the boss or a benefits person any questions at all that come up while you're studying your specific situation.

You're *entitled* to get answers to everything from simple questions like "When did I become eligible?" to complex ones like "Where's all the dough in the plan being invested?"

If you don't get up to speed on pension plans, you'll feel like a pilot who makes great landings at the wrong airport—unharmed, but where in the world are you?

The bottom line is that your "longest vacation" won't be worth a hoot if you can't finance it. Your mission, no ducking it now: to find out what your payoff will be from your current employer's plan *and*, just as important, from any plans of previous employers.

**Benefits alert:** For information on how to monitor a pension plan, send for a copy of "How to Obtain Employee Benefits Documents from the Labor Department" from the Pension and Welfare Benefits Division, Department of Labor, Public Disclosure Facility, Room N5507, 200 Constitution Ave. NW, Washington, DC 20210.▼

## GETTING DOWN TO THE NITTY GRITTY

A common kind of plan is called a *defined benefit plan*. When you meet certain age and length-of-service requirements, such a plan will pay you a definite sum of money, a "defined" benefit, starting at some future date. You'll get X dollars a month for the rest of your life, for instance. Or you could get a lump sum that an actuary calculates, if the plan allows this kind of payout. There are many variations of payment in between these two. No matter what, you definitely get a definite benefit.

The good news about defined benefit plans is that even if your employer goes out of business, a federal agency, the Pension Benefit Guaranty Corporation, will step in to pay you—up to a certain amount per year. Defined benefit plans are the *only* kind that the PBGC insures.

The bad news: Defined benefit pension plans may be going the way of the dodo bird. Government regulations are getting so complicated and costly to meet that many employers are throwing in the towel and cashing them in. Few employers are starting up new ones.

### ACTION IDEA

If you don't have the security of a defined benefit pension plan, ask why. If the answer is simply the economics of the situation (in other words, it costs too much money, puts too much pressure on the company to make payments to the plan each year, and takes too much time and effort to meet changing federal regulations), suggest that management set up such a plan in this way: Take some of the matching money the company has already contributed this year to another plan, like a 401(k) or profit sharing plan, to buy annuities in each participant's name. An annuity will pay a specific benefit at retirement. That route switches a lot of the regulatory headaches to the insurance company that writes the annuity contracts.

Management might also consider reducing future matching contributions to other plans so that it can make annual payments to the new defined benefit pension plan. The additional security this kind of plan offers you may be worth more than the future value of cash contributed to other benefits.

---

A *defined contribution plan* says your employer will set aside some sums each year in an account earmarked for you. The administrators invest the money to increase its value along the way to your retirement date. And, as noted earlier, you may be making decisions on how to invest that money.

A *profit sharing pension plan*, which is one kind of defined contribution plan, has money set aside each year by the employer. Sometimes the amount is related directly to profits through a formula. Sometimes it's just what the employer is inclined to put in. Profit sharing plans are quite iffy when it comes to building up retirement money. Few companies are consistently profitable. Moreover, management is likely to play it safe by shuffling less money into the plan than is really needed to pay good pensions. Some firms use profit sharing plans because they feel they can't commit to funding pensions in any other way.

---

### ACTION IDEA

If your company uses profit sharing as the *only* method to provide retirement benefits, swing into action right away. Mobilize interest among other employees in getting the company to start another kind of plan—a 401(k) or a Simplified Employee Pension (SEP), for instance. Get management to think of profit sharing not as *the* retirement plan but as a *supplement* to another type of pension plan.

---

Companies contribute a fixed percentage of your compensation when they set up a *money purchase pension plan*. This kind of plan allows greater contributions than SEPs or profit sharing—up to 25% of your pay to an annual max of $30,000, resulting in bigger pensions. The possibilities for better pensions are great if you can persuade management to put the maximum allowable amount of money into the plan.

*401(k) plans*, which are covered in chapter 7, get contributions from you, and these are usually supplemented by employer matches. You decide how much you'll sock into the plan each year up to certain limits.

These plans normally let you turn the money in your account at your retirement into a monthly pension for life. Or they let you sweep your account clean and take out all the cash that's built up. There are numerous variations between these two extremes.

Main differences: Defined benefit plans virtually guarantee you a specific amount when you retire. Defined contribution plans, however, give you only what's in your account—the contributions and earnings—and there's no totally accurate way to tell you how much that'll be.

## ANOTHER SCENE IN THE RETIREMENT ACT: SEPS AND SARSEPS

In 1978 Congress created Simplified Employee Pensions (SEPs). They allow employers, usually small ones, to more easily provide a retirement benefit for the owner and for all employees in the company.

Though SEPs resemble Individual Retirement Accounts (IRAs), they differ in two main details:

1. Contributions are generally made by employers, not employees.
2. The amounts contributed to SEPs can be much larger than those contributed by individuals to IRAs.

As a general rule, the boss can contribute up to 15% of everyone's pay, including his or her own, to a SEP each year for a maximum of $30,000 for each. In addition the Tax Reform Act of 1986 allows a salary reduction feature (these plans are called SARSEPs) for employers that have twenty-five or fewer individuals on the payroll.

## BENEFITS CHECKOFF: *SEP ADVANTAGES AND DISADVANTAGES*

If your company has a SEP, you'll find lots of advantages:

✔ The money chipped in to the SEP and its earnings from investment belong to you, even if you stop working for the company. You *can* take this benefit with you.

✔ Whatever your employer contributes to the SEP for your account isn't included in your income for income tax or Social Security tax purposes. (If you have a SARSEP, which calls for a salary reduction as your contribution to the plan, then you'll pay Social Security on the amount you put in, as will your employer.)

✔ You pay no tax on the money or its investment earnings until you start taking it out. If you start drawing it out before age 59½, you'll be slapped with a 10% penalty.

✔ The SEP money goes into a financial institution like a bank or brokerage, but you can change where your money goes if you don't like your employer's choice.

✔ If you die, your assets in the SEP will be paid to someone you've chosen.

✔ Your employer can continue to contribute to your SEP account until you retire. But you don't have to draw cash out until you reach age 70½.

✔ Your employer is not limited to contributing $2,000 a year to the SEP, and neither are you to a SARSEP, the way you are with an IRA.

On the negative side of the ledger:

✔ Your employer can vary the amounts contributed and doesn't need to make contributions every year. He/she can skip payments to the SEP when times are tough. Employers are often very careful with benefit bucks. They skip payments at the least sign of trouble.

✔ Your employer decides how much to put into the SEP each year, unlike other plans which may lock in contributions of certain amounts.

✔ You don't have any government watchdogs to see if the SEP is run for your benefit.

## STEPPING INTO A SEP

Generally, the company must include you and all other employees in the SEP, with these exceptions:

- employees who haven't worked for the company for two out of the last five years;
- employees who earn less than a pittance in a year (the figure was under $400 as this book was written, though it increases each year);
- employees who aren't 21 years old;
- employees covered by a collective bargaining agreement if retirement benefits were a part of the bargaining;
- nonresident aliens.

If your company hasn't yet included you in its SEP (and you don't fall into one of these categories), find out why. Even an innocent oversight by the company can cost you money.

When your company sets up a SEP and you become eligible, it'll give you a copy of Internal Revenue Service form 5305-SEP, part of which is shown in figure 23. In it the company agrees to make contributions when it can to Individual Retirement Accounts for all eligible employees. The company also agrees to kick in the same percentage of total compensation for every employee.

## NEW SPROUTS ON THE PENSION PLAN PLANT

Some companies haven't been entirely satisfied with either of the two major types of plans—defined benefit or defined contribution. They've taken cuttings from both kinds and bred some hybrids. The *target benefit plan* is one such type.

*Figure 23*

## Form 5305-SEP
### Simplified Employee Pension–Individual Retirement Accounts Contribution Agreement

Under Section 408(k) of the Internal Revenue Code

*(Business name/employer)*

makes the following agreement under the terms of section 408(k) of the Internal Revenue Code and the instructions to this form.

The employer agrees to provide for discretionary contributions in each calendar year to the Individual Retirement Accounts or Individual Annuities (IRAs) of all eligible employees who are at least ———— years old (not under 21 years old) (see instruction "Who May Participate"). This ☐ includes ☐ does not include employees covered under a collective bargaining agreement and ☐ includes ☐ does not include employees whose total compensation during the year is less than $363*.

The employer agrees that contributions made on behalf of each employee will:

• Be made only on the first $222,220* of compensation.

• Be made in an amount that is the same percentage of total compensation for every employee.

• Be limited to the smaller of $30,000 or 15% of compensation.

• Be paid to the employee's IRA trustee, custodian, or insurance company (for an annuity contract).

*This amount reflects the cost-of-living increase under Section 408(k)(8) effective 1-1-91. This amount is adjusted annually. Each January, the IRS announces the increase, if any, in the Internal Revenue Bulletin.

Signature of employer                    Date

By

## Information for the Employee

The information provided below explains what a SEP is, how contributions are made, and how to treat your employer's contributions for tax purposes . . . .

Please read the questions carefully. For more specific information, see also the agreement form and instructions on page 1 of this form.

Questions

1. What is a Simplified Employee Pension Plan or SEP?

2. What must my employer contribute to my IRA under the SEP?

3. How much may my employer contribute to my SEP-IRA in any year?

4. How do I treat my employer's SEP contributions for my taxes?

5. May I also contribute to my IRA if I am a participant in a SEP?

6. Are there any restrictions on the IRA I select to deposit my SEP contributions in?

7. What if I don't want a SEP-IRA?

8. Can I move funds from my SEP-IRA to another tax-sheltered IRA?

9. What happens if I withdraw my employer's contribution from my IRA?

10. May I participate in a SEP even though I'm covered by another plan?

11. What happens if too much is contributed to my SEP-IRA in one year?

12. Do I need to file any additional forms with the IRS because I participate in a SEP?

13. Is my employer required to provide me with information about SEP-IRAs and the SEP agreement?

14. Is the financial institution where I establish my IRA also required to provide me with information?

A target benefit plan is a defined contribution plan that gets the employer off the hook of making specified payments to a trust to buy a defined benefit for each participant. In a sense, the target plan copies a major feature of a defined benefit plan: It aims to build an account for every member that will provide a specified amount of money—a target—at retirement.

The plan uses a formula to reach that goal. It includes years of service, age, annual pay, etc. Actuaries stir this pot to calculate a figure that the company must contribute to hit the target for each participant.

---

### ACTION IDEA

If your company has a SEP and you want to add money to your account to boost tax deferred earnings for retirement, try to get at least half of the other employees to sign up for a SARSEP, which will allow you and them to do so. None of you has to contribute any fixed dollar or percentage amount, though there is a minimum. A salary reduction contribution from at least half the employees will be enough to get a SARSEP going, though you may want to consider contributing as much as the law allows to your own account. There's gold in those tax deferred savings!

If you have an IRA, keep it going. You can participate in a SEP and contribute to an IRA at the same time—a double dose of savings.

---

## WHY YOU MAY NOT GET YOUR PENSION THE "OLD FASHIONED WAY"

You may recall hearing about people who got their pensions the old fashioned way. They'd spend thirty-five or forty years with one company, pick up a gold watch at the retirement dinner, and then sit back and collect their monthly checks for life.

Corporate cultures have changed, and companies no longer recognize employee loyalty the way they once did. It's true, too, that many individuals prefer to work two years here, four years there, and five years at some other place. The culture of employees has changed. They're refusing to stagnate.

But "job-hopping," if that's the right term for it, has its disadvantages. When you don't stay in one place long enough, you can't build up enough credits to earn a reasonable pension for yourself. Worse yet, you may not get any credits toward a pension at all if you never reach the stage where your benefits are fully "vested," a term that is described more fully later in this chapter.

Check out the scenario in figure 24 to see this dilemma in action.

## THE CASE OF THE JILTED JOB-HOPPER

*Ted Smythe had been in the work force for nearly forty years and was now ready to hang up his spikes. It's time, he thought, to step down and look at the world of work from the sidelines.*

*Ted's wife, Helen, was a schoolteacher. After their kids had grown to school age, she went back to her job and put in nearly thirty years teaching sixth grade. Only a year younger than Ted, she was as ready as he was to find out if the so-called "golden years" were really as bright as advertised.*

*Ted's talents as a first-class draftsman were always in demand. Unlike Helen, who stayed put in one job, Ted had always reached out for better opportunities when they came along. He'd worked for four different companies during his career. Each time he moved to a new job he'd improved his lot and brought home more dough in his weekly paycheck.*

*"Maybe I'm a little ahead of my time," Ted once said to Helen. "All these new baby-boomers move around from job to job every few years. I guess I'm a job-hopper, too, just like they are."*

*Ted and Helen sat down one night to figure out how much money they'd get from their pensions. Ted knew that each company he'd worked for had a pension plan. Helen was covered by the teachers' union pension plan. After some spade work, Ted was able to dig up the numbers in figure 24, on the next page.*

*Helen, whose salary over the years approximately kept pace with Ted's, was in a 403(b) plan. Her money was invested in TSAs—Tax Sheltered Annuities. She was allowed by law to contribute a slightly higher amount to her 403(b) than Ted could to* *the 401(k) he'd been in, though she'd worked fewer years. Her pension came to $24,000 a year according to the trustees of the plan. That was substantially more than Ted was going to get, even though he'd earned as much and worked more years.*

Figure 24. A thought-provoking retirement scenario

| Job | Years served | Average annual salary | Kind of Plan | Pension benefit |
|-----|------|------|------|------|
| First | 8 | $12,000 | Defined Benefit | None: the plan called for 10 years of service before vesting—okay in those days |
| Second | 4 | $18,000 | Profit Sharing | Two years to become eligible; his account plus interest would buy an annuity for life of $180 a month |
| Third | 12 | $30,000 | Defined Benefit | $480 per month |
| Fourth | 13 | $40,000 | 401(k) | $620 per month estimated |
| | | | Total pension = | $15,360 a year |

*What's going on here? A case could be made that Ted's job-hopping caused him to sacrifice $8,640 a year ($24,000 minus $15,360) in pension benefits.*

*Some people get the elevator. Some people get the shaft.*

You have to check carefully the kind of plan you're in to figure out how much pension you're likely to get. That's especially true of plans you participated in before 1986. The federal government has been constantly upgrading the private pension system with laws and regulations aimed at a squarer deal for prospective retirees. Unless you're in the same boat as Ted Smythe was, with your work experience going many years back, you're not likely to lose as much as he did by moving from one job to another. Still, you may sacrifice some pension money by job-hopping.

## WHAT IS "VESTING"?

The word "vesting" has popped up from time to time. How you're vested in pension plans might affect your planning for retirement.

Vesting has to do with the principle that if you work for a specified period of time that's laid out in every benefit plan, you have a legal right to collect what's coming to you according to what the plan says. In a pension plan, when you're vested, you're guaranteed at least some payment at retirement whether or not you've continued to work for the same employer.

Keep in mind, though, that the value of your vested benefit depends on how long you've been in the plan, not how many years you've worked for the employer. You may have worked for twenty or thirty years for one or several employers. But you may have been in their pension plans for many fewer years. That's less likely to be true today, as the number of years for vesting has been shortened. Ask your benefits person how many years you've been in your current plan, if you're unsure. Go back to former employers to find out how many years you were in their plans. You'll need that data to estimate your pension benefits.

Some retirement plans require you to make contributions to them. Your contributions, plus the interest they've earned, are always 100% vested. That means that you're entitled to get back every penny you've put into the plan and the interest that money has earned while it was there. Your employer may also contribute to the plan. You have a right to the employer's contribution *only for that amount which has become vested*, plus the interest that amount has earned.

If the plan you're in covers only people employed by your company, you get vested at least as rapidly as either of these two methods:

- Cliff vesting—you're fully vested, 100%, after you've been in the company's plan for five years.
- Graded vesting—you're at least 20% vested after three years in the plan, and you'll receive another 20% vesting for each of the next four years. That means you'll be 100% vested after no more than seven years in the plan.

A booklet from your employer called a Summary Plan Description (SPD) tells you which vesting method the company uses. There's not much you can do to change it from one method to the other, except to complain. If enough employees do complain, though, maybe that'll persuade the company.

Sometimes companies do change their vesting schedule from one of the above methods to the other. If you've got three or more years of service, you're entitled to keep to the schedule you're already under, if that's what you want to do.

## FIGURING HOW MUCH TIME YOU HAVE IN THE PLAN

Usually, for vesting purposes, plans define a "year of service" as a twelve-month period during which you give at least one thousand hours of your time to working. Those hours are generally defined as:

- hours for which you're paid or entitled to be paid, including pay for vacation and sick leave;
- hours for which you're awarded back pay.

Some of an employee's service may be excluded when his or her vesting is calculated, such as:

- years of service before age 18;
- periods when an employee refuses to contribute to a plan for

which contributions are required;
- periods when the employer didn't maintain the plan;
- years when the employee had a break in service;
- certain periods preceding a break in service.

A pension plan may define a "break in service" as a year when an employee doesn't work more than five hundred hours. This may mean that the employee gets less credit for vesting purposes.

However, when employees take leaves of absence for pregnancy, birth, adoption of a child, or care for a child following birth or adoption, up to 501 hours of that leave must be counted as hours of service to the extent that those hours prevent a real "break in service."

Also, absence from a job for certain types of military service can't be counted as a "break in service."

## PENSION DOCUMENTS: WHAT YOU'RE ENTITLED TO

"Get it in writing" is always good advice. It's one thing you're entitled to when it comes to your status in your organization's retirement plan.

Federal law requires your organization to give you a Summary Plan Description within ninety days after you're in the plan. It tells you how the plan operates, when you're eligible to get your pension, how you can calculate your pension, and how to file claims (check out chapter 2).

You're normally given a Benefits Statement once each year. But you're entitled to ask for one at any time. You have to make your request in writing to the plan administrator, and you can ask for it only once a year.

The Benefits Statement shows a current estimate of the amount of money you'll get each month based on your current earnings, which may, of course, change. It also shows what you can expect to get each month from Social Security, though that amount will likely change, too.

The Benefits Statement also tells you what percentage you're vested and how many years of service you have for retirement plan purposes. Check out these numbers, and question those you don't understand or think may be wrong. You saw in chapter 2, figure 2, an illustration of one company's actual Benefit Statement.

Some organizations give their employees a form (check out figure 3) that helps them estimate how much of a pension they'll get when they retire. It's only an estimate, of course, because things like your pay and years of service that count toward retirement can change between the time you make the estimate and the date you actually retire.

You're also going to receive an annual financial report, which will give you an idea about the plan's investments. It's called a Summary Annual Report (SAR). You can ask your benefits person to give you a copy of form 5500, which the company files with the government. It's not the kind of reading that'll bring a lump to your throat like a first sighting of the Statue of Liberty. Still, it's yours if you want it. Your main purpose in asking for form 5500 is to keep tabs on your employer to make sure he's filing all reports the federal government requires.

## *YOUR GAME PLAN FOR COMFORTABLE RETIREMENT*

Just as every coach creates a game plan to win, so must you put one together to be sure you can retire comfortably. Benefits like pensions, Social Security, etc. are one part of your plan. Your financial position—current and what you're looking at for the future—is another. Take these steps:

1. Find out just how much you're worth today—your "net worth." You can't get to the retirement goal line unless you know where you're starting from.
2. Find out what your current "cash flow" is—your income less spending.
3. Analyze your spending to see what you can squeeze out of it so you can have something left over to put away for your "longest vacation" years.
4. Check out how much money you'll need for each big cate-

gory of spending *after* you retire.

5. Take a look at your after-retirement spending against your retirement income. Any difference you find will be the gap that your game plan must fill.

Take care of the first step by making copies of figure 25, Net Worth Calculator, and filling one out. You ought to recalculate your net worth every year to see what progress you're making.

*Figure 25. Net worth calculator*

| | |
|---|---|
| 1. Cash on hand $ \_\_\_\_ | 1. What you owe |
| 2. Checking account \_\_\_\_ |    a. Credit cards $ \_\_\_\_ |
| 3. Savings accounts \_\_\_\_ |    b. Bills on hand \_\_\_\_ |
| 4. Stocks, bonds, \_\_\_\_ |    c. Other \_\_\_\_ |
|    securities | 2. Loans |
| 5. Cash value of life \_\_\_\_ |    a. Balance of \_\_\_\_ |
|    insurance |      installment |
| 6. Money owed to you \_\_\_\_ |      payments |
| 7. Real estate |    b. Car loans \_\_\_\_ |
|    a. Home \_\_\_\_ |    c. Life insurance \_\_\_\_ |
|    a. Other Properties \_\_\_\_ |      loans |
| 8. Value of vested \_\_\_\_ | 3. Mortgages |
|    pensions |    a. Home \_\_\_\_ |
| 9. IRA/TSA/401(k) |    b. Other \_\_\_\_ |
|    thrift plans, etc \_\_\_\_ | 4. Taxes owed |
| 10. Annuities \_\_\_\_ |    a. Federal \_\_\_\_ |
| 11. Business interests \_\_\_\_ |    b. State \_\_\_\_ |
| 12. Other things owned |    c. Local \_\_\_\_ |
|    a. Furnishings \_\_\_\_ |    d. Property \_\_\_\_ |
|    b. Hobby/sports \_\_\_\_ |    e. Other \_\_\_\_ |
|    c. Art/antiques \_\_\_\_ | 5. Other money |
|    d. Furs/jewelry \_\_\_\_ |    owed (specify) \_\_\_\_ |
|    e. Boats/RVs \_\_\_\_ | |
|    f. Other \_\_\_\_ | |

**Total value of things**
  **owned (assets)  $ \_\_\_\_**

**Total value of what you**
  **owe (liabilities)$ \_\_\_\_**

**Total assets minus total liabilities equals NET WORTH $ \_\_\_\_**

*Figure 26. Cash flow calculator*

## ANNUAL CURRENT EXPENSES

**Essentials**

| | |
|---|---|
| Housing—rent, repairs, maintenance, etc. | $ _____ |
| Gas/electric, phone | _____ |
| Food—at home | _____ |
| Real estate/personal property taxes | _____ |
| Automobile—gasoline, maintenance, etc. | _____ |
| Commuting to work | _____ |
| Clothing | _____ |
| Medical/Dental not covered by insurance | _____ |
| Insurance | |
|    Life | _____ |
|    Health and medical | _____ |
|    Car/property/casualty | _____ |
| Other | _____ |
| | |
| **Total essential expenses** | $ _____ |

**Elective expenses**

| | |
|---|---|
| Vacations, travel | $ _____ |
| Entertainment—including eating out | _____ |
| Charitable contributions/gifts | _____ |
| Furnishings | _____ |
| Savings | _____ |
| Hobbies/sports/leisure | _____ |
| Other | _____ |
| | |
| **Total elective expenses** | $ _____ |

For step two in your game plan, make copies of figure 26, Cash Flow Calculator, and fill one out. If you're not keeping a budget, take a look at your checkbook stubs, your last income tax return, any credit card receipts on hand, etc., to help in getting numbers on expenses. To get an accurate fix you may have to keep a written record of spending for a full month.

Step three: Analyze your spending. No one's asking you to cut everything to the bone. But most people find wasted spending—

too many subscriptions to magazines they don't read any more; too-small insurance deductibles on cars, furnishings, and homes; too many meals at too-expensive restaurants; and that kind of thing.

Step four is a tough one. How can you estimate what you'll need for money when the "longest vacation" is many years away? Take a look at the following chart.

### AVERAGE ANNUAL SPENDING FOR PEOPLE OVER 65

| Category | % of total expenditures |
|---|---|
| Housing | 33% |
| Transportation | 16 |
| Food | 15 |
| Health care | 11 |
| Entertainment | 4 |
| Charitable contributions | 6 |
| Clothing | 5 |
| Insurance and pension | 4 |
| Other | 6 |

Source: U.S. Department of Labor, Bureau of Labor Statistics, Consumer Expenditures Survey.

Now take your own current expenses and squeeze them into the same categories given on the chart. Calculate your percentages in each category.

For the fifth step in your game plan, compare the percentages between your current spending and the Department of Labor averages. From that comparison you'll get an idea of how you'll have to adjust spending when you're no longer working. Apply the percentages to your estimated retirement income, and you'll have a rough but ready "retirement budget"—how much you'll have on hand to spend in each category. The comparison will also highlight the gap between expected income and retirement expenses that you must fill to be comfortable.

## PLUGGING THE INCOME GAP

Plugging income gaps is what this book is all about. To be sure, you'll have to do some personal saving that'll provide income after you retire.

More important, though, is to boost your benefits to pay off bigger and better than they currently do. That means making smarter choices when investing your 401(k) so that your account grows bigger to provide more retirement income.

But it also means becoming a "benefits activist." You want to get your management to increase matching contributions to your account. To add new benefits like profit sharing to the mix, and to increase the share of profits that go into the plan. Jacking up retirement income calls for you to persuade management to sock away a bigger percentage of your income into your account if you're in a money purchase pension plan, to start an ESOP, to offer an employee stock purchase plan and other income-producing benefits.

You should also tackle the subject of better health and medical coverage, with less sharing of premiums and lower deductibles. That'll put more money in your pocket now to funnel into personal savings, IRAs, and maybe annuities that'll pay you back in after-retirement income. It's not easy, and there are pitfalls aplenty. Here are just a few:

## BENEFITS CHECKOFF: SIX COMMON MISTAKES IN RETIREMENT PLANNING

✔ Not taking inflation into account. You may estimate your food expenses for your retirement years as being close to what they are today. But there's almost a guarantee they'll be at least twice as high ten years from now.

✔ Not starting to plan soon enough. It's an easy thing to put off. It's never too soon to plan, nor is it ever too late.

✔ Overestimating how much you'll get out of each pension benefit plan you've been in.

✔ Underestimating your health and medical costs after you retire. Even the best insurance coverage has some gaps, and that assumes you'll be covered without picking up the insurance costs after you retire.

✔ Spending too much money trying to plug up the health/medical insurance gaps, and getting too much duplicate coverage that won't pay off.

✔ Not planning for enough money to cover hobbies, sports, travel, and entertainment expenses after you retire. Having fun is one of the best parts of the "longest vacation."

## THE SOCIAL SECURITY INTEGRATION WRINKLE

Read your SPD carefully, for your plan may include a wrinkle that'll take some of your retirement benefits away from you. It's called "integration with Social Security."

Suppose your company's plan would provide you with a monthly payment on retirement of $1,200 a month. At the same time you'd be eligible for $600 a month from Social Security. An "integrated" plan calls for an offset. The administrators will subtract some percentage of the Social Security amount from the benefit you'd otherwise get from your employer's plan. Say the offset is 50%. You'd lose 50% of the Social Security amount, or $300, from your monthly payment from the plan. Instead of getting $1,200 from the plan, you'd get $900.

There was a time when every time the Social Security payment went up, the plan payment would go down. It's true that the pensioner would get a net increase, but not as great a one as he or she would have received if the plan had not been integrated.

### ACTION IDEA

Fortunately the feds have clamped down on the practice of integrating Social Security with private pension plans. If your plan is still integrated, check with the Social Security Administration to find out what your rights are now. Get a bulletin or other publication from SSA. Make sure your company is following the rules when it sends you (or you ask for) the annual "Benefits Statement" estimating your retirement benefit.

## BENEFITS CHECKOFF: OPTIONS FOR DRAWING
## YOUR PENSION MONEY

Most pension plans give you several options to choose from when you want to start drawing money from the plan at normal retirement age. The following ones are common to most plans:

✔ **Life only:** You get checks for the rest of your life. You usually can choose to get them monthly, quarterly, semiannually, or annually. This may be your best choice if you don't need to provide for a spouse or other dependent, and if you need a regular flow of cash for living expenses.

✔ **Life with term certain:** You get payments for your life, with checks to continue to your beneficiary if you die before the number of years you pick, usually five, ten, fifteen, or twenty. This is a choice for people who are concerned about their life expectancy; the disadvantage is that the payments may end during the life of the beneficiary.

✔ **Joint and survivor life option:** You get payments for your life, and payments of the same or lesser amount will continue to your spouse, or another person, for their life. When there's a big difference in age between the pensioner and beneficiary, payments may be substantially reduced; this option does provide income for the beneficiary who may not have other income sources.

✔ **Lump-sum payment:** You get all the money in your account in one big chunk. In a defined benefit pension plan, the amount will be calculated by an actuary to be the present value of monthly payments that would have been made to you if you'd chosen the life-only option. This option poses severe income tax questions (call in the tax experts). It also calls for you to plan carefully how to invest the lump sum as well as to keep watch over the investments. Some plans don't allow lump-sum payments. Those that do normally require you to pick this option at least a year before you retire or to pass a physical exam.

Keep in mind that your pension payments are taxable income. You may be able to defer paying taxes on a lump-sum payout by rolling it over into an IRA. But you must start drawing out your pension and paying taxes on the payout after you reach age 70½, even if you're still working.

*Ryan Baerga learned a hard lesson the easy way. Many employees find out too late that timing is everything when it comes to planning for their "longest vacation." Make sure you don't get dumped in that boat. Start putting the strategies from this chapter into action today.*

# 13

▼

# FAMILY BENEFITS

## Insuring the Best Deal for You and Your Dependents

### THE CASE OF THE BABY BROUHAHA

Jonas Kelston had never felt uncomfortable at work—until now, that is. Sure, he was just about the only male face for as far as the eye could see in the public relations department of his company. And sure, he took a fair amount of riding from his chums when the subject of being surrounded by women all day came up.

But he knew his job and did it well enough to become top dog in his department. And his co-workers all treated him professionally, so he never had a complaint—until now.

"I still don't understand it," he argued with the company VP, who happened to be female. "Just about everyone else here has the opportunity to take time off for an important event like the birth of a child. But when I ask for leave, I get stonewalled. How come?"

Eve Ferrante, Kelston's boss, was just as uncomfortable. "You know our former leave policy was for maternity only," she explained stiffly. "With the new Family and Medical Leave Act, we're reevaluating. But with our company size and your key status, we just can't automatically rubber-stamp your request. Yet."

Ms. Ferrante had better get her stamp warmed up. That Family and Medical Leave Act (FMLA) is on the books and raring to be implemented, backed by the full force of the federal government. Here are some of its main provisions:

- A female or male (are you listening, Jonas Kelston?) employee may take up to twelve weeks of unpaid leave in any twelve-month period for the birth of a child or an adoption; for the care of a child, spouse, or parent with a serious health condition; or for a health condition that limits the employee's own job performance.
- If you take that leave, you must be restored to your old job or an equivalent position upon your return. That doesn't mean just similar. It has to be the same in terms of pay, responsibilities, and benefits.
- While you're on leave, your employer is responsible for providing you the same health care benefits as if you were still at work. But if you don't come back, your employer can hit you up for the health care premiums it paid while you were on leave.
- Unless it's an emergency situation, you must give thirty days' notice of your intent to utilize family leave.
- While you're on leave, you can't collect unemployment or other government compensation.

There are a few other twists you should be aware of, especially those regarding eligibility, which were at the crux of Jonas Kelston's delay.

For one, the Act doesn't cover companies with fewer than fifty employees, and it allows companies to deny restoration rights to salaried employees within the highest 10% of its work force if it can prove that letting the worker take the leave would create substantial and grievous injury to its business.

For another, a company can ask for second and third medical opinions, and it can force you to use up other paid leaves as part of your twelve weeks before the unpaid leave kicks in.

Note: You don't have to take all twelve weeks consecutively, if you can work out an intermittent-leave plan with your employer. But if you do, you may be asked to transfer temporarily to an equivalent position that offers more flexibility in making the intermittent schedule work successfully.

## FAMILY MOVES INTO THE WORKPLACE

The quick passage of the FMLA reflects the growing importance attached to family matters at work, especially in the benefits area. But employers aren't suddenly family friendly in their benefits offerings out of the goodness of their hearts. It's more like out of the goodness of their pocketbooks.

Many of them, at long last, are beginning to realize that employees without family worries get more work done, with fewer hassles, and grow to be more loyal. They miss fewer days of work, concentrate more on their jobs, and come back to work faster from illnesses and other absences. Employers also get a break from less turnover, easier recruiting, and enhanced ability to retain good employees.

What's in this new look for you? If you're like Jonas Kelston and most other employees today, you're confronted with more and more family responsibilities that place demands on your physical, mental, and free-time resources. Companies are becoming increasingly cognizant of, and sensitive to, that fact of employment life.

## BENEFITS CHECKOFF: IMPORTANT FAMILY PERKS:

- ✔ child-care centers
- ✔ sick-child care programs
- ✔ various types of leave including parental, maternity, adoptive, bereavement, emergency, eldercare, sick, disability
- ✔ various time arrangements, like flextime, part-time, work at home, job sharing
- ✔ discounts with local providers of family assistance
- ✔ Employee Assistance Programs (EAPs)
- ✔ education
- ✔ eldercare

✔ housing and relocation assistance
✔ sabbaticals

## REDEFINING THE AMERICAN FAMILY

When it comes to benefits, expanding definitions of both family and dependents is now the name of the game. Unmarried couples, both same and opposite sex, are getting benefits opportunities just like those extended to traditional married couples. Prime example of that change: The 1990 census allowed respondents, for the first time, to identify themselves as domestic partners, meaning persons of the opposite sex sharing living quarters.

One benefits consulting company defines potential domestic partners this way:

1. Relationship resembling a family or household with close cooperation between the parties and each having specified relationships.
2. A committed nonplatonic, family-type relationship of two unrelated partners.
3. Two unrelated individuals who share the necessities of life, live together, and have an emotional and financial commitment to each other.
4. Two individuals who have an intimate and committed relationship and are jointly responsible for basic living expenses.
5. Cohabitating partners, significant others, spousal equivalents, nontraditional dependents, live-in companions.

**Benefits alert:** Some benefit areas still cling to traditional definitions of family. Example: When it comes to the extended health care coverage required by the Consolidated Omnibus Budget Reconciliation Act (COBRA), the law only covers qualifying beneficiaries who are spouses or dependents. Example: In a Flexible Spending Account (FSA) program, spouses may have premiums paid with pretax dollars. But "domestic partners" aren't recognized by the IRS, so their FSA money is taxable.▼

Some employers require affidavits of spousal equivalence to prove commitment of same-sex partners when it comes to benefits eligibility. To verify that two people of the same sex are each other's sole spousal equivalent, they want proof that (a) the individuals are not related by blood; (b) they are living together; and (c) they are jointly responsible for each other's general welfare and financial obligations.

The New York State Court of Appeals spelled out its expanded definition of "couples" when it ruled in a legal case involving maintenance of rent-controlled apartments. In that decision, homosexual and unmarried heterosexual couples passed legal muster if:

1. their relationship was exclusive and long-term;
2. they had a deep level of emotional and financial commitment to each other;
3. they exhibited public and private conduct typical of life partners.

## IT'S TRADITION: STATE FAMILY LEAVE LAWS

About a dozen states preceded the federal Family and Medical Leave Act with legislation of their own, sometimes more generous than the federal law. States like California have taken the lead. Its Family Rights Leave Act of 1991 demands employers offer up to four months of unpaid leave with guaranteed reinstatement for birth or adoption of a child or to care for a seriously ill child. It also contains other family clauses in its laws.

**Example:** California employees get up to four hours per child per school year to attend school conferences. The employee must give reasonable notice and use up other time off (vacation, comp time) first.

Laws usually define the family leave benefit as time off for the specific purpose of taking care of the needs of family members. That includes newborn or adopted children, family members suffering from a serious illness, and those who require constant or intermittent care.

Generally family leave is unpaid and comes with the guarantee that the same or similar job will be available upon return from it. New leave laws and their interpretation come and go. Consider:

- A state appeals court ruled Wisconsin's Family and Medical Leave Act allows employees to substitute any type of paid leave for part of unpaid family or medical leave.
- Dade County, Florida, guarantees unpaid sick or parental leave to all employees of private companies or municipalities with fifty or more workers.

---

**Benefits alert:** If you're a male and your company grants personal time off for child rearing to its female employees, it must offer you the same option. (Jonas Kelston, are you listening?) Employers who do offer leaves for personal reasons, including family responsibilities, must do so in a nondiscriminatory way according to civil rights laws that impact benefits.▼

---

Details of state laws vary and change (check out figure 27), but comprehensive leave policies generally apply to both sexes and are available for a wide range of family emergencies. Some specific benefits, such as maternity leave, are available only to women and usually cover childbirth and recovery.

Sometimes traditional leave options may bump up against modern leave opportunities—in court. One company offered a generous paid sick leave package of seventeen days per year. One stipulation: That paid leave couldn't be tied to another type, like maternity, unless the individual was disabled.

A female employee of that company wanted to spend more time with her new child. She claimed the Pregnancy Discrimination Act required pregnancy benefits to be treated like disability benefits, thus allowing her to tack the paid sick leave on to her maternity sick leave. A court ruled against her. The choice to stay home after a pregnancy is not a medical one, and thus not a disability, the court said. (*Maganuco v. Leyden Comm. H.S. Dist.*, CA 6, No. 90-2277, 1991)

*Figure 27. Sampling of state leave law*

## A Sampling of State Leave Laws

### CALIFORNIA

Eligibility: All women.

Leave period: Up to four months. If necessary, must transfer to less strenuous job.

Allowable reasons: Pregnancy, childbirth, related medical conditions.

Reinstatement: Same or comparable job.

### CONNECTICUT

Eligibility: All employees who have worked at least twelve months or one thousand hours in the previous year.

Leave period: Up to sixteen weeks in any two years.

Allowable reasons: Family leave for birth, adoption, or serious illness of any family member.

Reinstatement: Original or comparable position; less demanding job if necessary.

### ILLINOIS

Eligibility: All women.

Leave period: No more restrictive than other forms of disability leave.

Allowable reasons: Pregnancy, childbirth, and related medical conditions.

Reinstatement: None required.

### IOWA

Eligibility: All women.

Leave period: Up to eight weeks where other leave is not available or is insufficient.

Allowable reasons: Pregnancy, childbirth, and related medical conditions.

Reinstatement: Must match reinstatement policies with other forms of disability.

### MAINE

Eligibility: All employees with at least twelve consecutive months with the same employer.

Leave period: Up to eight consecutive weeks in any two years.

Allowable reasons: Family leave; childbirth; adoption; serious illness of employee, child, parent, or spouse.

Reinstatement: Same or comparable position.

**NEW JERSEY**

Eligibility: All persons employed for at least twelve months and working at least one thousand hours per year.

Leave period: twelve weeks in any two-year period.

Allowable reasons: Family leave for birth, adoption, or serious illness of a family member.

Reinstatement: Former or comparable position, unless intervening conditions such as a layoff mean the employee would have lost that position.

**OREGON**

Eligibility: All employees except seasonal and temporary workers.

Leave period: Up to twelve weeks.

Allowable reasons: Parental leave for birth or for adoption of a child aged five or younger.

Reinstatement: Former or comparable position without loss of any accrued benefits. If changed conditions make this impossible, reinstatement to any other suitable position.

---

## ACTION IDEA

While not a direct aspect of family leave, sabbaticals are often used for family purposes. They may be dress rehearsals for retirement, or they may be for recharging personal batteries in the face of stress or burnout conditions.

Sabbaticals are getting more popular in high-tech, fast-paced employment scenes. Try running them up the flagpole with your boss as a potential benefit.

---

**Benefits alert:** Speaking of time off, if you're looking for extra time for religious observances, you'll probably have to settle for unpaid leave. One employee wanted to combine his three policy-mandated religious days with three policy-mandated personal days. Unluckily for him, the policy also said that the two couldn't be combined; personal couldn't be used for religious. That policy was upheld. (*Philbrook v. Ansonia Bd. of Ed.*, CA 2, 54 FEP Cases 1614, 1986) ▼

## DEPENDENT CARE ACCOUNTS

One of the main family financial strategies that today's employers and employees are hooking up on are dependent care accounts, also known as reimbursement accounts, flexible spending accounts, salary reduction plans, or set-aside programs.

As you read in chapter 3, with a dependent care account you allocate a certain amount of money (up to a maximum of $5,000) to be used by you to take care of expenses you run up in caring for dependents both young and old.

**How it works:** Before the start of your company's fiscal or calendar year, you estimate your dependent care expenses for the next twelve months. Payroll deducts that amount in equal installments from your paycheck, and it escapes the clutches of IRS reporting. When you incur expenses, you report the amount to your employer and are reimbursed.

Setting aside the full $5,000 max for dependent care can save a family in the 28% tax bracket around $2,000 come April 15. To be eligible, you and your spouse must both work, or you must be a single working parent. If your spouse earns less than $5,000, whatever that annual pay is becomes the max you can put into the account.

Two more caveats: If your company offers the reimbursement account and you earn less than $5,000, only half of your earnings can go into the dependent care account. And if the dependent care is done in your home, you must pay Social Security taxes.

Among the expenses you can claim:

- child's day care
- preschool tuition
- nanny or babysitting
- home nurse care for elderly parents who spend at least eight hours per day in your home
- tuition for summer camp if it's not overnight.

More "can't" caveats: Children must be under the age of thirteen. You can't alter the amount you designate for the account after you set it, unless a so-called life event or change in job status occurs. You can't use a dependent care reimbursement account if you claim a dependent care tax credit when you file your income tax. But if your annual income is at least $25,000, you're almost sure to save more with a reimbursement account than with a tax credit.

## FAMILIES IN COURT

Familial obligations and demands have sparked litigation in which benefits were the bottom-line reward. (The FMLA is sure to add to that caseload.)

**Example:** In a case that could have far-reaching impact, a woman quit her job to relocate with her male domestic partner (not husband) of thirteen years. A court decided she was entitled to receive unemployment benefits. Why was she eligible for those benefits? Because she demonstrated that the reasons for leaving were necessary and made separation from her job involuntary. (*Reep v. Comm. of Dept. of Employment & Training*, MA Sup. Jud. Ct., No. HS-5798, 1992)

As is often the case, what the law gives, it also takes away. A Virginia court was asked to rule on the question of "sexual equity" in unemployment benefits. A female worker quit her job because her spouse was transferred. Denied unemployment benefits, she claimed the law discriminated against women, since they were the most likely to be forced to voluntarily quit jobs in a transfer situation.

Practically speaking, you're right, ruled the court. But legally speaking, the language of the law, denying benefits to anyone who voluntarily quits, is gender neutral. (*Austin v. Berryman*, CA 4, No. 91-1750, 1992)

**Case:** A woman racked up a record of poor attendance that finally drove her employer to dismiss her. She applied for unemployment, and the company protested. Her claim: My child was sick, and I couldn't afford any available child care options.

The court heard the evidence and came to the conclusion that the employee had made a determined effort to find care, that she was concerned about her job, and that her absenteeism did not amount to job-related misconduct. Also, she wasn't guilty of willful disregard of her employer's interests. She won. (*McCourtney v. Imprimis Tech. Inc.*, MN Ct. App., No. C6-90-2000, 1991)

## FAMILY BENEFITS AND SEXUAL PREFERENCE

Vermont has passed a gay rights bill that affects employment. Wisconsin, Connecticut, Hawaii, and New Jersey already have laws protecting the rights of their residents regardless of sexual orientation.

A new ingredient for benefits lawsuits is sexual preference discrimination, outlawed in employment conditions by certain states and localities.

**Example:** In Minneapolis, three librarians claimed the city discriminated against them because it refused to provide health insurance for their lesbian partners. The workers had applied for dependent health care coverage for their long-term partners and were denied each time they applied. They were told they didn't qualify because their partners were not spouses. The upshot: a commission ruling that they had been illegally denied benefits, contrary to the city's antidiscrimination statute, on the basis of "affectional preference." (*Anglin v. Minneapolis*, MN Comm. on Civil Rights, No. 88180-EM-12, 1992)

## BENEFITS CHECKOFF: FAMILY BENEFITS IN ACTION

While many companies have jumped on the family benefits bandwagon, many are still standing on the sidelines. After you read about some of the companies that are taking the lead, try taking the lead yourself by suggesting to your benefits people that they consider a program or two from among these ideas. It can't hurt.

✔ One large hotel chain places heavy emphasis on family benefits. It offers the maximum $5,000 in its dependent care plan, on-site day care centers for children of employees, joint ventures with extended child care providers, and a coaching program for teaching mothers how to protect the health of their unborn babies, with cash rewards for women who complete the program.

✔ A Massachusetts company started a corporate intergenerational center. Both children and the elderly receive care there. And each group is encouraged to interact with the other, bringing added personal and family benefits. They go on trips and expeditions together, share family experiences like cooking and gardening, and spend time together telling stories and reading.

This company has been on the family benefits bandwagon for more than two decades, with day care programs leading the way. It has even expanded its efforts to include community children and elderly, and arranged for a private, nonprofit organization to run its workplace facility.

✔ One major computer company offers midday flextime options as well as a three-year leave of absence and national child care and eldercare referral services.

✔ An insurance firm restructured to allow for flexible work arrangements and was one of the first to establish a work/family coordinator.

✔ A manufacturer provides all of its employees with a "Career and Family Book & Kit," a thorough review of the company's work/family policies and a list of external providers.

---

**Benefits alert:** Time is an increasingly important commodity when it comes to employees and their families. So some companies are trying "on-site strategies" to help employees spend more time at home. These include setting up workplace sites for grocery shopping, dry cleaning, banking, and video rental. Another example: Take-out service from a company cafeteria.

One company came up with what it called an Employee Convenience Center after surveying its employees about what benefits they
wanted most. Time was a crucial commodity. The result: a structure resembling a mobile home in the company parking lot. Workers can rent
videotapes, drop off film and dry cleaning, and shop for groceries
through order forms from the local supermarket.▼

To see what a leading-edge, family-friendly firm offers, check
out figure 28.

## GOT PERSONAL PROBLEMS? HELP IS HERE

Many companies' Employee Assistance Programs (EAPs) deal
with family matters. If your company offers an EAP as a benefit, check it out thoroughly. Some employees cling to the
stereotyped and outdated notion that EAPs are meant to deal
strictly with drug and alcohol problems.

Not so. EAPs today can cover a wide range of personal concerns including emotional, psychological, family, and financial
matters. Among the common EAP offerings for treatment and
counseling are:

- alcohol and drug abuse;
- emotional problems and stress;
- pre-retirement planning;
- termination;
- marital problems;
- career development;
- monetary problems;
- legal problems;
- compulsive gambling;
- eating disorders;
- spouse abuse.

You're usually guaranteed confidentiality and no harassment
or loss of employment opportunity if you are considering an
EAP for a personal problem. Other family members can receive help too, so it's well worth the effort to investigate.

*Figure 28. A leading-edge family benefits company*

## JUST DESSERTS: ICE CREAM MAKER OFFERS LIP-SMACKING BENEFITS

Vermont-based Ben & Jerry's Homemade Inc. has received a lot of publicity for its social conscience when it comes to corporate decisions. That philosophy also extends into the benefits area at Ben & Jerry's, making its program an enviable one.

For example, the company has offered "domestic partner insurance" for several years, rejecting unmarried, heterosexual, or homosexual considerations.

When a benefits issue arises, employees' opinions are always a key ingredient. The company has a group that serves as a communications vehicle, absorbing workers' suggestions and passing them on to management. Focus groups were used to elicit worker input when the 401(k) plan was expanded, for instance.

Employees enjoy a profit sharing program based on length of service and a spot bonus program, and can even volunteer for work in the community and get paid by the company.

While you may never be offered the range of benefits that Ben & Jerry's provides its employees, you may get some ideas for changes at your firm from this **Benefits Checkoff:**

- ✔ 401(k) plan;
- ✔ profit sharing plan;
- ✔ unmarried partner benefits;
- ✔ health and dental insurance for hourly and salaried workers (health coverage includes mammograms and well-baby care);
- ✔ financial counseling;
- ✔ life insurance (two times salary);
- ✔ sabbatical leave;
- ✔ four weeks off with full pay to an employee who adopts a child, if he or she is the primary care-giver; two weeks off with pay if he or she is the secondary care-giver;
- ✔ six weeks' full pay after delivery to women who give birth, plus 60% of salary for as long as six months;
- ✔ twelve-week paternity leave for new fathers, with the first two weeks paid in full and the remaining ten unpaid;
- ✔ $1,500 company contribution toward adoption costs;
- ✔ children's center;

✔ Employee Assistance Program;

✔ cholesterol and blood pressure screening on-site;

✔ smoking cessation classes.

---

## *BENEFITS CHECKOFF: SEVEN CRUCIAL QUESTIONS TO ASK ABOUT EAPS*

Offering access to an EAP is almost required for any company that has to comply with the federal Drug-Free Workplace Act. Many EAPs have structured their preventive and educational aspects to meet the demands of that act.

As with all benefits, study your EAP options and opportunities carefully. Ask these questions:

✔ Are both full- and part-time employees covered?

✔ Are there programs for relatives of employees, or are they strictly for immediate family?

✔ What are the referral procedures?

✔ Can you be referred by yourself or by your supervisor?

✔ Does the EAP use in-house resources or outside organizations?

✔ Are job security and future opportunities protected in writing?

✔ Does the program distinguish between personal and job-related problems? Which are covered?

## *ELDERCARE*

The graying of America has focused new concern on eldercare. One survey reported that as many as one in every four workers spends from six to thirteen hours a week taking care of responsibilities for an older person. Another report claimed that one-third of all employees missed work as a result of eldercare responsibilities.

**ACTION IDEA**

The American Association of Retired Persons (AARP) is very active in the area of eldercare. Recommend to your employer that it check out the AARP's "Caregivers in the Workplace Kit." Or you can take it one step further and organize a support group in your company that deals with issues surrounding eldercare.

The main options you can look for in this area to give you time to take on responsibilities for caring for your elderly parents or relatives include:

- part-time work;
- flextime;
- extended leave;
- job sharing;
- work at home.

One reason for increased focus on eldercare: It is just as likely to affect a company president as an entry-level clerk, a CEO as a maintenance person.

Most companies don't provide direct help. They'll make contributions to community agencies that provide assistance to the elderly, allow extended leaves for employees, provide options in part-time work and flextime, or even sponsor counseling programs.

Among the companies that had programs offering referral services were IBM and AT&T. Personalized referral services were available to both IBM retirees and its employees with elderly relatives, for example. You may not work for an IBM-sized company. But if you can convince the powers that be to investigate this avenue of employee benefits, you can also give them some direction. Health Resources Publishing puts out the *National Directory of Adult Day Care Centers* from its Wall Township, New Jersey, location.

**Benefits alert:** Flexible Spending Accounts are an increasingly popular way to tap company benefits for eldercare. But in order for you to utilize one, the "patient" in question must live with you and be a dependent, and you must need the assistance purchased with FSA dollars in order to stay employed. ▼

---

You can tell that eldercare has come of age when it gets dragged into employee lawsuits. Case in point: A secretary asked for a more flexible schedule to take care of her ailing father. Her request was denied, and she was terminated. At that point she pulled out a local statute that barred bias on the basis of "family responsibilities." One court disagreed with her, but another said she could take her suit to the next level. (*Sampson v. D.C. Office of Human Rights*, D.C. Ct. App., No. 90-49, 1991)

## *EDUCATIONAL BENEFITS*

Many companies have programs that offer scholarship money for children of employees and tuition money for employees who pursue higher education or extra training in job-related skills. New twist: An employer may offer "scholarships" for employees who get laid off and then pursue a teaching certificate. The company might even offer financial help to schools that hire such employees.

## *TESTING FOR FAMILY FRIENDLINESS*

To see how "family friendly" your company's benefits package is, check off items on the checklist in figure 29. If you get more than half of the benefits on the list, you're in good shape. Under one-third, seek some more. Over two-thirds, send a thank-you note to the board of directors.

*Figure 29. Judging the family atmosphere at your company*

---

### HOW FAMILY-FRIENDLY IS YOUR FIRM?

| | |
|---|---|
| _____ | Work/family task force or representative |
| _____ | Written company commitment to family issues |
| _____ | Support for community family resources |

| | |
|---|---|
| _____ | Seminars or workshops on work/family issues |
| _____ | Employee Assistance Program |
| _____ | Housing/relocation assistance |
| _____ | Education/tuition programs (two checks if you can get money for both yourself and dependents) |
| _____ | Adoption assistance |
| _____ | Legal assistance (in areas like wills and house buying) |
| _____ | Flexible Spending Accounts for dependent care |
| _____ | In-house child care or external options |
| _____ | Sick child programs |
| _____ | Summer camp, before- or after-school programs |
| _____ | Family time at work (visiting day, company picnic) |
| _____ | Eldercare programs, including external support |
| _____ | Parental, maternity, or paternity leave |
| _____ | Personal leave |
| _____ | Sabbaticals |
| _____ | Adoption or family emergency leave |
| _____ | Corporate discounts for external family service providers |
| _____ | Flextime, job sharing, or compressed work week |
| _____ | Work at home or part-time work |

*Jonas Kelston may not be able to fill out this figure with a lot of checkmarks. But more and more companies are making family-oriented benefits a priority. Check to make sure your employer is one of them.*

# 14
▼

# LEGAL BENEFITS RIGHTS

*Getting the Lowdown on ERISA and COBRA*

## THE CASE OF THE OUTSPOKEN SPOKESPERSON

D*on't worry," Leesa Edalman heard over and over. "Our pension plan will take good care of you once you decide to retire. And our health coverage, as you know, is one of the best in the business. So relax."*

*Leesa couldn't relax. She had read too many headlines about employees being smacked with huge uncovered medical expenses . . . about pensioners having to scrape by on reduced post-retirement paychecks . . . about seemingly secure workers suddenly losing their jobs before the plum part of their pension kicked in.*

*So instead of relaxing, Leesa took the benefits bull by the horns and demanded her rights. She asked for an update of the company's Summary Plan Description. She investigated the plan date of the pension plan she qualified for. She checked the language of the medical options offered for both pre- and post-retirement.*

*In fact, she checked and demanded and investigated so much that she became the unofficial spokesperson for her department, including her supervisors and managers. The company began to be more forthcoming in its pronouncements on benefits, and the employees began to feed back more input to top brass.*

*Small glitches in passing out documents were cleared up. New benefits programs favorable for both management and employee sides were started up. And no legal problems in the employee benefits area reared their heads in the entire year.*

Couldn't happen in real life, you say? Too Pollyanna-ish, you claim? Doesn't reflect the actual workplace relationship between management and employees?

Don't be so sure. In fact, the more you know about your legal rights in employee benefits, the less likely it is you'll have to exercise them. Plus, the more your employer knows that you know, the more likely it will steer a straight and narrow legal path.

So don't be daunted by the plethora of federal law acronyms or the case citations attached to court decisions you'll find in these two legal chapters. Get cozy with your legal rights. You never know when they'll come in handy. Start with the two major federal laws that affect benefits—the Employee Retirement Income Security Act (ERISA) and the Consolidated Omnibus Budget Reconciliation Act (COBRA).

## THE BIG DADDY OF BENEFITS ACRONYMS: ERISA

The most important single piece of legislation dealing with employee benefits goes by the moniker of ERISA, the Employee Retirement Income Security Act. As suggested by the name, it focuses mostly on pension plans for private companies. But in reality it holds sway over two types of employee benefits packages.

Briefly, one is pension plans that provide retirement income or deferral of income by employees. ERISA imposes rules regarding eligibility, vesting, employee rights, and employer obligations.

ERISA also covers employee welfare benefit plans, which provide benefits to you in the event of sickness, hospitalization, surgery, accident, death, disability, or unemployment. For those types of benefits, ERISA doesn't set standards.

The number-one requirement of ERISA is dissemination of facts. Your company's "plan administrators," who should be named in your benefits booklet, must give you all the facts about your plans. Those facts must be written in a language you can understand, they must be accurate and comprehensive, and they must advise you of all your rights and entitlements. You saw many of the documents you must be given back in chapter 2.

## ERASING ERISA CONFUSION

You know the old saying about what happens when you ASS-U-ME. So don't assume anything about ERISA. There's a lot of confusion surrounding it.

**Assumption No. 1:** Employers are required by ERISA to provide employee benefits. Not so. Employers are not legally required to provide benefits by ERISA. However, once they do provide certain benefits, then ERISA insists that they be fair, nondiscriminatory, and consistent.

**Assumption No. 2:** ERISA only regulates pension plans. Not so. ERISA actually covers two types of benefits, as you just read. In technical terms, they are "employee pension benefits plans" and "employee welfare benefits plans." The first type includes the traditional plans involving your retirement income, such as defined benefit plans or defined contribution plans like salary reduction 401(k) plans, profit sharing plans, and employee stock ownership plans.

The second type—"employee welfare benefits plans"—includes a surprisingly broad range of benefits such as medical, hospital, surgical, disability, death, accident, severance pay, prepaid legal services, day care centers, and scholarship funds.

**Benefits alert:** Some forms of compensation provided by employers are not ERISA-covered, such as overtime pay, shift premiums, holiday premiums, weekend premiums, vacation pay, paid military leave, and paid leave for jury duty.▼

**Assumption No. 3:** ERISA mandates the type of welfare benefits that have to be provided to employees. Not so. ERISA does not specify the type of welfare benefits. Employers are free to determine the type and amount of welfare benefits that they'll provide to you. (**Note:** Congressional legislation could be tossed into the hopper at any time to restrict that discretion and mandate certain benefits. That's what minimum health insurance benefits for employees are all about.)

To some extent state laws have already filled this gap and ordered certain benefits for employees. Some states, for example, have laws that call for employers to provide coverage for specific medical conditions or to pay for services from specified health care providers, such as psychiatrists. If you think you could be affected, by all means check out requirements with the state commissioner. Then check in with your company benefits person if there's a discrepancy.

**Assumption No. 4:** An organization can "do what it wants" as long as it does not have a written employee benefits plan. Not so. ERISA requires employers to interpret and apply a benefits plan or policy, written or unwritten, in a consistent and uniform manner according to the terms of the plan or policy. Employers cannot escape the requirements of ERISA by having unwritten and informal benefits practices.

Result: They can't make exceptions for certain employees and provide them with less—or more—benefits than allowed for in the plan or policy. They also can't provide different benefits to a particular employee because of his/her circumstances, or make oral commitments about benefits that differ from the information provided in writing, or inadvertently create a benefit through a particular practice.

**Note:** If you find out that some people in your organization are getting better benefits than others, do some snooping to find out why. It could be legal; for example, there could be differences between a union member and a supervisor. If you find differences, see if you can get on the gravy train.

---

**Benefits alert:** What your employer says can be as important as what it does. Case in point: An automobile body-shop owner told his

employees that his retirement bonus compared favorably with retirement benefits at a nearby competitor. That bonus: $1,000 for every
year worked based on five years of employment and continuous service. A twenty-five-year vet laid claim to the bonus. No soap, replied
the owner. You broke the rules of no moonlighting, and anyway you've
got nothing in writing to make it an ERISA-regulated benefit.

   Wrong, said the judge. Federal law doesn't say you have to have a
pension plan. But if you do promise one, you'd better come through.
(*Moeller v. Bertrang*, D.C. SD, No. 90-1045, 1992) ▼

---

**Assumption No. 5:** A company does not have to honor
promises and commitments made by managers, supervisors, or
personnel staffers. Not so. You may be able to use any communications about benefits to obligate the company to provide you
with those benefits. Plus, if your manager tells you one thing,
and it turns out to be inaccurate or inconsistent with the terms of
the written benefits documents, you still may be able to collect.

**Assumption No. 6:** Employers need not conform employee
benefits plans/policies/practices to any special requirements.
Not so. ERISA has reporting and disclosure standards requiring certain uniform characteristics, such as a procedure for filing a benefits claim and the appeal of a benefits claim denial.
ERISA also requires decisions about awarding benefits to be
made according to the terms of the benefits plan or policy.

   You can see that ERISA doesn't take the place of management prerogative. It doesn't set benefit levels or specify precisely how benefits must build up. It deals in generalities, like
providing that employees accrue benefits in some fair and or-
derly fashion, without laying down the exact blueprint for how
that is to be accomplished.

## *BENEFITS CHECKOFF: SEVEN MAJOR CONCEPTS OF ERISA*

✔ Workers must become eligible for benefits after a reasonable
  amount of service.
✔ Adequate funds must be set aside for promised benefits.

✔ Standards of conduct (fiduciary responsibility) must be met by those in charge of such funds and plans.

✔ Information must be made available in order to determine whether the law's requirements are being met.

✔ Pension plans must be operated solely in the interests of participants—that's you—and their beneficiaries.

✔ Employees must be allowed to participate if they're 21 and have completed a year of service (two years may be required for full and immediate vesting), and they can't be excluded because of advanced age.

✔ No matter what vesting requirements are applicable, the employee must always be fully vested for his or her contributions to the plan.

## FIVE DOCUMENTS ERISA DEMANDS YOU GET

The people in your company responsible for administering any plan under ERISA must provide you with the following material:

1. A Summary Plan Description (SPD)—This booklet must be written in language you can understand. It should tell you how the plan operates, when you're eligible to receive your pension, how to calculate the amount of your benefits, and how to file claims. You get this within ninety days of becoming a participant.

2. A summary of the annual report—This material covers the financial activities of the plan. It's only a summary, but you can put in a written request for a full report.

3. Survivor coverage data—This information deals with survivor coverage and tells how it affects you and your spouse.

4. A benefit statement—You can request one of these in writing, not more than once a year. It details your total accrued benefit and the earliest date on which you become vested.

5. A Summary of Material Modification (SMM)—If material changes are made in your plan, you must get a report detailing them.

**Benefits alert:** Your employer can maintain different types of plans under ERISA, such as one for production workers and one for office staff. But antidiscrimination laws still hold. No age, sex, race, national origin, religion, or disability factors may enter into the benefits equation when those differences come into play. Your employer may offer benefits that attract a specific group (such as family benefits that are more enticing to younger workers). But it can't offer different benefits to different groups, such as young versus old or men versus women.

The IRS also nudges its nose into discrimination aspects of benefits plans. Your employer can't claim the tax advantages of benefits plans if, say, its retirement plan discriminates in favor of senior executives or other highly compensated individuals. Example: Your employer can't allow senior managers to contribute 10% of their salaries to a retirement plan while capping lower-ranking employees' contributions at 5%. ▼

## KNOWING YOUR ERISA RULES AND RIGHTS

In general, ERISA prohibits any employer from changing a plan to directly or indirectly reduce already accrued benefits. An amendment is generally considered against the law if it eliminates or reduces an early retirement benefit or retirement-type subsidy.

Under ERISA, vesting has to do with when you acquire legal rights to your accrued retirement benefits. Chapter 12 discusses different types of vesting schedules. ERISA's regulations set minimum standards for defining years and hours of service under pension plans. For the purposes of participation and vesting, an ERISA year is a twelve-month period during which an employee has one thousand hours of service, for example.

**Benefits alert:** Check out your company's plan year and its definitions for hours of service, years of service, and breaks in service. They may seem like technicalities, but they have a lot to do with what you're owed and what you're not owed. You don't want to lose pension benefits just because you don't completely understand those definitions. So check back with chapter 12 if you're not crystal clear on this.

Also, ERISA standards are minimums. Your company's plans could very well be more liberal. If you want to know more about the subject, write the U.S. Dept. of Labor and ask for the booklet "What You Should Know about the Pension Law." ▼

---

## *BENEFITS CHECKOFF: DO'S AND DON'TS WITH ERISA*

You don't need to become an ERISA expert to protect your benefits rights. But the more you know about what the law does—and doesn't—cover, the better able you'll be to take full advantage of what your employer has to offer.

✔ ERISA **doesn't** require a pension plan to provide for early retirement (ER). But it **does** demand that ER benefits be at least the actuarial equivalent of normal retirement benefits. So a plan may first compute the expected monthly benefits payable at normal retirement age, and then reduce that monthly amount to take into account the age of the early retiree.

✔ ERISA **does not** require pension plans to provide you with disability benefits, so such plans are generally free to establish their own rules for eligibility.

✔ ERISA **does** permit (under special conditions) private pension plans to have pension formulas that integrate them with Social Security payments. So your private plan may be affected by your public one.

✔ ERISA **does not** require pension or profit sharing plans to provide lump-sum distribution options. And under ERISA, a plan may provide that it will cash out the vested benefits of a participant who leaves employment, usually if the present value of that vested benefit is under $3,500. Over that amount, other rules kick in, and an employer may not have to provide the benefit until a set retirement age.

✔ ERISA **does** protect your pension and welfare plans from financial losses due to mismanagement or misuse of assets. That means those who have "fiduciary responsibility" for your plan had better take care of business.

## *ERISA RIGHTS WHEN YOU'RE WRONGED*

ERISA also governs claims procedures if you feel your initial claim has been unfairly denied. If you think you are entitled to some benefit from a pension or welfare plan, file the claim with the appropriate person in your company. That filing procedure should be spelled out clearly in your original employee benefits booklet.

If your claim is denied, you must be notified in writing, generally within ninety days. You must be given the specific reasons for the denial, and the specific provisions on which the denial was based. You must also be told what additional information may be required. Then you get sixty days to appeal, and the decision on the appeal usually must be made within another sixty days.

## *BENEFITS CHECKOFF: SIX BASIC RIGHTS UNDER ERISA*

✔ Age and service requirements for your pension plan eligibility must not be unreasonable.

✔ If you work for a specified minimum period, you must get at least some pension at retirement.

✔ Your money must be available when it comes due to you through prudent handling by the company.

✔ You and your beneficiaries must be fully informed of your rights and entitlements.

✔ In certain cases, your pension must be protected in case of termination or insolvency.

✔ You may appeal any deserved benefits, exercise your rights without harassment, and sue in federal court to recover benefits.

## *WHEN YOU NEED TO GO TO COURT*

Because of the complex issues, legal fees, and bitter feelings, lawsuits under ERISA are often no-win situations for both sides. But you can't let your legal rights get lost in the benefits shuffle. Be on the lookout for these five situations that could give you a legal claim under ERISA:

(a) You depend—to your detriment—on misleading, inaccurate, or ambiguous language in employee benefits documents.
(b) Your employer seizes on inconsistencies between verbal and written material to deny benefits.
(c) Your company does something not solely in the best interests of participants in its ERISA-controlled plans.
(d) You don't get full, complete, correct, and timely information on your plans.
(e) A company representative gives you incorrect information that causes loss of benefits.

## SHIFTING GEARS TO COBRA: YOUR HEALTH WATCHDOG

The Consolidated Omnibus Budget Reconciliation Act (COBRA) of 1986 is another major player on your employee benefits legal team. It applies to all group health plans that provide medical, dental, vision, or prescription drug coverage. It doesn't affect disability coverage. Its basic job: making sure you get continued health coverage after you leave one employer and before you are covered by another plan. Naturally, there are guidelines and restrictions, but basically you can't be shoved out from under the COBRA umbrella until:

• you reach the end of the designated COBRA coverage period, either eighteen, twenty-nine, or thirty-six months;
• you fail to make timely payments of your premium;
• you become entitled to Medicare; or
• your former employer decides to terminate its health plan.

Employers must offer terminated or laid-off workers and their dependents the option to continue their group health plan coverage under the provisions of COBRA. Health care continuation coverage also must be extended to employees whose work hours have been reduced to the point where they no longer would be covered by the employer's group health plan, and to employees' dependents following certain "qualifying events" (such as a divorce or death of the employee) that cause the dependents to lose coverage under the employer's plan.

## COBRA COVERAGE: GETTING THE FACTS STRAIGHT

Group health plans for employers with twenty or more employees who worked at least 50% of the working days in the previous calendar year are subject to COBRA.

To understand COBRA, you've got to understand what a QB is. That's not a quarterback, as in football, but a qualified beneficiary.

A **qualified beneficiary** (QB) generally is any individual covered by a group health plan on the day before a qualifying event. A qualified beneficiary may be an employee, the employee's spouse and dependent children, and in certain cases a retired employee and the retired employee's spouse and dependent children.

Then you have to know what a QE is. That's not the cruise ship *Queen Elizabeth* but a qualifying event.

**Qualifying events** (QE) are those events that would cause you or a dependent to lose coverage under your employer's health plan if there were no continuing-coverage requirement under COBRA. The type of qualifying event will determine who your qualified beneficiaries are and the length of coverage, i.e., the amount of time the plan must offer coverage under COBRA.

Here's a chart divided into three parts that lays out for you what events trigger COBRA coverage, the amount of time the coverage must extend, and who falls under the coverage.

| Trigger Event | Coverage Period | Affected Individuals |
|---|---|---|
| Voluntary or involuntary termination of employment for reasons other than "gross misconduct" | 18 months | Employee, spouse, dependent children |
| Reduction in the number of hours worked | 18 months | Employee, spouse dependent children |
| Covered employee's becoming entitled to Medicare | 36 months | Spouse and dependent children |
| Divorce or legal separation of the covered employee | 36 months | Spouse and dependent children |
| Death of the covered employee | 36 months | Spouse and dependent children |
| Loss of "dependent child" status under the plan rules | 36 months | Dependent children |

## COMMUNICATION RULES AND REGS

When a qualifying event occurs, your employer must notify its plan administrator within thirty days of your death, termination, or reduced hours of employment. The plan administrator then must notify you and family members of your election rights within fourteen days, either by first-class mail or in person.

**Benefits alert:** You have notification obligations, too. If you have a QE, such as divorce, legal separation, or loss of dependent child status, you or your spouse or child must notify the plan administrator within sixty days.▼

Although COBRA specifies certain minimum required periods of time that continued health coverage must be offered to qualified beneficiaries, it does not prohibit plans from offering continuation of health coverage that goes beyond the COBRA periods.

That means your company could cut you a break and offer you longer coverage. If it doesn't, it can't hurt to ask if it will.

## PAYING THE COBRA PIPER

If you get hit by a qualifying event and COBRA coverage kicks in, you may be required to contribute the entire premium for coverage. But that amount cannot exceed 102% of the cost of the plan for participants who are still employed. Premiums reflect the total cost of the group health coverage, including both the portion paid by employees and any portion paid by the employer, plus 2% for administrative costs. No matter what you pay, a group plan is almost invariably cheaper than any you could find on your own.

## WHAT TO DO IF A COBRA CLAIM IS DENIED

You should submit a written claim for benefits to whomever is designated to operate the health plan (employer, plan administrator, etc.). If your claim is denied, you must be given a notice of denial in writing, generally no more than ninety days after the claim is filed. The notice should state the reasons for the denial, any additional information needed to support the claim, and procedures for appealing the denial.

You have sixty days to appeal a denial and must receive a decision on the appeal no more than sixty days after that, unless:

- the plan provides for a special hearing; or
- the decision is to be made by a group that meets only on a periodic basis, like a board of directors.

## BENEFITS CHECKOFF: MORE COBRA NEWS

The Revenue Reconciliation Act of 1989 (P.L. 101-239) put a few more teeth in the COBRA law. It:

✔ Prohibits employers from terminating continuation coverage for COBRA beneficiaries who become covered under other plans that do not cover previously covered conditions. That means if your previous plan covered blood transfusions and your new plan doesn't, you can count on the previous plan for that coverage.

✔ Restricts a group health plan from requiring payment of any COBRA premium until forty-five days after you make the initial election coverage. This gives you some breathing room for decisions and payments.

✔ Requires that employers provide COBRA coverage for an employee's spouse or dependents for thirty-six months from the date the employee becomes entitled to Medicare (unless the spouse is also eligible for Medicare). That gives you more peace of mind as you enter the senior group health coverage.

✔ Expands the COBRA rights of disabled employees from eighteen months from their date of termination of employment to twenty-nine months. During this special extended period of coverage, an employer may charge up to 150% of the applicable premium. If you're disabled, you get almost an extra year of coverage.

**Benefits alert:** COBRA doesn't demand that your company offer you a health plan after you've been separated from employment. It only governs plans already in effect. Also, if you are covered and you do choose the same coverage you had before you were separated, then you can't be required to prove insurability.▼

## COBRA COVERAGE IN ACTION

You've got to be aware of lots of ins and outs in the COBRA coverage game. For example, suppose you lose your job, fall under COBRA for two months, then obtain coverage from a new employer. But that new plan contains exclusions or limitations on coverage of pre-existing conditions for one of your qualified beneficiaries. Then, depending on the plan year of your old plan (remember, that's the effective date that it came under the COBRA mantle), you may be able to continue coverage for those conditions under the old plan.

Here are some simple sample scenarios to review to get a feel for how COBRA works at work.

**Example 1**

John Q. participates in the group health plan maintained by the ABC Co. John is fired for a reason other than gross misconduct, and his health coverage is terminated. John may elect and pay for a maximum of eighteen months of coverage by the employer's group health plan at 102% of the group rate.

**Example 2**

Day laborer David P. has health coverage through his wife's plan, sponsored by the XYZ Co. David loses his health coverage when he and his wife become divorced. David may purchase health coverage with the plan of his former wife's employer. Since in this case divorce is the qualifying event under COBRA, David is entitled to a maximum of thirty-six months of coverage.

**Example 3**

RST, Inc. is a small business that maintained an insured

group health plan for its ten employees in 1987 and 1988. Mary H., a secretary with six years of service, leaves in June 1992 to take a position with a competing firm that has no health plan. She is not entitled to COBRA coverage with the plan of RST, Inc. since the firm had fewer than twenty employees in 1987 and is not subject to COBRA requirements.

**Example 4**

Jane W., a stockbroker, leaves a brokerage firm in May 1990 to take a position with a chemical company. She is five months pregnant at the time. The health plan of the chemical company has a pre-existing condition clause for maternity benefits. Even though Jane signs up for the new employer's plan, she has the right to elect and receive coverage under the old plan for CO-BRA purposes because the new plan limits benefits for pre-existing conditions.

## *BENEFITS CHECKOFF: COBRA IN A NUTSHELL*

✔ *What continuation coverage (CC) must be offered to qualified beneficiaries?*

**A.** Each QB has the right independently to elect continuation of the coverage he/she had at the time of the qualifying event. He/she cannot add or change coverage at this point, except that vision or dental coverage costing 5% or more of the total coverage cost can be deleted.

✔ *What is the election period for a beneficiary to elect continuation coverage?*

**A.** The election period begins no later than the date when coverage would be lost under the terms of the plan and runs until sixty days after that date or until sixty days after the election notice is sent to the QBs.

✔ *Who has the right to elect continuation?*

**A.** Each qualified beneficiary has an independent right to elect continuation coverage. But an employee or spouse who is a QB and so elects is deemed to elect for other beneficiaries who would lose coverage by reason of the same qualifying event. A parent or guardian may elect for a minor child and a spouse or legal representative may elect for an incapacitated QB.

✔ *If continuation coverage is elected, when is it effective?*

A. Continuation coverage is effective as of the date on which coverage would have been lost. The statute says that the regular premium payments may be monthly if the beneficiary wishes, and that a regular payment is timely if made within thirty days of the due date. It also says that if election of CC is made after the qualifying event, payment for coverage in the period up to the election need not be made until 45 days after the election.

✔ *What happens if an unmarried covered employee terminates employment, elects individual coverage under COBRA, and subsequently marries?*

A. The employee can choose to have the spouse covered under the group health plan or whatever terms apply to covering new spouses of active employees. The spouse, however, does not thereby become a qualified beneficiary. Consequently, the spouse does not have to be offered the opportunity to elect COBRA continuation coverage if the former employee dies, divorces, or legally separates while the COBRA coverage is in effect.

For more information on COBRA election or notification rights, employees of private companies can contact the U.S. Dept. of Labor, Pension and Welfare Benefits Administration, Division of Technical Assistance and Inquiries, 200 Constitution Ave., NW, Room N-5658, Washington, DC 20210. Public employees can contact the U.S. Public Health Service, Office of the Assistant Secretary of Health, Grants Policy Branch (CO-BRA), 5600 Fishers La., Room 17A-45, Rockville, MD 20857.

*It's no picnic to get up to speed on your legal benefits rights. As Leesa Edalman found out, it takes a lot of time and effort. But it paid off for her. It can for you, too.*

# 15
▼

# MORE LEGAL RIGHTS

## Understanding Benefits Discrimination by Age, Sex, Etc.

### THE CASE OF THE LEGAL WHIPLASH

Mara Speare's head was spinning as her lawyer whipped through a mind-boggling assortment of legal remedies he had proposed to, as he put it, "make her whole" after her recent discharge.

All Mara Speare had wanted to know was whether her boss, Rob Kaufman, had the right to hand her her walking papers in the heavy-handed way he had.

"I don't know that I want to sue anyone," Mara began. "It's just that it seems unfair to me the way things turned out. First they assured my department that our jobs were safe. Then they offered a great early-retirement deal to a bunch of male managers from another division. Finally they kicked me out just as I was getting within hailing distance of my pension."

"That all adds up to a legal swift kick in the pants," retorted her lawyer, "and you have every right to demand your rights. By the way, did they ask you to sign any waivers before you left?"

"They gave me a bunch of papers," Mara remembered, "and said I should sign them before I picked up my paycheck and final benefits information. So I signed. What else could I do?"

As you'll see in this chapter, Mara could—and should—have done plenty to protect the rights and benefits she had earned in her employment.

While ERISA and COBRA are the major players on your employee benefits legal team, they're supported by a number of other federal laws, state legislation, and judicial decisions. Take a look at each area to see how it impacts your particular situation, either now or in the future.

Again, don't be put off by the legal technicalities or citations given in this chapter. Depending on legal avenues to obtain deserved benefits should be your last recourse. But you must know how to go about it if you're forced into that position. The explanation of these laws and judicial decisions will give you a basis to (a) decide if you really have a case and (b) investigate further with the help of a competent professional in the field.

## GETTING OLDER DOESN'T MEAN GETTING STUCK

The Age Discrimination in Employment Act (ADEA) says that your employer can't discriminate in offering benefits because of your age. It can't set up a system for covering people over 40 completely different from the one that covers those under 40. But the act doesn't prohibit legitimate differences.

For instance, to keep premium costs level, your employer may reduce life insurance benefits for older workers. Or to keep costs uniform in disability insurance, your employer may adjust benefits offered to older workers by reducing either the amount of the benefits or the duration of the benefit payments.

The Older Workers Benefit Protection Act (OWBPA), an amendment to ADEA passed in 1990, has set in legal concrete that equal-benefit or equal-cost concept. The bottom line: Covered employers must provide older workers with benefits equal to those provided to younger workers. The only exception: If the employer can prove that the cost of providing those equal benefits is unequal, that it is greater for older than younger, then a discrepancy is permitted. So if $100 buys $50,000 of coverage for a 30-year-old and only $25,000 of coverage for a 60-year-old, that difference in coverage is legal.

**Benefits alert:** Various amendments to ADEA have added Benefits Equivalence Provisions. Examples: If under-65 employees are offered spousal coverage, it must be offered to over-65s. An over-65 must be able to select any group health plan offered to under-65s. Also, an employer must tell over-65s how Medicare coverage complements its benefits plans. ▼

## YOU'RE SUPPOSED TO SQUAWK UNDER ADEA

Here are some examples of how ADEA affects employee benefits:

**Suppose** your company falls on hard times. It falls back on a reduction-in-force (RIF) strategy and offers a severance plan that calls for one week's pay for every two years of service. The pension plan allows for early retirement at age 55. You happen to be 56. The company announces that your severance pay for the RIF will be offset by the retirement pension benefits to which you're entitled.

Your move: Squawk. Denial of severance-pay benefits based on pension eligibility is age discrimination. Severance pay and pension benefits are different animals. Your employer can't leash them together. You're entitled to both.

**Suppose** you've put in a long and healthy twenty years at your firm but develop kidney problems around your 60th birthday. You qualify for disability retirement. But your company has no specific feature in its retirement plans for that. In fact, it doesn't have any long-term disability provision on the books. The only thing your employer does have is a disability clause in its life insurance plan. One problem: You are told that you're ineligible because employees 60 and over are excluded from the plan. It's too costly to cover them.

Squawk again. While companies can equalize costs and benefits for older/younger workers, the total elimination of disability benefits for older workers would probably cross over the legal line of bias. You may have to muddle through with reduced benefits, but you should get something.

**Suppose** your company implements a plan that denies accruals of service and salary credits after the age of 65. It also cuts profit-sharing contributions after employees hit that magic number.

Squawk. If a company goes out of its way to make it unattractive for its protected senior employees to work beyond 65 and essentially forces them to quit, it could be vulnerable to an ADEA lawsuit. (*AARP v. Farmers Group*, CA 9, No. 90-55872, 1991).


## *BENEFITS CHECKOFF: EIGHT REQUIREMENTS FOR LEGAL WAIVERS*

The Older Workers Benefit Protection Act also toughened another tender zone by setting forth eight requirements that employers must meet when asking employees to sign waivers of age discrimination claims. (Mara Speare should have known about these.) No matter what benefits rewards you're promised, don't sign anything unless these eight conditions are met:

- ✔ The waiver must be part of a written agreement between you and your employer. The agreement must be written "in a manner calculated to be understood"—by you.
- ✔ The waiver must specifically refer to rights or claims arising under ADEA.
- ✔ You must not be forced to waive rights or claims that may arise after the date you sign the waiver.
- ✔ There must be consideration for the waiver—that is, you must be given something over and above everything you're already entitled to.
- ✔ You must be advised in writing to see a lawyer before you sign the agreement.
- ✔ You must be given twenty-one days in which to consider the matter if you're an individual employee negotiating a waiver, or forty-five days if you're part of a group or class of employees let go in connection with an exit incentive or other mass employment-termination program.
- ✔ In addition to the time given to consider the agreement, the company must allow you seven days to revoke or repudiate the agreement after you've signed it. The agreement cannot become effective before the end of seven days.

✔ In case of an exit incentive or other mass termination program, the employer must provide you with three pieces of information, in writing: (a) the class, unit, or group of employees covered by the program, the eligibility requirements for the program, and any time limits (for accepting or participating in the program); (b) the job titles and ages of all individuals eligible or selected for the program; and (c) the job titles and ages of all individuals in the same plant or unit who are not eligible or selected for the program.

## ABOVE AND BEYOND OWBPA: BE ALERT

You'll probably also see other provisions in the waiver document you'll be studying. Check them for accuracy and completeness. If there's an inconsistency or incorrect statement, don't just sit there and sign. Demand a change. A waiver document, especially the most common ones that deal with termination, include:

- An acknowledgement that the termination was voluntary. Was it?
- A statement of the circumstances that caused the termination. Are they exaggerating?
- A statement of whether you'll be eligible for future reemployment. Are you in their future plans?
- Your agreement not to sue or to file a complaint with any federal or state administrative agency, like the EEOC. Have they fulfilled all the previous waiver requirements?
- Provisions for the return of company property and confidential documents. Is anything yours?
- The dates you'll be terminated, retired, or otherwise given a new status. What are the normal due dates for pay and other benefits and for vesting of pension rights?
- The amounts of salary, bonuses, or other benefits, when they are to be paid, and the dates of any remaining service. Are they buying time with your money?

If you're really angry about a suspected benefits violation, especially if you're over 40, and you think something fishy is going on, you may want to consider seeking legal counsel. But before you do, investigate the ten areas outlined in figure 30.

## *GETTING BENEFITS EQUALITY WITH THE EQUAL PAY ACT*

The formal bottom line: The Equal Pay Act (EPA) prohibits unequal wages for women and men who work in the same "establishment" for equal work on jobs that require equal skill, effort, and responsibility and that are performed under similar working conditions.

The practical bottom line: The word *wages* covers a lot more than the traditional definition. That's why EPA affects benefits as well as your weekly paycheck. According to the act, wages include all payments for employment. That includes vacation and holiday pay and fringe benefits, among them medical, hospital, accident and life insurance, retirement benefits, profit sharing, bonus plans, and leave.

As you can see in figure 31, one of your biggest "wage" benefits, your vacation time, has gotten a lot of legal scrutiny.

The Equal Pay Act wasn't designed to prohibit all differences in wage rates, just those based on sex and not on other factors. So it lays out four exceptions to the general standard of equal pay across sex lines. They are:

- seniority systems;
- merit systems;
- systems measuring earnings by quantity or quality of production;
- a general rule of thumb if the differential is based on any factor other than sex.

Importantly, the employer must be able to prove that its use of one of those exceptions is valid.

*Figure 30. Steps to take before you hurl age charges*

## AGE LAWSUIT INVESTIGATION

**If you're thinking about a lawsuit involving age and benefits, run through this checklist first.**

_____ Does the company have specific grievance procedures and complaint processes? Have you used them? Have you been stonewalled?

_____ Did you talk with your boss about your problem? No acceptable response? Did you check with Personnel and not receive satisfactory answers?

_____ Document, document, document. No matter what your eventual claims will be, get as much in writing as you can: letters you sent to your company reps and vice versa, notes on your conversations, all benefits documents and communications.

_____ Ask around. See if anyone else has run into similar problems. See if others were treated differently in similar circumstances. Get co-workers' help.

_____ Become an expert on the policies or benefits in question. Know all the specifics. Check federal, state, and local requirements. Understand how and when your company may be exempt from the law.

_____ Find out whether the company has consistently followed its internal policies and avoided legal taboos. Uncover exceptions. Document them. Scare up witnesses if you can.

_____ Keep track of all meetings, both those you attend and those called without you to discuss your problem.

_____ Check the company's economic condition. If it's pleading poverty and just trumpeted a lucrative contract signing, factor it in. Read up on how the industry is doing.

_____ Review the makeup of the company with an eye toward how it might show age bias. Have a lot of older workers been cut? Has average employee age plummeted? Does recruiting emphasize "new blood"?

_____ Listen for age bias in the workplace. Do older workers suffer verbal harassment? Do they get belittled? Are they the brunt of jokes and sarcasm?

*Figure 31. Legal rights in vacation benefits*

## TAKING A VACATION IN THE COURTROOM

One of the most sensitive areas in employee benefits involves vacations. A basic question: Must an employer provide vacation time to employees? The basic answer: There is no state or federal law that requires an employer to provide vacation time. However, once it is offered, vacation pay is considered an employee welfare benefit subject to federal law.

Another sensitive question: Must a terminated employee be paid for unused vacation?

The general rule of law is that earned or accrued vacation time is treated as wages subject to EPA and must be paid on termination. For instance, Massachusetts state law sets criminal sanctions against officers of corporations who fail to pay wages. When a bank refused to cough up vacation pay to two fired employees, the state filed criminal actions. (*Mass. v. Morash*, U.S. Sup. Ct., No. 8 88-32, 1990)

Your main concern should be whether vacation is earned or not, how it accrues, and whether it's forfeited under certain circumstances. Ask:

1. How is vacation earned at your firm? Do you accumulate vacation in stages, or do you earn it all at once?
2. Can unused vacation be carried forward?
3. When do you forfeit the right to take or receive pay for vacation?
4. Does the policy specify time periods when employees can and can't take vacations?

State laws also poke their heads into the "use it or lose it" vacation controversy. A California court ruled that state law prohibited forfeiture of vested vacation pay at termination. It emphasized the difference between a "use it or lose it" vacation policy and one that restricted additional accrual. Under the first, you lose earned vested vacation pay if it's not used within a designated time period. Under the second, the amount of unused vacation you can save up is limited.

So under California state law, an employer who has an established vacation policy must pay an employee for all unused accrued vacation at termination. But that employer can also place limits on the amount of unused vacation time that can accrue. (*Boothby v. Atlas Mech.*, CA App. 3d, C009284, 1992)

## *BENEFITS CHECKOFF: DO YOU HAVE AN EPA CASE?*

Keep these key points in mind if you think you're being discriminated against in benefits on the basis of sex:

✔ The OWBPA "equal-benefit, equal-cost" concept doesn't cut the mustard here. Your employer can't hide behind the excuse that the cost of benefits is greater for one sex than for the other.

✔ An employer is flirting with legal disaster if it uses factors like "head of household" or "chief wage earner" in its determination of benefits. A court shot that system full of holes.

✔ Your pension or retirement plan can't have different optional or compulsory retirement ages based on sex. In fact, no aspect of such benefits programs can differ by sex.

✔ Your employer must make the same benefits available for the spouses and families of employees without regard to whether the employee is male or female.

---

**Benefits alert:** One employer ran afoul of the rules in offering increased pay to its employees who were heads of households. That's bias, said a court. "So we'll change," replied the company, "and eliminate the salary sweetener for those male 'heads.'" That's not what the law calls for, said the court. EPA says you must increase the lower rate to the higher, not vice versa. (*EEOC v. First Baptist Church*, U.S. D.C. N.IN, No. S91-179M, 1992) ▼

---

## *BENEFITS CHECKOFF: WHEN YOU'RE PREGNANT*

The Pregnancy Discrimination Act of 1978 (PDA) amends Title VII of the Civil Rights Act of 1964 and forbids discrimination on the basis of pregnancy, childbirth, or related medical conditions. The basic principle: Women affected by pregnancy and related conditions must be treated the same as other disabled employees in all conditions of employment, including benefits.

The way your employer treats workers who have short-term disabilities should give you an appropriate yardstick for determining whether you're getting your just due when you're pregnant. Here are eight key practical points to be aware of when dealing with the benefits aspects of pregnancy.

✔ If your employer holds jobs open for workers on sick or disability leave, then you've got a right to have your position held open for you (unless you tell your boss that you don't plan to return to work).

✔ The time credited for vacation, seniority, and pay increases must be the same for pregnancy leave and other types of disability leave.

✔ If your employer continues to contribute to a profit sharing plan for employees who take disability leave, then it must do the same for you while you're on pregnancy leave.

✔ You can't be forced to use up your vacation benefits before receiving sick leave or disability payments, unless your employer demands the same system for all employees who go on disability leave.

✔ While your employer isn't directly obligated by PDA to grant leave for child care after you're medically able to return to work, the rule of thumb is that it must offer you the same options it offers other employees seeking nonmedical leave.

✔ If your employer offers choices among several different health plans, each one must include coverage for pregnancy and related conditions.

✔ Your medical expenses for pregnancy, childbirth, and related conditions must be reimbursed in the same manner (i.e., fixed or percentage) as expenses incurred for other medical conditions.

✔ You can't be forced to pay an additional or larger deductible to cover the costs of pregnancy.

# WHEN PREGNANCY CASES REACH THE COURTS

The best way to get a handle on the legal aspects of pregnancy and benefits is to consider a couple of cases:

**Case #1.** A company had a sick leave policy that demanded one year of service before an employee could get time off for sickness. That policy had a negative effect on women. During one period, of the fifty-three first-year employees fired on the basis of the policy, fifty were women. And twenty of them were pregnant.

Court: Working women must be protected against all forms of employment discrimination based on sex. This policy had a disproportionately negative impact on women, especially pregnant ones. It had to go. (*EEOC v. Warshawsky & Co.*, D.C. N.IL, No. 90-C-1352, 1991)

**Case #2.** An organization came under the legal gun when it put a pregnant employee under its discipline gun. Just four days after announcing her pregnancy, a secretary was counseled for her unwillingness to pitch in and work long hours. That had been a condition of the job for her and others in her office.

The employee was eventually fired, and she sued under PDA. Her claim: The company had given other employees fewer hours when they requested them, so she was treated differently just because she was pregnant. A court agreed. What a company grants to some of its employees, it must not deny to its pregnant ones. (*EEOC v. Ackerman, Hood, & McQueen*, 758 F. Supp.1440, W.D. OK, 1991)

# ADA AND EMPLOYEE BENEFITS

The Americans with Disabilities Act (effective dates: 6-27-92 for employers with twenty-five or more employees; 6-27-94 for employers with fifteen or more) states that an employer may not limit, segregate, or classify an individual with a disability on the basis of disability, in a way that hurts the individual's em-

ployment. This law applies to health insurance and other benefits, such as life insurance and pension plans. In plain English,
it means that if you suffer from a covered disability, you can't be
discriminated against when it comes to benefits.

## WHAT'S A DISABILITY UNDER ADA?

Under ADA, an individual with a disability is a person who:

- has a physical or mental impairment that substantially limits
  at least one major life activity;
- has a record of having such an impairment; or
- is regarded as having such an impairment.

To be a disability covered by ADA, an impairment must **substantially** limit at least one major life activity—like walking,
speaking, breathing, seeing, hearing, and learning—compared
to an average person in the general population.

The regulations provide three factors that determine
whether a person's impairment substantially limits a major life
activity:

(a)  its nature and severity;
(b)  how long it will last or is expected to last;
(c)  its permanent or long-term impact or expected impact.

## BENEFITS CHECKOFF: INSURANCE BENEFITS
## AND ADA

The benefits area hardest hit by ADA is likely to be insurance.
Here are some general points to keep in mind:

✔ If an employer provides insurance or other benefits plans to
  its employees, it must provide the same coverage to employees with disabilities.
✔ An employer cannot deny insurance to an individual with a

disability or subject that individual to different terms or conditions of insurance based on disability alone, if the disability doesn't increase insurance risks.

✔ An employer cannot fire or refuse to hire an individual with a disability because its current health insurance plan does not cover the individual's disability, or because the individual may increase the employer's future health care costs.

✔ An employer cannot fire or refuse to hire an individual (whether or not that individual has a disability) because the individual has a family member or dependent with a disability that's not covered by its current health insurance, or that may increase current or future health care costs.

✔ Employers must offer health insurance to employees with disabilities on the same basis they offer such insurance to other employees. Employers are allowed to maintain all significant aspects of the program (deductibles, caps, exclusions, and restraints on pre-existing conditions), even if they have a negative effect on individuals with a disability. The key point is that all employees must be subject to the same factors.

✔ An employer may continue to offer health insurance plans that contain pre-existing condition exclusions, even if this adversely affects individuals with disabilities, unless these exclusions are being used as a subterfuge to evade the purpose of ADA.

✔ An employer may continue to offer health insurance plans that limit coverage for certain procedures and/or limit particular treatments to a specified number per year, even if these restrictions adversely affect individuals with disabilities, as long as the restrictions are uniformly applied to all insured individuals, regardless of disability.

---

**Benefits alert:** ADA is sure to provoke lawsuits in the benefits area, especially when it comes to costly disabilities like AIDS. Several courts have already weighed in with benefits discrimination decisions on reducing or capping benefits.

Facts: A self-insured company saw the financial handwriting on the wall and reduced its lifetime benefits for treating AIDS from $1 million to

$5,000. An employee sued, claiming ERISA protection. The court disagreed, ruling employers are free to change plans if it is not done to retaliate or deliberately discriminate and if it is based on a need to cut costs. That's true even when the benefit reduction falls most heavily on an identifiable group of employees or beneficiaries. (*McGann v. H&H Music Co.*, CA 5, No. 90-2672, 1992)

On the other side of the AIDS-capping coin, the EEOC came out with a strongly worded policy statement that places the burden of proof on employers when it comes to discrimination claims by people with specific illnesses when the insurance provisions of the ADA are in question. Court tests will eventually decide just how much room employers have to maneuver when it comes to cutting the costs involved with major-league illnesses.▼

## *DISABILITY NONDISCRIMINATION IN OTHER BENEFITS*

If you have a disability, you must have an equal opportunity to attend and participate in any social functions or recreational activities conducted or sponsored by your employer. Functions such as parties, picnics, shows, and award ceremonies should be held in accessible locations, and interpreters or other accommodation should be provided when necessary.

You must also have equal access to break rooms, lounges, cafeterias, and any other nonwork facilities that are provided by your employer for use by your co-workers.

The same goes for access to an exercise room, gymnasium, or health club provided by your firm. At the same time, your company doesn't have to eliminate facilities provided for its other employees because you, an employee with a disability, can't use certain equipment or amenities because of your disability. For example, an employer would not have to remove certain exercise machines simply because an employee who is paraplegic could not use them.

Employees with disabilities must be given an equal opportunity to participate in employer-sponsored sports teams, leagues, or recreational activities such as hiking or biking clubs. Again, an employer doesn't have to discontinue such activities because an employee with a disability cannot fully participate due to his/her disability. For example, if you were blind and unable to ride a bike, your employer wouldn't have to discontinue the company biking club.

Transportation provided by an employer for use by its employees must be accessible to employees with disabilities. This includes transportation between employer facilities, transportation to and from mass transit, and transportation provided on an occasional basis to employer-sponsored events.

## ADA AND LEAVE

Consistency and fairness also apply to leave benefits for employees with disabilities. An employer may establish attendance and leave policies that are uniformly applied to all employees, regardless of disability. But it may not refuse leave needed by an employee with a disability if other employees get similar leaves.

Employers are also required to adjust leave policy as a reasonable accommodation. While not obligated to provide additional paid leave, accommodation may include leave flexibility and unpaid leave.

Just because a uniformly applied leave policy has a more severe effect on an individual who is disabled, that doesn't mean it violates ADA. However, if an individual with a disability requests a modification of such a policy as a reasonable accommodation, an employer may be required to provide it, unless it would impose an undue hardship.

**Example:** If an employer has a policy providing two weeks of paid leave for all employees, with no other provision for sick leave and a "no leave" policy for the first six months of employment, an employee with a disability who cannot get leave for needed medical treatment couldn't successfully charge that the employer's policy is discriminatory.

However, this individual could request leave without pay or

advance leave as a reasonable accommodation. Such leave should be provided, unless the employer can show undue hardship.

## WHEN BENEFITS GO ON TRIAL

Hundreds of cases have weaved their way through the American judicial system based on problems generated by benefits practices and policies and the way they've been interpreted. One big problem: Different courts have viewed similar problems from different angles, making any attempt to lay down hard and fast rules an exercise in futility. The following cases, though, may give you some ways to measure whether you have been on the short end of the legal benefits stick.

**Tension point:** Is there any such thing as lifetime benefits?

One major company notified retirees that it was requiring them to share in the cost of their health coverage through co-payments and deductibles. A group of retirees objected to these changes, claiming that they had been promised medical benefits for life as an inducement to retire. Said a court: You've got a case. (*Sprague v. GMC*, U.S. Dist. Ct., E.D. MI, 1991)

Lifetime benefits also were an issue in a case involving formal versus informal documentation. Seems retirees at one company thought their health insurance benefits were set in concrete for life. They even had a couple of letters from company reps promising lifetime coverage and payment of all premiums.

Imagine their consternation when they learned the company had decided to reduce some benefits and eliminate others, while adding deductibles and coinsurance payments. Peeved, they sued. Sorry, said the court. The formal company documents retained the right of the company to change its plans. That's exactly what it did. (*Arndt v. Wheelabrator Corp.*, D.C. N.IN, No. S89-360, 1991)

Another court gave *carte blanche* to a company to change its retiree health plan and demand that beneficiaries contribute a portion of the premium. Why? The company had a written clause that said it could do so. (*Pierce v. Security Trust Life Ins., Co.*, CA 4, No. 90-1101, 1992)

**Benefits alert:** There's only one person who's going to take care of number one, and you see that individual's reflection in the mirror every day. That's why you bought this book. And that's why it keeps hammering away at the fact that you have to take your benefits by the throat; you have to plan for coverage and costs; you have to be prepared to act if your employer pulls any part of the corporate benefits rug out from under you. Even the courts can't always supply you with an out. ▼

Another court expressed its "sympathy" for the plight of retirees who thought their company was going to pay the cost of life and health benefits for their lifetimes. That didn't change the legal fact that the company was not required to continue retiree welfare benefits after the collective bargaining agreement between the company and its employees had expired. (*Senn v. United Dominion Ind. Inc.*, CA 7, No. 90-3100, 1992)

Similarly, a federal judge declared that a company could unilaterally change or eliminate medical benefits for its retirees because, unlike pension benefits, medical benefits were not automatically vested or guaranteed. (*John Morrell & Co. v. United Food & Comm. Workers Int'l Union*, U.S.D.C. SD, No. CV-91-4184, 1993)

Note: The trend of companies socking more costs to retirees is likely to expand as the FAS 106 rule takes hold. That financial requirement demands that companies show the future cost of health benefits promised to retirees on their current bottom lines.

**Benefits alert:** Keep your eyes open for news or information about actions your company may take in the big scheme of benefits, before it notifies you. And give your health and medical care documents another once-over to see if your company can make unilateral changes that can cost you money. ▼

## EARLY RETIREMENT PROVOKES LATE LAWSUITS

Early retirement has become another tension point for lawsuits. In one instance, the company implemented a middle-manager reduction-in-force it dubbed MIPP (Management Income Protection Plan). To get managers to resign and take early retirement, the company offered generous benefits like separation pay of 5% of annual salary plus 5% for each year of service after the first.

The window for choosing the plan was open for only two months. The company was adamant that this was a now-or-never, take-it-or-leave-it proposition. But some managers held back, hoping for a better deal.

During the next two years, a number of those managers quit or retired. Funny thing happened then. The company offered a new MIPP with even better terms. The individuals who had left in the interim period cried foul, claiming the company had breached its fiduciary responsibility by misrepresenting its intentions about a second MIPP. A court agreed. (*Berlin v. MI Bell Telephone Co.*, 858 F.2d 1154, 6th Cir., 1988)

On the other hand, a court of appeals ruled that an employer that offered a "one time only" retirement bonus and then later sweetened its early-retirement package didn't breach its fiduciary responsibilities under ERISA.

The bonus plan was known as VERO (Voluntary Early Retirement Opportunity), and employees had three weeks to take advantage of it. Two years later, along came VRIP (Voluntary Retirement Incentive Program), offering bigger benefits than VERO. Those who had retired under the earlier plan launched a lawsuit, based on that "one time only" company announcement.

That "one time only" referred to the three-week period during which VERO was available, retorted the company. We never promised we'd never have another early-retirement program. Court: The company didn't intend to mislead, so the ex-employees are out of luck. (*Barnes v. Lacy*, CA 11, No. 90-7288, 1991)

On the other hand, a federal appeals court determined that another company had misled a group when it offered them a less lucrative early retirement plan than was offered to other workers. The U.S. Supreme Court refused to review, thus leaving the company open to over seven million dollars in potential damage awards. (*GMC v. Drennan*, U.S. Sup. Ct., No. 92-1607, 1993)

## *BENEFITS BY STATE*

Besides the alphabet of federal laws governing employee benefits and judicial decisions you've read about, you've also got to be aware of how states are involved.

The primary focus of state benefits legislation is on health benefits. Virtually all states impose some requirements on group health insurance plans. Hawaii and Massachusetts have gone so far as to enact legislation that requires—or provides financial incentives to encourage—employers to provide health care coverage for employees.

Treatment for alcoholism or mental illness is frequently mandated under state law; so is coverage for drug abuse, to a lesser extent. Many states have also mandated coverage for pregnancy and child care, including preventive health care for children and even fertility treatment. Illinois, for instance, demands that companies offering health insurance to cover pregnancy costs must extend that coverage to treatments for fertility problems.

Other states have enacted provisions requiring coverage for certain specific diseases, like Alzheimer's; for specific medical or surgical procedures, like organ transplants; or for the services of certain health care professionals, like chiropractors.

To get just a taste of these state health provisions, check out figure 32. Laws like these can change at the drop of a hat. So just read through them as appetizers, and make sure you review the entire menu of the most up-to-date information from your particular state if you need to investigate this area.


## *NEGOTIATING A SEVERANCE PACKAGE*

Keep in mind that discrimination laws, both federal and state (some cities have them, too), are very strong and well known to employers. They cannot discriminate in hiring, disciplining, promoting, paying, or discharging on the basis of age, sex, religion, race, color, national origin, disability, or pregnancy.

*Figure 32. A sampling of state-mandated health requirements*

## A SAMPLING OF STATE HEALTH LAWS
### Coverage for Alcohol/Drug Abuse Treatment

Alaska has mandatory coverage, with $7,000 minimum inpatient/outpatient coverage for twenty-four months and a $14,000 lifetime maximum. Nebraska requires insurance companies to offer alcoholism treatment as a benefits option, but employers can choose not to cover their employees for it. If they do, minimum coverage is thirty days for inpatient, sixty visits for outpatient.

### COVERAGE FOR MENTAL HEALTH

Illinois requires it as an insurance option employers can choose to provide or not provide. It sets a minimum yearly inpatient/outpatient combination of 25% of lifetime policy limits. Massachusetts has mandatory coverage, with a sixty-day-per-year minimum for inpatient aid and a $500-per-year minimum for outpatient. The lifetime maximum for inpatient care in this area must be the same as for physical illness. New Jersey, Pennsylvania, and Rhode Island are among the states with no statutory requirements.

### COVERAGE FOR MATERNITY AND DEPENDENTS

Arizona mandates coverage for newborns and for adoptions if they occur within one year of birth. There is no pregnancy care, fertility treatment, or preventive care for children. Florida covers newborn and adopted children and does have preventive-care requirements for children up to 16 years of age.

### COVERAGE FOR SPECIFIED DISEASES/MEDICAL CONDITIONS

California demands coverage for Alzheimer's, unless it's a pre-existing condition; diabetic education programs are a required option (i.e., insurance companies in the state must offer employers this benefit option, but employers may choose not to cover employees for it), as is footwear needed by people suffering foot disfigurement. The District of Columbia mandates coverage only for AIDS. Missouri does the same.

### COVERAGE FOR SPECIFIED PROVIDERS

California mandates coverage for psychologists and social workers, as well as for marriage, family, and child counselors; speech pathologists; acupuncturists; and psychiatric nurses. Delaware demands coverage for nurse midwives, while Florida does the same and adds optometrists, chiropractors, dentists, podiatrists, and acupuncturists.

You don't have to take a layoff or permanent discharge lying down—unless it's for some kind of misconduct that's been clearly spelled out. You can, and should, negotiate for better terms than you're offered. Even when you quit voluntarily, perhaps to take another job, you should try to get the best deal you can from your employer. After all, the benefits you've been earning most likely make up 30% to 40% of your total compensation. It makes no sense to toss them away without some stiff negotiating before you leave.

Your first step should be to make up a list of the benefits you're getting. Then classify each one as absolutely essential, very important, nice to have, or can get along without. Work out a negotiating strategy for each one. Take the list with you when you go to discuss your severance. The following checklist will help you get started on developing your own strategy for negotiating a better deal for a few of the most common benefits.

## BENEFITS CHECKOFF: SIX KEY NEGOTIATING IDEAS TO SWEETEN YOUR SEVERANCE DEAL

✔ **Severance pay:** Find out if anyone has ever been given more than you're offered. If anyone has been given a better deal, make that severance pay your minimum demand. If no one has been given a better deal, base your upping the ante on length of service, results you've achieved, responsibilities, and any extra unpaid hours you've worked.

✔ **Pension benefits:** The pension plan spells out your rights when you leave the company. Don't rely on the Summary Plan Description of those rights if you're not satisfied with the deal as it's laid out. Instead, take advantage of your right to examine the plan document itself in the company's offices. The gobbledegook in the plan won't read like it was written by Hemingway. But you may find a hidden nugget like some discretion on payouts allowed to the plan's administrators for hardship cases or other circumstances.

✔ **Health/medical insurance:** The feds stepped in during 1985 with COBRA (Consolidated Omnibus Budget Reconciliation

Act). Your employer is required (1) to continue identical coverage for eighteen months if a worker becomes unemployed for any reason other than misconduct, and (2) to continue coverage for thirty-six months to dependents of deceased workers. That's the good news. The bad news is that your employer can charge you 102% of the premium. Negotiate a better deal—ask for the same premium sharing, if any, you had as an employee for the first six months after you've left the company.

✔ **Profit sharing:** Ask for an immediate rollover of the sums in your account to your IRA.

✔ **Stock purchase plan:** Ask for an immediate redemption of your stock; if that's not possible, accept immediate issuance of the stock certificates, which you can sell in the open market, unless you want to keep them as an investment.

✔ **ESOP:** Offer your allocated shares to the company for redemption.

### Let's make a deal

Mary Kay Hernandez had seen the red flags of warning snapping in the breeze for several months. A new CEO had slapped everyone with nitpicking cost-cutting rules. Then she saw workers laid off, even line and staff supervisors. Finally, the ax fell on her.

She went right to her boss to ask about severance pay and benefits. He bucked her to Personnel, which put her on hold for a few days. That gave her time to find out what kinds of severance packages other dismissed people had gotten and to read up on industry layoff practices.

Mary Kay typed up a neat list of benefit items she felt were negotiable and marched into Personnel. Personnel buttoned itself up like it was in a bunker: three weeks of severance pay and continuation of health/medical insurance under COBRA at a cost of 102% of the company's group rate. "Policy," Personnel said.

"Listen to me," Mary Kay replied. "I'm the only woman out of more than five hundred supervisors in this company. I'm black, Hispanic, and I was born in Cuba. I'm 52 years old, and here's what I want in my severance package."

Visions of lawsuits began to dance before the eyes of Personnel as Mary Kay ticked off her demands:

- a month's severance pay for each year of service;
- all her earned vacation pay;
- medical/health insurance at no cost for six months, and at 50% of cost until she got covered in a new job;
- her annual performance bonus prorated to date of discharge;
- her profit sharing account rolled directly into her IRA within six months;
- a guarantee that her pension benefit would be transferred to a new employer's plan when she became eligible;
- letters of recommendation that told of her effectiveness as a supervisor and the awards for efficiency she'd won.

Outcome: A negotiated settlement that fell about two-thirds of the way between what she was told was "policy" and what she'd demanded. Her haymaker punches delivered a TKO.

---

*In most employment lawsuits, neither side wins. The stress, time, out-of-pocket expenses, embarrassment . . . it all adds up to a bad deal from both ends. But you can't allow yourself to be pushed around, as Mara Speare was. So don't be eager to initiate a lawsuit . . . but be prepared.*

# GLOSSARY

**Accidental Death and Dismemberment (AD&D)**—A provision in a health insurance plan that pays a specific cash sum if you should lose a limb (an arm or leg) or lose your life as a result of an accident. (chapter 4)

**Administrator**—The company that administers your health benefits plan. In most cases it is a health insurance company; however, it may also be your employer or a third party.

**Age Discrimination in Employment Act (ADEA)**—A law that protects you from discrimination if you're over the age of 40. (chapter 15)

**Americans with Disabilities Act (ADA)**—A law that protects you from discrimination in employment if you're disabled. (chapter 15)

**Annual benefit maximum**—The total amount your benefits plan will pay for your health costs in a given year. If your costs exceed this total amount, you usually must pay for the rest of the costs yourself.

**Annual benefits statement**—A statement of deferred vested benefits furnished to each employee. You should get one each year, but especially if you are separated from service. It'll show whether you have vested pension rights, the amount of accrued vested benefits or the earliest date on which they will accrue, and your total accrued benefits. (chapters 2 and 12)

**Annuity**—A series of equal payments from a pool of money. The amount of each payment may be based upon your life expectancy, and it terminates at death. The different types of annuities are:

> **Certain**—An annuity that guarantees payment for a minimum time period, usually five, ten, or twenty years.

> **Deferred**—A contract that compounds earnings on a tax-deferred basis. You don't receive payments until a later date.

> **Fixed**—A deferred annuity that compounds earnings at a fixed rate, usually pegged to a U.S. Treasury security interest rate.

> **Variable**—A deferred annuity that's invested in one or more mutual funds. You usually get to make the choices. Your return depends upon performance of the fund(s). (chapter 9)

**Beneficiary**—A person (or people) that a particular insurance plan covers. You are a beneficiary of your employer's health plan, and your family members may also be beneficiaries of the same health plan. If you have life insurance, you name your beneficiary.

**Benefits**—In equal employment opportunity law, nonsalary items provided to employees, such as vacation pay, sick pay, health and life insurance, pensions, etc.

**Cafeteria plan**—A flexible benefit plan in which your employer provides you with a range of options in cost, coverage, and providers. You make selections based on how much you want to pay and your needs. It's called a cafeteria plan because you pick and choose your own benefits package, the way you'd decide on a meal from a menu, one item at a time, according to what you want. (chapter 3)

**Case management**—The review and monitoring of your medical care by a health professional. For example, a hospital or insurance company might assign a single clinician to your case. This "manager" is responsible for determining how you use what's available to you (e.g., whether you should see a specialist, whether you should go to the hospital, how long you should stay in the hospital). (chapter 4)

**Claim**—Your request for reimbursement from your health insurance company for medical costs you have incurred. (chapter 4)

**Coinsurance**—A form of cost sharing between you and your health insurance company. After you meet your deductible, you must pay a percentage of each additional bill you submit to the insurance company. So you pay a percentage of your health costs and your insurance company pays the rest. A typical coinsurance ratio is 20% (what you pay) to 80% (what your insurance pays).

**Consolidated Omnibus Budget Reconciliation Act (COBRA)**—An act requiring that group health plans offer continuation of health coverage to certain beneficiaries upon the occurrence of such qualified events as:

1. termination of employment (for reasons other than gross misconduct) or reduction of hours of employment;
2. death of employee;
3. divorce or legal separation;
4. entitlement of the employee to Medicare benefits;

Typically, COBRA requires employers to offer to employees who are being terminated up to eighteen months of continual health care coverage for up to 102% of the premium cost. (chapter 14)

**Coordination of benefits**—A health insurance provision restricting the total medical expense reimbursement from more than one plan. In dual-career families, for example, it may be up to 100% of allowable medical expenses so as to avoid duplicate payments. It also provides for the sequence in which coverage will apply when a person is insured under two plans.

**Copayment**—A form of cost-sharing between you and your health insurance company that requires you to pay a fixed fee toward the cost of each service you use. (Note that you pay a fixed fee and not a fixed percentage as with coinsurance.) For example, a prescription drug benefit might require you to make a copayment of $10 per prescription, regardless of the cost of the prescription.

**Deductible**—A specific dollar amount that you must pay for covered services in a year's time before your insurance kicks in.

**Defined benefit plan**—A plan that uses specific formulas to determine how your benefits will be accrued and measured. (chapters 2, 3, and 12)

**Defined contribution plan**—A plan that provides for an individual account for each participant and for benefits based solely on the amount contributed to that participant's account. Any income, expense, gains, losses, and forfeitures of accounts of other participants are factored into the participant's account. (chapters 2, 3, and 12)

**Denial**—A refusal by an insurance company, or an outside review firm hired by an insurance company, to reimburse you for specific services. For example, in a traditional health care indemnity plan, you may submit a claim for an annual checkup with the doctor. Since most traditional insurance plans don't pay for preventive care, the insurance company may issue you a denial and refuse to pay for your checkup.

**Dependent**—Anyone who relies on you for his or her primary financial support. Your spouse and your children are usually considered your dependents. In many plans, your dependents can be covered by your benefits plan at an additional charge, should you request it. Usually there is an age limit for dependents (for example, after your kids reach 18, the plan may not cover them).

**Disability insurance**—Generally, an employer-provided plan whereby payments are made to guarantee your security during periods in which you cannot work due to illness or accident. (chapter 4)

**Effective date**—The date you begin to be covered by your insurance, but not always the same as the date you begin employment. Sometimes there is a thirty-day or ninety-day waiting period, so be sure you know the date your insurance becomes effective when you join a new plan.

**Elimination period**—The first days of confinement that are not covered by a policy. Can be seven, twenty, or one hundred days or more.

**Employee Retirement Income Security Act (ERISA)**—A law that protects you by setting rules and guidelines for "welfare benefits programs" so you don't get shortchanged in areas like pensions. (chapter 14)

**Employee Stock Ownership Plan (ESOP)**—A qualified contribution plan that is designed to be invested primarily or exclusively in your employer's stock. (chapter 8)

**Employee stock purchase plan**—An option given to employees under which you can have a certain percentage of your salary deducted and accumulate it in an account from which purchases of employer stock may be made. (chapter 8)

**Equal Pay Act (EPA)**—A law that protects you from discrimination based on sex in wages and remuneration.

**Exclusions**—The health problems or situations your plan will not cover. Many plans will not cover what are called "pre-existing conditions"—health problems that began before you joined the plan. Some policies limit or exclude coverage for specific diseases or conditions, such as organ transplants or mental illness. Or they put a cap on AIDS payments, for example.

**Face amount**—The dollar amount of a policy that is payable in a claim.

**Fee-for-service**—A kind of medical plan in which health care costs are paid for as they are incurred, usually after you pay a deductible amount. It usually has a cap on the maximum amount it'll pay. (chapter 4)

**Fiduciary**—Under ERISA, a person who:

1. exercises discretionary authority or control over the plan or its assets;
2. renders investment advice for a fee or other compensation; or
3. has discretionary responsibility in the administration of the plan.

**Filing claims**—A procedure required by some plans, in which you pay for your health care first and then submit your receipts with a claim form to the health insurance company. (chapter 4)

**Flexible Spending Account (FSA)**—Also called a reimbursement account. A system in which you store up an untaxed cache of money to pay for costs not covered under other benefits plans or for care of a child or dependent disabled parent.

You fund individual accounts, either with flex dollars from your budgeted balance or with payroll deductions. (chapters 3 and 4)

**401(k) plan**—A cash or deferred arrangement allowing employees to use their tax-free contributions to a fund, and sometimes their employer's, to build up a nest egg. (chapter 7)

**Guaranteed renewable**—An agreement to continue insuring a policyholder up to a certain age, or for life, as long as the premium is paid.

**Health Maintenance Organization (HMO)**—An organized system of health care that you can join, usually for a set monthly fee, to receive a comprehensive array of basic and supplemental health services. In most cases, you may see only the physicians who belong to the HMO, or you will not be reimbursed. (chapter 4)

**Increasing Premium Whole Life (IPWL)**—Term life insurance that automatically becomes whole life insurance after it's been in effect for fifteen or twenty years.

**Indemnity plan**—One of the most common types of health insurance plan, in which an insurance company agrees to indemnify, or reimburse, you for a specific amount of your actual hospital and medical expenses. (chapter 4)

**Individual Retirement Account (IRA)**—An account that is established by an employee or self-employed person to which contributions are made and then deducted, subject to certain restrictions, on the individual's income tax return. The money you set aside and the earnings on it are not taxed until the money is withdrawn. There are specific rules governing the amount that can be contributed, how much can be deducted, and when the proceeds of the account can be distributed. (chapter 9)

**Life insurance**—A contract under which an insurance company agrees, in exchange for a specified amount (the premium), to pay a certain amount (the face value of the policy) to one or more people (the beneficiaries of the policy) upon the death of the insured individual. (chapter 10) Types of life insurance include:

**Annual renewable term (ART)**—Also known as term insurance. A type of policy that is issued for the number of years stated in the contract, usually until age 65 or older, and is renewable annually at a predetermined premium. That amount increases each year as you get older and become a greater risk. But you usually don't have to have a medical examination or provide evidence of insurability. It does not build cash value and can be canceled at the option of the insured.

**Convertible term**— Term life insurance that you can convert to whole life insurance without offering evidence of insurability.

**Decreasing term**—A type of life insurance in which the benefit is reduced each month or year while the premium remains unchanged. Mortgage insurance, which covers a decreasing liability, is a decreasing term policy.

**Single premium**—A type of whole life insurance that entails the payment of a single premium, usually a minimum of $5,000, and builds immediate cash value that can be borrowed against without tax consequence.

**Universal**—A type of whole life insurance in which the cash value (savings account) portion of the policy builds at a rate tied to current market interest.

**Variable**—A type of whole life insurance in which the cash value is invested in a mutual fund.

**Whole (also known as ordinary or straight life)**—A policy that combines term (pure) life insurance with an investment/savings account, so that the policy can be surrendered for cash or borrowed against.

**Long-term disability income insurance**—A plan that provides you with income if you become disabled due to sickness or accident and are unable to work for six months or longer. It usually pays a specified percentage of earnings that continues to retirement age or for a specified period of time. (chapter 4)

**Long-term health care**—A system of health and custodial care provided to support people who have chronic long-term physical or mental conditions that prohibit them from taking care of themselves.

**Major medical**—The portion of your benefits plan that covers many nonhospital expenses, such as outpatient procedures and laboratory tests (e.g., mammograms), incurred if you visit a hospital or physician as an outpatient.

**Managed care**—The general term for a system that seeks to ensure that the treatments you receive are medically necessary and provided in a cost-effective manner. HMOs and PPOs are prime examples. Usually a managed care plan requires you to get advance permission to receive major medical treatment. Failure to comply with requirements of managed care programs may reduce your health coverage. (chapter 4)

**Mandated benefits**—Specific minimum health benefits that insurance carriers must offer to all policyholders, in states that have passed legislation outlining such minimums.

**Medicaid**—A federal/state cooperatively funded and state-operated program of health benefits to eligible low-income people, established under Title XIX of the Social Security Act. States determine program benefits, eligibility requirements, rates of payment for agencies and institutions that provide services, and methods of administering the program under broad federal guidelines. (chapter 11)

**Medical necessity**—Health insurance companies often require that hospital stays and other medical treatments be deemed medically necessary before they will agree to cover the costs of that care. Under many plans today, you have to get advance approval for certain types of care or certain procedures.

**Medicare**—A federal health insurance program for people aged 65 and over who are eligible for Social Security or Railroad Retirement benefits, and for some people under age 65 who are disabled. Medicare was established under Title XVIII of the Social Security Act. There are two parts: hospital insurance (Part A), covering inpatient hospital care and skilled nursing care, and supplementary medical insurance (Part B), covering physicians' and others' services. The latter part is voluntary and requires payment of a monthly premium. (chapter 11)

**Medigap insurance**—Private health insurance purchased to cover the gaps between Medicare payments and physician and hospital charges, and often some additional services, not covered by Medicare. (chapter 4)

**Out-of-pocket payments**—Costs you pay directly that are exclusive of insurance payments.

**Pension plan**—A plan providing you with retirement income, or deferring some income to a period extending to the termination of covered employment or beyond. Also known as a retirement plan. (chapter 12)

**Portability**—The ability of employees, upon termination of employment, to transfer their account balances to another employer without restrictions or penalties.

**Pre-existing conditions limitation**—A waiting period before a medical plan will provide coverage for health conditions that a policyholder had prior to becoming insured.

**Preferred Provider Organization (PPO)**—A group of health care providers that agrees to offer health care to groups of employees at a negotiated rate. A normal PPO will provide you with a list of doctors or other licensed health professionals and providers to choose from, and you choose your doctors and specialists from that list. (chapter 4)

**Premium**—The monthly payment you make to your insurance company. Usually your premium is taken directly out of your paycheck. Insurance companies typically offer different premium rates for single people, married people, and married people with children.

**Profit sharing plan**—A plan established and maintained by an employer to provide for your participation in company profits.

**Qualified beneficiary (QB)**—Generally, any individual covered by a group health plan on the day before a qualifying event. A qualified beneficiary may be an employee, the employee's spouse and dependent children, and, in certain cases, a retired employee and his or her spouse and dependent children. (chapter 14)

**Qualifying event (QE)**—An event that would cause you or a dependent to lose coverage under your employer's health plan if there were no continuing coverage requirement under COBRA. (chapter 14)

**Renewable**—A type of insurance offering you the right, during a specified period of time, to renew your policy without evidence of insurability. (chapter 10)

**Second opinion**—Some health plans require that you consult a second doctor when your primary physician recommends surgery or a hospital stay. The goal is to make sure that the prescribed medical treatment is necessary and appropriate.

**Simplified Employee Pension (SEP)**—An Individual Retirement Account (IRA) or individual retirement annuity that meets certain requirements relating to participation, discrimination, withdrawals, and an employee allocation formula. (chapter 12)

**Summary of material modifications (SMM)**—A summary of any material change or modification of a benefits plan or the information contained in the Summary Plan Description that must be furnished to each participant and beneficiary. (chapter 2)

**Summary Plan Description (SPD)**—A report describing the contents of a benefits plan, which must be provided to each plan participant and beneficiary who is receiving benefits under the plan. (chapter 2)

**Target benefit plan**—A defined contribution plan that gets the employer off the hook of making specified payments to a trust to buy a defined benefit for each participant. In a sense, the target plan copies a major feature of a defined benefit plan: It aims to build an account for every member that will provide a specified amount of money—a target—at retirement.

**Third-party administrator (TPA)**—A firm selected by your employer to administer medical claims or conduct employee wellness and safety programs.

**Thrift plan**—A hybrid savings plan that usually contains two related provisions requiring contributions by participants and by their employer. The employer's contributions are usually based on the amounts contributed by employees.

**Vesting**—The timing schedule that determines when you obtain a nonforfeitable right to contributions and benefits derived from plan contributions made by your employer. (chapter 12)

**Waiver of premium**—An extra-cost option that allows your coverage to continue without any payment of premiums if you become totally disabled for more than a specific period. (chapter 4)

**Wellness program**—A program that can range from educational classes or seminars to on-site exercise facilities. It's designed to encourage improved health and a healthful lifestyle for employees through education, exercise, nutrition, and health promotion. (chapter 4)

**Workers' Compensation**—A program of cash payments funded by employers and mandated by state law for employees who are injured on the job or who become temporarily or permanently disabled due to on-the-job injuries or illnesses. (chapter 11)

# INDEX